THE ARABS' NEW FRONTIER

The Arabs' New Frontier

ROBERT STEPHENS

Westview Press·Boulder·Colorado

Library of Congress Cataloging in Publication Data

Stephens, Robert Henry, 1920-
  The Arabs' new frontier.

  Includes index.
  1. Arab countries—Economic conditions.
2. al-Sundūg al-Kuwaytī lil-Tanmiyah al-Iqtisādīyah
al-'Arabīyah. I. Title.
HC498.S8 1976   338.91'17'4927   76-27890
ISBN 0-89158-644-X

Printed and bound in Great Britain by
Billing & Sons Ltd,
Guildford, London & Worcester

Contents

Foreword

This book is about an institution whose work has hitherto not been widely known but which was until recently unique in the Arab world and in some ways in the world as a whole, the Kuwait Fund for Arab Economic Development. The first edition, published in 1973 was intended primarily as a description and analysis of the first ten years of the Fund's operations.

It seemed to me then that the Fund's work could best be understood by placing it where possible in the broader context of the economic and social background of the Arab countries where it was being carried out. In the course of collecting material for the book I travelled to almost every country in the Arab world, including two countries, Libya and Saudi Arabia, which had not received Kuwait Fund loans since they had large oil revenues of their own. The resulting work was meant not only to give a comprehensive account of the Fund's operations and its special character, but also to convey a picture, not of course by any means intended to be complete, of some of the problems of economic and social development in the Arab world and the efforts being made by many Arab countries to overcome them.

The first edition then appeared just as the 1973 Middle East war and the accompanying oil 'crisis' had brought a spectacular increase in the oil money available for development and a revolutionary change in the economic prospects of the Arab world. The change also led to the quintupling of the capital of the Kuwait Fund and an extension of its role from the Arab world to all developing countries.

It is too soon to attempt to give a full account of the impact and likely consequences of the great increase in oil revenues and the new development possibilities they open up, but it seemed worthwhile to try meanwhile to bring this book up to date as far as possible in the light of these latest developments, while preserving what is still valid of the general picture of the Arab world given in its first version. And that is what I have tried to do.

I should like to repeat here the thanks I expressed in the first edition to all those in the countries I visited, ministers, officials, businessmen, farmers, economists, journalists and others, who generously gave their time to talk to me or show me projects. Once again I also wish particularly to thank the Director-General of the Kuwait Fund, Mr Abdulatif Youssef Al Hamad, and his colleagues who, in preparing both editions, were immensely helpful in placing at my disposal the Fund's own studies and documentation, as well as their own writings and the fruits of their personal experience.

The book and its revision were made possible by financial support from the Fund, but I was left entirely free in my treatment of the subject and in my comments on the Fund's operations. For the final contents of the book and its judgements and conclusions I alone am responsible.

1 The Arab world, oil and development

Behind the Arab world of the newspaper headlines, with its flavour of exotic political melodrama and its clichés about multi-billionaire oil sheikhs holding us all to ransom, there is another Arab world the West still knows very little about, but is now being forced for its own sake to discover.

It is the bread-and-butter, everyday world of the Arab countries where people have to earn their living, the world of farmers, factory workers, businessmen, civil servants, engineers; where tractors and trucks have long been replacing camels, where giant dams and diesel pumps are taking over from water-wheels, where more and more villages rely on power stations instead of kerosene lamps, where hundreds of thousands of students go to modern universities instead of Koranic schools, where more and more girls work computers and run clinics instead of staying behind veils and shutters at home, and where even oil sheikhs are likely to have graduated from Harvard or the London School of Economics.

It is a world in the throes of mighty change, pressed forward sometimes too fast for its own comfort and taste, not only by the impact of industrial civilisation, but also by its own inner demands for modernisation, independence, unity and social justice. It is the part of the developing Third World that is nearest to Western Europe (if one excludes Greece and Turkey) and the most closely linked with Europe historically, culturally and economically.

Nevertheless, even in Europe public ignorance of this close and important neighbour remained profound and the public image of the Arab world was extraordinarily distorted and out of date. Then came the shock of the Middle East war of October, 1973, and the accompanying oil crisis. Apart from demonstrating the supreme importance of the Arab world in the international balance of power and for the economic survival of the industrialised countries, especially in Europe, the 1973 events showed that the Arabs were capable of mastering the advanced technology and large-scale organisation required both for modern warfare and modern industry. The increase in oil producers' association – indicated the determination of the Arabs fully to control the exploitation of their most valuable but expendable economic resource.

OPEC (Organisation of Petroleum Exporting Countries), the oil producers' cartel – indicated the determination of the Arabs fully to control the exploitation of their most valuable but expendable economic resource.

These changes, together with the dramatic reallocation of international resources implied by the tremendously increased Arab oil revenues after 1973, have led to a new and more evenly balanced relationship between the Arab world and the West. They have also led to at least the beginning of a Western public reappraisal of the old picture of the Arabs, albeit new and equally misleading clichés have sometimes taken the place of the old: the picture of the primitive, incompetent, camel-borne Arab is apt to be replaced by the sinister stereotype of the arrogant, Cadillac-borne oil blackmailer who will either ruin the industrialised countries or buy up their key industries – and at the same time selfishly ignore the increased poverty of the non-oil countries of the Third World. In fact, apart from the limited use of the oil embargo as a political weapon in the Arab-Israeli conflict, both Arab and non-Arab oil producers have encouraged close cooperation with Western governments and business so as to use Western technology and surplus oil-money to modernise and industrialise the oil countries themselves, their region and the developing countries as a whole.

Aid from the OPEC countries to the poorer developing countries has been quick and substantial, several times bigger in percentage of GNP (Gross National Product) than that from the industrialised countries.

According to OECD (Organisation for Economic Cooperation and Development) figures, the major OPEC donor countries gave about £1,143 million (2,400 million dollars) in overseas development aid in 1974. This was the equivalent of 1.8 per cent of their combined GNP and 2.7 per cent of their combined oil income for that year. The seventeen countries of OECD's Development Assistance Committee gave 11,300 million dollars (£5,000 million) or 0.33 per cent of their GNP. But these figures were for actual disbursements of money; the commitments were much bigger. Commitments and promises by OPEC countries in 1974 totalled 7,500 million dollars and, together with pledges to the World Bank and the International Monetary Fund, investments and commercial rate loans, amounted to 14,000 million dollars. The total net outflow of non-military resources from OPEC countries to the developing countries in 1974 was 4,750 million dollars or 3.4 per cent of the donors' combined GNP. This compared with 26,350 million dollars or 0.77 per cent of GNP from the DAC countries.

The biggest share of aid from Arab members of OPEC has gone to other Arab countries, especially Egypt, Syria and Jordan, the states most affected by the conflict with Israel, but a substantial amount has been given to other developing countries in various forms. Apart from direct government-to-government bilateral aid, there has been an expansion of existing development institutions and a proliferation of new ones, both national and multi-national, financed primarily by the Arab oil states and giving aid not only to other Arab states but also to non-Arab developing countries.

Some details of new Arab development institutions will be given later in this chapter. But meanwhile let us look briefly at the Arab world and its development problems as its new oil wealth opens up prospects of accelerated economic and social progress.

The twenty independent states which now form the Arab world stretch across North Africa and the Middle East from the Atlantic to the Indian Ocean and from the borders of Turkey to Equatorial Africa. They embrace more than 100 million people and they are widely different in size, character and degree of development. They range from Egypt with a population of 36 million to the newest Union of Arab Emirates in the Persian Gulf with some 300,000; from highly sophisticated Lebanon with seventy per cent literacy to Yemen only just emerging from the Middle Ages. Their political and economic systems vary from republics to monarchies or principalities, from local varieties of socialism or state-control to free enterprise, from countries with substantial industries such as Egypt, Syria and Algeria to others which are either almost entirely agricultural, like the Sudan, or largely pastoral, as was the case until recently in Saudi Arabia. But they also have enough in common – over and above the fact that most of their people are still very poor and live on the land – for the term 'Arab World' to be justified as a unifying label. Unlike 'Europe' which claims a similar label for itself, they have the great advantage of a common language in Arabic. They also share to a large extent a common religion in Islam – though there are substantial religious and other minorities, a common culture, and a similar historical experience which has included for most of them a period under European colonial rule, usually in the form of a mandate or protectorate. They also share common aims and ambitions though they do not always agree on the best way to fulfil them.

They share essentially in the modern Arab revival. This movement has stemmed from two things: a reassertion of the Arab cultural identity which had been submerged in most of the Arabic-speaking lands for many centuries; and the general reaction, shared by Arabs, of the peoples of Asia and Africa to the outward thrust of European power and modern technical civilisation. The fact that this power and this civilisation went together has sometimes created a psychological dilemma for the Arabs in their attitude towards Westernisation since the fruits of the civilisation were desired, indeed appeared indispensable, while the power and its wielders were resented.

From the beginning – in the last century – the approach to asserting, saving or rebuilding the Arabs' own civilisation took several forms. One was to try to cling as closely as possible to the threatened culture – which in this case meant Islam as much as Arabism, since Islamic ethics and institutions were the framework of Arab society until the nineteenth (and in some respects the twentieth) century, rather as Christianity and the Church shaped the policy of medieval Europe before the Reformation.

The second way was to go all out to adopt Western ideas and methods, even as far as abandoning Islam if it stood in the way of material progress and political change. The third method was to try to modernise without destroying the ethical and spiritual traditions founded in or inherited from Islam. This third way – fortified sometimes by the argument that there is no necessary clash between a science-based civilisation and Islamic ideas – has been the predominant path towards modernisation in the Arab world. It has been challenged constantly by the other two schools of thought whose modern manifestations may be seen in Islamic right-wing movements such as the

Muslim Brothers, and in Marxists and liberals on the left.

The final emphasis has usually been on modernisation rather than conservation, and has led to the increasing divorce of the state from Islam and the spread of secular nationalist politics. This struggle and the ambivalence in Arab attitudes from which it springs affected the speed and type of economic development in some Arab countries. Its effect was more obvious in those which started late in the race from the basis of isolated and traditional societies, such as those in the Arabian peninsula and Morocco. But it has also been felt to a lesser degree in more developed countries such as Egypt and Algeria. Sometimes development was slowed down because of its social impact, and in most cases the state has been obliged to take an increasingly active role as a promoter of development. But even in Saudi Arabia where modernisation and Islamic tradition have had perhaps their sharpest confrontation, the pace of development has suddenly begun to quicken enormously and the commitment to a far-reaching transformation of society now appears irrevocable.

Indeed, all Arab societies, including the most backward are now committed to some degree of modernisation. In their aspirations for development they share four motives:

1 They hope to modernise Arab society without destroying its cultural identity and uniqueness; indeed, they see the modernising process as part of the revival of Arab culture.
2 They seek to consolidate national independence – for the Arabs in their separate lands and for the Arab world as a whole.
3 They believe that development and independence go together, because development cannot be fully achieved under foreign rule and because without development independence may be lost again.
4 They are convinced that both development and independence require greater cooperation and unity among the Arab peoples, since division hinders their economic progress and weakens their political and military resistance to outside control.

Since the watershed of 1973 the Arabs have also become more conscious of their position in the Third World of developing countries. Some of them, especially Algeria, have seen themselves as having a special role to play in bringing about a restruc-

turing of the world economy to share resources more fairly
between the industrialised and developing countries. In their
colonial experience, their national revival, their general poverty and psychological reactions, they feel part of the Third
World. They see their own development as part of a general
movement to redress the economic balance between the rich
and poor nations.

'Development', in the sense of modernisation and industrialisation and a more intensive exploitation of economic
resources, began in the Arab world at the beginning of the
nineteenth century, especially in Egypt, the Levant and North
Africa, under the impact of European expansion and intervention.

It was a mixed blessing, for even where it did not bring
immediate colonial conquest and direct exploitation, as in
Algeria (where the French seized land and crops) and eventually in Morocco and Tunisia, European 'aid' of the nineteenth
century kind – investment and technical advice – led to debts,
to tighter European financial and political control, and eventually to the loss of independence, a process of which Egypt was
the chief example. Egypt lost her independence for seventy-five
years basically because successive Egyptian rulers from
Mohammed Aly onwards tried to modernise too fast. Consequently it was not surprising that President Nasser was sus-
picious about the terms of Western aid for the High Dam and at
one point feared that the President of the World Bank, Eugene
Black, was turning out to be another Ferdinand de Lesseps.

But it has now become widely accepted by the Arabs that
their only hope of maintaining an independent identity and
political existence lies in equipping themselves to compete
effectively in economic and technical terms in the modern
world. This lesson has been driven home to them by the outside
pressures to which they have been subjected as the occupants of
coveted strategic areas and of the world's richest oil lands. It
was instilled into them most forcibly by their conflict with the
technologically modernised state of Israel, which has resulted
in the expulsion of over a million Palestinians from their lands
and the conquest by Israel of the whole of former Palestine as
well as adjacent parts of Egypt and Syria.

These are challenges to which the Arabs know they have not
yet found an adequate response (although the 1973 war

increased their confidence that they were on the way to finding it), but which they increasingly believe can be met successfully only by their own more rapid economic and social development. The drive for development is, therefore, not, as is sometimes suggested in the West, a desirable but neglected alternative to Arab political nationalism but rather an integral part of it.

The difficulties in the way have hitherto been enormous – problems of scarce resources and cultural, political and geographical obstacles. The Arab world is not a compact land mass like Germany or Italy which also were once welded together out of many smaller states. It is strung out over 3,000 miles from Morocco to Oman. If on the map the deserts were coloured blue like the sea, one would be able to observe more clearly that the settled areas of the Arab countries are like a chain of long thin islands, following the lines of sea coasts and river valleys, an archipelago like Indonesia and presenting some of the same problems of communication, control and political unity. The population is also erratically distributed, with half of it concentrated in the Nile valley and half the Arab countries having populations of under five million, six with less than a million. Most of the land is poor, indeed the greater part desert, water is scarce and so are raw materials (except oil and phosphates), technical skills and, until recently, capital. Seventy per cent or more of the labour force is still employed – much of it under-employed – on the land in Egypt, Sudan, Algeria, Syria, Iraq and Morocco. Among the peasants and workers, where changes of attitude are most needed, there has been a cultural inertia resisting innovation.

At the same time, several Arab countries, especially Egypt, the states of the Fertile Crescent, Sudan and North Africa, inherited from the colonial period a useful legacy of an infrastructure and an administrative framework – railways, roads, power and other public works, education and health services.

Into this rather forbidding equation there was thrown in the twentieth century a powerful new factor – oil. Production of oil did not begin on a large scale until mid-century, but between 1946 and 1973 it rose from 32.5 million metric tons a year to 926.7 million, dropping slightly in 1974, after the big price increases, to 914.3 million, but still accounting for nearly a third of all world production. By 1974 oil was being exploited in varying quantities in thirteen of the twenty Arab League states – Jordan, Morocco, Lebanon, Somalia, Mauritania and North and South Yemen were still net importers of oil. The production of each country varied greatly, from 3.5 million tons a year in Tunisia to 407.8 million in Saudi Arabia. By 1972 the oil revenues of the Arab states had reached a total of over £3,500 million a year. With the price increases the figure leapt up to over £6,000 million in 1973 and more than £23,000 million in 1974.

The demand for Arab oil from Western Europe, the chief customer, had been increasing by seven to ten per cent a year up till 1973. Through a combination of high prices, economic recession and conservation measures, the demand slackened off in 1974 and 1975, but calculations of Western Europe's energy requirements and means of satisfying them, including alternative fuels and sources of oil, showed that by 1980 Europe would still be dependent for some 60 per cent of its fuel supplies on Middle East and North African oil. The European Community Commission's energy plan drawn up in 1974-5 aimed to reduce this figure to thirty per cent by 1985, but this would still leave 70 per cent of oil consumption to be provided from outside Europe, mostly from the Arab countries. The plan envisaged European oil consumption reaching a peak in 1980 and then declining to the 1973 level by 1985 as other fuel resources such as coal and nuclear energy were developed.

For the Arabs the first phase of the oil boom up to 1973 had created both problems and opportunities. It opened up a new reservoir of capital for development and thus for strengthening their economic independence. At the same time it exacerbated some of their political difficulties. It embroiled some of the Arab states with the Great Powers and divided them among themselves between haves and have-nots.

The second phase of the oil boom from 1973 onwards gave vast new dimensions to this picture. It opened new horizons for more rapid economic development, and changed the nature of some of the political problems. It gave the Arabs both greater international influence and greater international responsibilities. The big price increases made by OPEC, combined with the Arab use of the oil embargo as a political weapon in the conflict with Israel, created a new source of friction with the Western industrialised countries, primarily political with the

United States and economic with Western Europe.

The threatened accumulation by the Arab oil producers of enormous surplus funds (which so far have proved smaller than expected) over the coming decade appeared to raise new problems for the international monetary system for which different experts and different countries produced conflicting solutions. The so-called 'recycling' of these surplus funds concerned especially three groups of nations – the oil producers, the rich oil-importing countries (particularly those with balance of payments deficits), and the developing countries with no oil production of their own. After a series of preparatory meetings during 1974 and 1975 these three groups were brought together into an international conference in Paris in December 1975 to try to work out some agreement that would link oil supplies and pricing with investment and development needs and with the price and supply of other raw materials and industrial goods. The Paris conference set up a number of committees to study these problems.

The new super-abundance of wealth of the Arab oil producers coincided with the greater inter-Arab solidarity born of the October war, and with the progressive assumption by the Arab oil states of control over the oil operations in their territory. As a result the Arabs were able to present a stronger and more united front in dealing with the Great Powers and the Arab have-states showed a greater readiness to share their wealth with the have-nots. This readiness extended also to the have-nots outside the Arab world among the developing countries, whose economic plight and political support were both recognised as important considerations.

The Arab oil producers had their own priorities for the use of the new oil revenues. They seemed to agree that the first claim was for the future of their own economies, whether through the development of their home resources or through the creation of income-earning investment in other areas. Second came the development of the rest of the Arab world, followed by aid to other non-Arab developing countries, with probably some preference shown to political friends and to Muslim co-religionists. Fourth, investment in or financial support for the industrial economies.

The broader thinking behind these priorities was set out succinctly in a speech by the Director-General of the Kuwait

Fund for Arab Economic Development, Abdulatif Youssef Al Hamad (see later).

'The oil-exporting countries, and for that matter other parts of the developing world (said Al Hamad), can no longer meekly accept to be confined to the role of mere raw material producers, or even at best be persuaded to remain agricultural economies under the pretext that there are so many things to be done on the land. More and more people – at least in the conditions prevailing in our part of the world – are coming to realise that the issues of development are not just those of poverty relief or the improvement of abject conditions. What we aim at now in the Middle East is the reconstruction of the Arab economy's secondary and tertiary sectors on modern standards. In fact, given our climatic conditions and demographic pressures no profound analysis is needed in order to realise that there are simply no alternatives for desert economies like ours.

' . . . We also well know that to rely exclusively in this connection on our own efforts under the slogan of "self-help" would almost certainly court rapid failure and frustration. What is needed above all . . . is for the various parties concerned to be willing to envisage a serious programme of multifaceted international cooperation on the basis of true and complementary partnership . . . over a broad spectrum of economic, social, cultural and even political fields.'

Al Hamad defined the first task as 'identifying – within the oil exporting countries, the Arab world, the developing countries and the industrial economies (perhaps in that order) – the most promising sectors, and consequently the most suitable projects for joint action and investments.' Second was the formulation of arrangements for joint ventures resting 'basically on a blend between, on the one hand, the provision of technology, know-how, marketing and other services, and, on the other, petrofunds finance.' Governments should introduce special measures, such as tax relief and tariff concessions to encourage joint ventures. The main instruments for these tasks should be public or semi-public corporations in the oil countries and the giant industrial and financial companies of the Western world.

There was one peculiarity about oil which had slowed down the application of oil revenues for development in the Arab world in the first phase of the oil boom up to the seventies. This peculiarity was that oil was found at first in the biggest quantities in the smallest or least populated and most backward Arab countries – the desert lands, which had virtually no resources of their own for development. At first, too, the most over-populated countries, such as Egypt and Jordan, and those which had the most resources for development but were starved of capital, such as Syria, had little or no oil. (Egypt has in the past few years found useful quantities, enough to make her self-sufficient in oil, and Syria has begun to do so, but neither country has yet become a substantial net oil exporter). So that while such countries were crying out for capital, hundreds, eventually thousands, of millions of pounds of surplus revenue from the main oil states were being kept in English or Swiss banks or invested in Canada, Germany or Japan. It was not surprising that when Arab leaders, such as President Nasser, talked of Arab unity, they were suspected by some of really having in mind a share-out of this wealth and of seeing a solution to problems such as Egypt's in acquiring control of the oil revenues of the Arab have-states. Nasser no doubt hoped that he could by one means or another get Arab aid for Egypt's development and also count on Arab markets for Egyptian manufactures and man-power. But, whatever his intentions, there was clearly an important economic aspect to Arab unity. If Arab political solidarity had any serious value for the various Arab states, as it appeared to have, then it was absurd that they should not use at least part of this wealth for developing and strengthening the Arab community rather than developing and strenthening other countries which were in some cases even actively hostile to some Arab states.

But money is not the only thing needed for development: there is also the ability to use it effectively, and the will to apply it also for social purposes, which involve risks of political change. In recent years and especially since they gained their political independence, almost all the Arab countries have drawn up development plans and have begun a conscious effort, guided by the governments, to direct investment into channels which will increase production and raise living standards. These plans have varied in seriousness or superficiality according to the stage of development of the countries concerned, their political systems or ideologies, their effective resources and especially the skills and experience of their administrations. Some development programmes or five-year plans are little more than hopeful lists of projects or outlines of government spending targets, especially in countries like the Lebanon which have predominantly free enterprise economies; like Morocco which lacks trained planning staff, or the Yemen which has only just begun to create any economic administration and still has scarcely any modern economic structures at all. The plans of other states, such as Egypt, Algeria, Tunisia and to a lesser extent Syria and Iraq, are both more comprehensive and more purposeful, though usually too ambitious. After 1973 Saudi Arabia vastly expanded its development programme with a five-year plan for 1975-80 calling for the expenditure of some £40,000 million, or more than twenty times the total planned development spending of all the Arab countries in 1971. The problem here may prove to be not finding the money but finding the goods and equipment to buy and providing the trained man-power and local political and social framework needed to conduct such a huge programme efficiently. Already in early 1975 the plan was reported to be undergoing drastic revision.

In most Arab countries, government action plays a large part in stimulating and financing economic development. This is the case not only in the countries with socialised or partly socialised economies – Egypt, Syria, Iraq, Algeria, the Sudan, Libya and, to a certain extent, Tunisia. Nor is it only in the oil-producing states with large revenues, small populations and few natural resources, such as Saudi Arabia and Kuwait. Even in Jordan, Lebanon and Morocco, which lean more to private enterprise, there is some government intervention for development purposes.

In the socialised countries, particularly Egypt, the motives for government intervention were not simply ideological. Even in these countries agriculture, the main occupation of the population, is still based chiefly on private land ownership and production. But the large-scale investment required for big irrigation schemes such as the Nile, Euphrates and Tigris dams could not have come from local private capital. Moreover, in most cases agriculture also required a restructuring through agrarian reform which could be achieved only through government action. Similarly, in Egypt and other Arab countries experience showed that the drive for industrialisation needed to create more jobs cannot rely on private capital, at least in its early stages. For both historical and economic reasons, private investors have preferred to invest in real estate or commerce rather than in industry. A third, primarily political, motive for socialisation or government investment was the fear that reliance on foreign private capital, even where it was on offer, might lead to a loss of political independence. Egypt especially was haunted by the spectre of her nineteenth-century experience.

In the socialised countries, structural changes, such as nationalisation of industry and commerce and land reform, delayed increases in output. War, political upheaval and heavy defence expenditures sometimes absorbing as much as half the national budget, were additional brakes on development in many Arab countries, especially those in the Middle East.

Government intervention has also sometimes led to waste through misjudged priorities, administrative inefficiency, technical ignorance and too great weight being given to large-scale prestige projects. Such shortcomings partly explain the trend in post-Nasser Egypt towards a greater liberalisation of the economy. (Other reasons for this trend under President Sadat, apart from ideology, were the desire to attract funds from Western sources and from the more conservative Arab oil states and to reduce Egypt's dependence on Soviet aid.) But it is probable that without government intervention a less serious development effort would have been made. Nor can the success of the effort at this transitional stage be judged solely by short-term production results. In industry, especially, there must also be counted the longer-term benefits of gains in experience, skill and self-confidence, changed social attitudes and the creation of a more dynamic economic climate. A greater awareness of development problems and how to handle them also leads to a better economic administration in both the public and private sectors, and this is one of the decisive factors in the development process.

But even on purely statistical measurement, most of the Arab countries achieved relatively high though uneven rates of growth in the decade of the sixties compared with the growth rates of most developing countries. In the last six years before the 1967 war, Arab growth rates averaged from five to eight per cent, representing a net gain over population increase of two to four or five per cent a year, compared with an average net growth rate of two and a half per cent for all developing countries.

Figures of growth for 1965-70 show a more uneven spread: six to seven per cent in the main oil-producing countries; four to five per cent in Syria and Morocco; four per cent or less in Egypt, Iraq, Jordan, Lebanon and Tunisia.

A similar pattern prevailed from 1970-73 but with increased growth rates in some of the oil states (for example 12.5 per cent in Saudi Arabia), usually attributable mostly to increased oil production, and also in Syria (7.4 per cent).

Apart from war, politics and the availability of foreign exchange, the main influences on growth rates have been crop fluctuations, due to weather or pests; oil production; and the state of world markets for export crops such as cotton.

Agriculture is still the mainstay of most Arab economies, though the farming situation varies widely. Egyptian agriculture, for example, is highly developed and nearing the limits of its resources of water and cultivable land, while Iraq, Sudan and to a lesser extent Syria, have great potential of unused land and water for agricultural expansion. Other countries, such as Saudi Arabia and Kuwait, have very little agriculture and no serious prospect of developing it economically.

All the first four countries mentioned above increased their agricultural output in recent years, in some cases and for some products, substantially. For example, between 1952-56 and 1967-68 Egypt increased her wheat production by 10 per cent, rice by 100 per cent and cotton by 50 per cent. Figures for the Sudan showed an increase of 200 per cent for wheat, barley and rice and an increase of 100 per cent for cotton. Iraq showed an increase of 20 per cent for wheat, 40 per cent for rice, 100 per cent for cotton, and a decrease of 10 per cent for barley. In Syria wheat increased by 15 per cent, barley by 40 per cent, cotton by 100 per cent, and rice decreased by 40 per cent. Taking agricultural production as a whole, average output for the years 1970-73 compared with the average for 1961-65 showed an increase of 28 per cent for Egypt, 53 per cent for the Sudan, 43 per cent for Iraq, and 4 per cent for Syria (affected by two severe drought years in 1970-71). For the world as a whole the increase for the same period was 24 per cent. But in most Arab countries average annual growth rates for agriculture have been about three per cent or less. So agriculture has remained in a desperate race with the increase of population, a race that explains the search for a way out through industrialisation. Although in most Arab countries the share of agriculture in the Gross Domestic Product has been declining relative to industry, trade and services, not one of them can yet be properly described as an industrial country. In Egypt, industry's share in the GDP increased to 23 per cent by 1971, while the share of agriculture dropped to 25 per cent. But even there farming still employs 55 per cent of the population, and cotton exports earn two-thirds of Egypt's foreign exchange.

Economic expansion has been accompanied and stimulated by social development. One striking measure of this social change can be seen in the rapid growth of education in most Arab countries. The figures for school enrolment for children aged 5 – 19 (percentage of the population of school age) increased between 1950 – 64 in the following Arab countries: Egypt 25 to 51 per cent; Syria 35 to 46 per cent; Lebanon 47 to 81 per cent; Jordan 27 to 73 per cent; Sudan 5 to 16 per cent; and Kuwait from 4 to 100 per cent. In Israel the comparable figures were 72 to 83 per cent; in Turkey 33 to 45 per cent; and in Iran 16 to 40 per cent. There has also been a spectacular expansion in the numbers of students at universities or other institutions of higher education.

It is difficult to give precise overall figures for the rate of development spending of the Arab countries as a whole; development budgets have been repeatedly revised upwards since 1973; in the case of the oil states, to astronomical levels.

Some orders of magnitude can be given both for the period before 1973 and for the years since then. In 1960-66 investment in the Arab countries was estimated at between 15 and 18 per cent of Gross National Product, and in 1970 gross fixed capital formation was nearly £3,000 million. Egypt's first five-year plan for 1960-65 involved a public expenditure of £1,577 million. Subsequently, until 1973, Egypt's development spending, reduced by the 1967 war and by preparation for the war of 1973, averaged between £250 million and £300 million a year. Egypt's 1974 budget allocated £E564 million for public investment, and in 1975 a new five-year plan for 1976-80 was being worked out with an anticipated total development expenditure of between £E7,000 and £E8,000 million. Algeria's 1970-73 plan provided for expenditure of over £2,000 million. This was more than doubled in the original version of the current 1974-77 plan, and doubled again in 1974 to a target figure of some £10,000 million. Morocco's plan for 1968-72 envisaged expenditure of £790 million over five years. The next plan for 1973-77 set an investment target of £1,300 million, but in 1973 this figure was doubled and was raised again the following year to £4,140 million. In 1972, Syria was spending on development at the rate of about £100 million a year. The figure increased to £350 million in 1974 and to £580 million in 1975. Iraq's development budget rose from some £350 million in 1973-74 to £1,500 million in 1975. In Saudi Arabia £1,500 million was allocated for development projects in the 1973-74 budget; this figure was doubled in 1974-75 as a prelude to the 1975-80 plan which calls for the investment of some £40,000 million. The development budget in Kuwait rose from £67 million in 1972 to over £200 million in 1975.

Altogether the planned development expenditure envisaged during 1971 in all Arab countries was in the region of £1,700 million. For 1975 it was about £10,000 million. In the public sector not all of past allocations were spent, and future spending is also likely to fall behind the targets; in some countries the funds were not available or projects were not ready in time for the money to be used, or after 1973, deliveries of imported capital goods were not fast enough to meet the vastly expanding demand. But a good deal of these sums represents real commitments and gives some measure of the investment involved.

Since those Arab governments without large oil revenues – and they include some of those most active in development – are short of foreign exchange, they are dependent on external financing for a large part of the foreign exchange element in their development spending. This they obtain, when they can, partly in short-term commercial credits and partly in longer-term official aid from foreign, including Arab, governments or international institutions, such as the World Bank or IDA (International Development Association), in the form of loans or grants. Since most of this financing was in loans, often at the high interest rates which have prevailed in the international money market in recent years, a serious and growing problem of external debt was created for some Arab countries, among them notably Egypt, Tunisia and Morocco. In early 1975 Egypt was estimated to owe Western countries and institutions about £1,400 million and another £500 million to Communist countries for civilian projects. Estimates for her debts for arms supplied by the Soviet Union varied from £900 million to £1,800 million. Most of the debts to the West were rescheduled by agreement after the 1973 war but the Russians refused repeated Egyptian requests for a moratorium on debts to them.

Foreign non-military aid to the Arab countries from non-Arab sources and from some Arab sources, has been politically selective and in most cases – at least before 1973 – on a fairly modest scale.

Among the Arab states of the Middle East most Western aid (from OECD countries) until the 1967 war went to Egypt and Jordan – and most of it came from the United States. American aid to Egypt up till then (from 1950 to 1966, when it was suspended) totalled 950 million dollars; and to Jordan between 1960-66 it was 357 million dollars. But Western aid was reduced to a trickle after the 1967 war. Per capita Western aid to Egypt between 1966-68 was only 1.4 dollars which put her 77th on the list of 82 countries receiving aid from OECD members. Iraq was 80th with 0.9 dollars a head, and Syria received only 0.6 dollars. Jordan was seventh on the list with 26 dollars a head.

Loans to the Arab countries from the World Bank and IDA (an affiliate of the Bank which gives 'soft' loans at long term with low interest) between 1950 and 1970 totalled 527 million dollars. Up to 1966 the biggest recipients were the Sudan, Egypt, Algeria, Morocco, Lebanon and Tunisia. During 1965-70 the Bank granted only four loans and credits to the Arab Middle East, a total of 60.5 million dollars to Egypt, Iraq, Jordan and Syria. No loans were made to Algeria but Tunisia and Morocco received increasing amounts.

Over a roughly comparable period – 1947-66 – Iran received 449 million dollars, Turkey 229 million and Israel 124 million dollars from the World Bank and IDA. Israel's total per capita foreign aid income amounted to thirty or forty times that of Egypt.

But in the past few years the World Bank has been increasing both its lending to and borrowing from Arab countries. In the period 1969-73 loans to Arab countries from the Bank and IDA totalled 1,189 million dollars or nearly four times the amount lent in the preceding four-year period. And in 1974 the total Bank lending to Arab countries for the year rose to 548.7 million dollars. At the same time the Bank borrowed 291 million dollars from three Arab oil states, Libya, Kuwait and Abu Dhabi.

Several Arab countries received economic as well as military aid from Communist sources, sometimes on a substantial scale. Between 1964-7 Egypt was estimated to have obtained 1,011 million dollars worth of non-military aid from the Soviet Union, and 1,679 million dollars worth from all the Communist countries, second only to India's receipts from the same source. Iraq received 184 million dollars worth of Communist aid and Syria 393 million. Some Communist bloc aid also went to Algeria, Morocco, the Sudan and North and South Yemen.

After 1967, with the suspension of American aid to many Arab countries, the Communist states became the main source of external, non-Arab aid for the Arab world. This situation began to change in the early seventies with the resumption of American aid to several Arab states, the cooling in relations between Egypt and the Soviet Union, the expansion of World Bank lending and, above all, especially since 1973, the big increase in inter-Arab aid.

In pursuit of their ideals of self-help, independence and unity, it was natural that the Arab states and Arab public opinion should have early begun to look to inter-Arab aid, especially to the investment of the growing oil wealth, and greater regional economic integration as ways of stimulating development without increasing Arab dependence on the outside world. It was, however, also to be expected, in the light of geography, history, temperament and the serious economic and administrative obstacles, that such aid and integration should have been slow in developing.

Given the wide and awkward geographical spread of the Arab world, some have seen more rational politico-economic units in smaller regional groupings such as the Nile Valley linking Egypt and the Sudan; the Maghreb, composed of Morocco, Algeria and Tunisia, with or without Libya; the Fertile Crescent bringing together Iraq, Syria, Jordan and Lebanon; and the Arabian Peninsula.

Between Egypt and the Sudan the advantages of economic union were not shared equally enough to outweigh the preference of the Sudanese for complete political independence. Economically most of the advantages of union would be on Egypt's side unless Cairo took special steps to redress the balance. The two countries are competitive in their main export of cotton; the Sudan has land which could be used by Egypt's surplus population and could be a protected market for Egypt's growing industries. But Egypt could not, without denying some of her own needs, supply the capital the Sudan requires for development. The missing element of capital might have been supplied, at least in part, if Egypt and the Sudan had also joined with Libya and its oil resources, as was contemplated for a time in 1971. But this combination was still-born because of political incompatibilities.

The Fertile Crescent area is a more natural economic unit, especially if it were extended to include Kuwait. It existed as such a unit under the Ottoman Empire without internal economic or political barriers until its liberation from the Turks in the First World War. But its later unity was prevented first by imperial rivalries between Britain and France (and now between America and Russia) and then by differences of ambition, foreign policy and political systems between the Arabs of the region themselves. Ironically, one of the chief obstacles to its unity in recent years has been the rivalry between two factions of the Baath party, which is more committed than any other Arab political group to the idea of Arab unity. The two factions, established in power in Damascus and Baghdad respectively, keep the two essential elements of the Fertile Crescent, Syria and Iraq, apart. The influence of Israel has also been exerted to prevent the formation of an effective alliance against her.

The idea of a unified Maghreb, even some kind of North African federation, was in the minds of the Arab nationalists of Morocco, Algeria and Tunisia when they were struggling for independence from French rule. Then their common colonial situation seemed the most powerful bond. But with independence came greater divisions: differences of ruling personalities, political systems and foreign policy. Monarchic conservative Morocco and republican Tunisia with its mixed economy turned towards France and America; radical, socialist Algeria under an army ruler sought greater help from Russia as well as from France. There also came the recognition that the three countries had parallel rather than complementary economies and that their separate economic ties with Western Europe and especially with France were still far greater than their trade and communications with each other. In 1970, for example, Morocco carried on four-fifths of her trade with industrialised countries, especially those of the European Common Market. Less than three per cent was with the other Maghreb countries and the percentage for the whole Arab world only a fraction more.

Yet there is obviously some scope for closer coordination between the development programmes of the Maghreb countries, as between the Arab states of the Middle East. They could improve their communications, avoid duplication and overproduction, especially in industrial investment intended to supply the local market and in agricultural export crops, such as wine and sugar-beet. So far little has been done in this direction – indeed even the disputed frontier between Morocco and Algeria which caused a brief border war in 1963 has not yet been completely demarcated and in February 1976 the same two countries came to blows over the former Spanish Sahara. But the economic ministers of the three Maghreb countries meet from time to time and have established a permanent consultative committee. There are also various specialist committees for industry, transport and communications, tourism and the coordination of postal, telephone, radio and TV services. In 1975 a programme was being worked out for a completely automatic telephone system between the Maghreb countries, with expected financial help from the newly created inter-governmental Arab Fund for Social and Economic Development.

Despite these difficulties, various bold but mostly ill-prepared attempts have been made to create bigger Arab groupings and sundry forms of regional economic cooperation, either on a scale embracing all the members of the Arab League or in smaller regional units. None of these regional groupings has so far been very successful. Their failure has been due partly to their having been often merely an opportunistic response to short-term political or military needs – springing from either local personal ambitions or the need for alliances against Israel or other foreign powers. Their political super-structures usually went too far ahead of the economic and social harmonisation below.

The most serious attempt – the merger of Egypt and Syria in the United Arab Republic under President Nasser – broke up in 1961 after three years. It failed because of the geographical separation of the two member-states, political incompatibilites between their ruling groups, and different economic traditions and structures. The Hashemite federation of Iraq and Jordan in 1958 was killed almost at birth by the Iraqi Revolution. The proposed tripartite federation of Egypt, Syria and Iraq in 1963 was an attempt to revive the UAR in a wider, looser form, but it never got beyond the stage of preliminary talks. The attempt at a confederation between Egypt, Syria and Libya, launched in 1971, for which Sudan was also at one time a candidate, appeared at first to be more promising because it was more flexible and cautious, and because of the complementary resources of oil capital, skilled man-power, and land and water that it could bring together. But the heart of it was really two alliances with differing purposes. The first was between Egypt and Syria for military purposes against Israel, and the other between Egypt and Libya for economic and social develop-ment, at least as far as Egypt was concerned. The grouping produced some useful results for the members in strengthening Egyptian-Syrian cooperation in waging the 1973 Middle East war. It also provided jobs for Egyptians in Libya which needed their skills, and some Libyan military aid to Egypt. But the young Libyan leader, Colonel Muammar al Qadhafi was too impatient for a closer political union; he also disagreed with Egyptian and Syrian military strategy against Israel. His pres-sure led first to Egyptian agreement in July 1972 to a complete merger with Libya, but the agreement was never carried out and after the 1973 war relations between President Sadat and Colonel Qadhafi grew rapidly worse – almost to the point of complete rupture. Nevertheless, from a purely economic point of view, a closer union between Libya and Egypt would make sense for both countries. It is also easier to envisage such a union than the development of a solidly-based regional union of the Arab states further east until there is a settlement between these states and Israel, if only because the inclusion or at least cooperation of Jordan is vital, and that also depends on agreement with Israel.

One small regional grouping which has so far managed successfully on a loose confederal pattern is the federation of the United Arab Emirates in the Gulf created in 1971, which unites Abu Dhabi with six other emirates of the former Trucial Coast. Another local union between North and South Yemen, agreed in principle in 1972, has remained only an aspiration because of ideological differences.

Meanwhile the Arab League made several more modest attempts to improve economic cooperation between its members. In 1953 it created two economic treaties, one on trade and the other on payments and the movement of capital. The trade treaty provided for an extension of preferential treatment between the signatories and for the regulation of transit trade. The payments convention left existing regulations more or less unchanged.

An agreement on Arab economic unity was drafted by the Arab League in 1962 and ratified by five Arab countries two years later. A Council of Arab Economic Union was then set up and it decided to form an Arab Common Market. The Market was to take effect from January 1965 and to be open to all who had signed the 1962 agreement on economic unity. Seven states have now signed and ratified both agreements.

In its present form the Arab Common Market is really a kind of free trade area, since it has so far affected only tariffs between the members and has not led towards a common external tariff. The agreement provided for tariff cuts on inter-regional trade of twenty per cent a year for agricultural produce and ten per cent for manufactured goods, as well as for a reduction of quotas. The agreement also calls, however, for the regional coordination of development plans and, in particular, of plans for industrialisation. But little or no coordination of this kind has taken place. Nor has the Arab Payments Union, agreed upon at the same time as the Common Market and due to take effect in 1969, yet materialised. But in 1975 it was agreed to set up an Arab monetary fund of some £400 million.

The Arab League also carried out a number of studies of regional economic integration and of projects designed to further it. These included civil aviation (almost every Arab country now has its own national airline), oil, transport, shipping, mining and tourism. Before 1973 only one of these projects got beyond the paper stage. This was the proposal for a joint Arab Potash Company in Jordan, first proposed in 1956, then left languishing until revived in 1966-7 with the help of the Kuwait Fund, but then blocked again by the June war. (In 1975 there was an Arab League project to set up an Arab Mining Company in Jordan with a capital of 338 million dollars.) Another regional project, not originating from the Arab League was the Arab-African Development Bank founded jointly in Egypt and Kuwait in 1964.

In the field of oil, an agreement between Kuwait, Saudi Arabia and Libya led in 1968 to the creation of the Organisation of Arab Petroleum Exporting Countries (OAPEC), to coordinate the dealings of the Arab producers with the oil companies. In practice, before 1973, most of this work, especially as regards price agreements, was done within the broader framework of OPEC which has non-Arab as well as Arab members. In 1973 OAPEC became more active and important as the coordinating body of Arab oil policies, including the embargo imposed during the October war and the progressive take-over of control of the oil companies. It has also set up three inter-Arab companies for oil tankers (the Arab Maritime Petroleum Transport Company with a capital of 500 million dollars), shipbuilding and repair (100 million dollars) and petroleum investment (1,014 million dollars).

Cooperation over oil matters was not the only sign that between at least some of the Arab states, especially those in the Middle East, there was a high and growing degree of interdependence which would inevitably lead to continued attempts at greater integration. Whenever this interdependence breaks down, as through the closing of the borders between Syria and Jordan or Lebanon, or the blocking of inter-Arab pipelines or restrictions on air space, it has the effect of a political crisis. Moreover, there is great mobility of labour and movement of people within the Arab world. Full exploitation of water resources also requires some regional cooperation: for example, Syria, Iraq and Turkey all have interests in the Euphrates river.

Greater regional integration may also in practice flow from a freer movement of capital between the Arab countries and its use to encourage joint inter-Arab ventures. To produce this result is the purpose of two recently created inter-Arab institutions which appear to have better chances of effective life than some of their predecessors. One is the Arab Fund for Economic and Social Development (see page 76), an intergovernmental body for promoting development in Arab countries, which began operations in 1973 from headquarters in Kuwait and has a present working capital of £600 million. The other is the Inter-Arab Investment Guarantee Corporation (see page 80) designed to insure Arab investors against non-commercial risks in Arab countries. Both institutions are intended to give special priority to joint inter-Arab projects. Support for regional development also comes indirectly from the development funds set up by the main Arab oil states, and aid from their governments, even though in practice their loans or grants have gone mostly to individual Arab governments or national projects.

As the post-war oil boom got under way in the Gulf and Arabia in the fifties and sixties, the idea gradually gained ground that the oil countries should share some of their wealth with the less fortunate Arab states. It was an obvious match – especially for those without oil. Some of the oil money began to find its way into 'have-not' channels by various means – through private investment, in Egypt, Syria and Lebanon especially, and through politically motivated grants and subsidies, at first mostly from Saudi Arabia. But the greater part of the oil money which was not spent at home in the oil states was salted away abroad where it served to finance development in the already developed countries. The enormous increase in oil surpluses after the 1973 price rises and the enhanced Arab self-confidence and solidarity created a new situation. The oil states were ready to divert more of their funds to the have-not countries, extending their help in the first place to fellow Arabs but also to non-Arab developing countries. They created several new national and inter-Arab institutions for this purpose. The Kuwait Fund for Arab Economic Development, which had led the way in this field, was joined by the development funds of Abu Dhabi (created in 1971) with a capital of £250 million, of Saudi Arabia with capital of £1,350 million, and of Iraq (£77 million). In addition there is now the Islamic Development Bank (capital £1,100 million) for aid to Muslim countries, to which the Arab oil states are key contributors, and several organisations specially designated for Arab financial and technical aid to African countries.

Although Saudi Arabia, the richest oil state with a 1974 revenue of 20,000 million dollars, (over £9,000 million), has now become probably the biggest Arab aid donor in absolute terms (her loans, grants and other overseas contributions had reached a total of 4,600 million dollars by the beginning of 1975), it was the small Gulf oil state of Kuwait which was the first to make a more serious effort to use oil money constructively in the Arab world. Kuwait's disbursements after she gained independence in 1961, began, like those of Saudi Arabia, as more or less straight protection money, such as her £25 million loan to Iraq. The Kuwait government has continued to lend or give money to Arab governments to support their budgets or balance of payments, with a basically political motive. But it has also been engaged during the past fourteen years in financing a more economically productive and politically neutral effort which is linked with national development plans, with the regional development of the Arab world, and more recently, with the development of other Third World countries. This effort has been made through the Kuwait Fund for Arab Economic Development, which for a decade was alone in this field.

Between 1961 and 1973 Kuwait gave aid at a rate varying between 15 and 20 per cent of its budget and between five and seven per cent of its GNP. This rate was far above the international recommended targets for aid of one per cent for donor countries for the total outflow of resources, or 0.75 per cent for official aid. It made Kuwait seventh on the list of world aid donors and sixth among non-Communist countries after the United States, Britain, Germany, Japan and France, and by far the world's biggest donor in relation to GNP. In 1974 Kuwait's commitments to Arab and African countries and in subscriptions to multilateral institutions were estimated to amount to more than 1,000 million dollars or more than one tenth of Kuwait's anticipated oil income in that year. This is a remarkable effort for a state of barely one million people whose wealth is in the form of depletable oil reserves, even though it has meanwhile a disproportionately large capital surplus. Of the total Kuwaiti aid over the past fourteen years, over £350 million has been provided through loans from the Kuwait Fund – about one-third of the amount of money lent to all Arab countries by the World Bank and IDA over the same period.

But before looking in greater detail at the operations of the Fund, let us look briefly at Kuwait itself, where the money comes from.

2 Kuwait

The flight from London to Kuwait is extraordinary perhaps because outwardly so routine: six hours, five or six miles up, far above the clouds, in a beautiful silent machine so vibrationless that one seems hardly to be moving, while invisibly down below a continent pours past at six hundred miles an hour – strange, as complete, physically simple but mentally complex as a chess move. The pure high sun burnt bright on the wing, then sank and went out. We landed in darkness past blazing oil flares and stepped out into a hot, dust-laden night.

It was May 1971. The next day the temperature was over a hundred and the tail-end of a sandstorm, the curse of Kuwait, was darkening the streets. As I set out from the American-style hotel, all glass, steel and air-conditioning, to explore the city, I recalled my first visit. It was towards the end of the Second World War. I flew in from Bahrain uncomfortably squeezed into an RAF torpedo bomber and stayed in a mud-brick guest house. The great oil boom had not begun, though it was on the horizon, its arrival delayed by the war. Kuwait was then a compact walled town of about 80,000 people, a port for the sea and the desert which both began immediately outside its crenellated, brown, mud walls. Pearling, fishing, shipbuilding and trade were still its main occupations. In the early years of this century Kuwait had over 800 ships and 30,000 sailors engaged in pearling – by 1956 only five boats were still working. The pearl industry had already been badly hit before the war by Japan's development of cultured pearls, but along the seashore you could still see men at work building and shaping the beautiful wooden ships that plied the Gulf coasts and the big *boums* which would carry cargoes of Basra dates beyond the Gulf and out across the Indian Ocean on voyages of many months to Indian and African ports, bringing back timber and spices.

Among Kuwait's mudbrick houses and narrow alleyways, the main public buildings were then a few simple whitewashed mosques and the modest palace of the ruling sheikh. On that first visit I sat in the sheikh's reception room and gazed with pleasure and surprise at the ceiling covered with framed copies of Victorian neo-classical paintings, including one that looked like a splendid Etty nude. Apart from such unexpected novelties in interior decoration, the airstrip and the town wall (which, four and a half miles long and ten feet high with round towers at intervals and four main gates, was hurriedly built only in 1920 to repel a threatened Wahabi invasion), Kuwait probably looked little different then from what it had looked like during most of the previous 200 years of its existence.

Although the adjacent island of Falaika still bears the Hellenic traces of the garrison established there by one of Alexander's generals, the foundation of Kuwait itself dates from the middle of the eighteenth century when two families of the Anaza bedouin tribe of Arabia, the Sabah and the Khalifa, arrived and settled there. (The word Kuwait is a diminutive of 'kut' meaning a fort.) The Khalifa did not stay but moved south and occupied Bahrain. The Sabah founded the dynasty which began with Sabah 1st in 1756 and has continued to this day.

Kuwait's chief advantage then was a fine natural harbour. In 1865 the Arabian traveller, W.G. Palgrave, noted its prosperity as the most active port of the modern Gulf. He attributed its pre-eminence to the 'skill, daring and solid trustworthiness' of the Kuwaiti mariners, the low import duties and friendly inhabitants, and the 'good administration and prudent policy' of the ruling family – some of the qualities still evident in Kuwait today.

At the turn of the century Kuwait was being talked of as the terminus of the controversial Berlin-to-Baghdad railway. Caught among conflicting Great Power pressures, the then ruler of Kuwait, Mubarak the Great, followed the example of other Gulf rulers and in 1899 signed a treaty of protection with Britain which lasted until 1961.

The British connection proved useful to Kuwait in preventing it being over-run by desert warriors during the rise of Ibn Saud, the creator of Saudi Arabia. The link also proved very profitable to the British, for it helped to ensure that in 1934 the concession to explore for oil in Kuwait territory went to a company in which the British-owned Anglo-Iranian Oil Company (now British Petroleum) had a half share, the other half being held by the American-owned Gulf Oil Corporation.

The Kuwait Oil Company, as the joint venture was called, first struck oil in large quantities in 1938 with the discovery of the Burgan field, possibly the biggest single oil field in the world. But drilling was stopped in 1941 because of the war. When it was resumed after the war, oil production rose from 800,000 tons in 1946 to 17 million tons in 1950. Then the oil boom began in real earnest. It was helped by the Abadan crisis in 1951 when the Iranian premier, Dr Moussadeq, nationalised the Anglo-Iranian Oil Company and encountered an international oil marketing boycott. By 1955 production had reached 54 million tons and by 1972 it was 151.2 million tons. But in 1973, as a result of the Kuwait Government's restriction of output for conservation reasons and because of the Arab oil embargo during the Middle East war, production fell to 138.4 million tons. In 1974 it was 114.4 million tons (to these latter figures there has to be added another 13-14 million tons a year representing Kuwait's half-share of the production of the Neutral Zone.) Kuwait was in 1974 the sixth biggest oil producer in the world, third in the Middle East after Saudi Arabia (407.8 million tons) and Iran (301.2 million tons), and second among the Arab countries after Saudi Arabia, though likely to be overtaken shortly by Iraq.

Kuwait's income from oil rose from about £4 million in 1950 to £863 million in 1973 and, following the quadrupling of oil prices by the end of that year, it made a huge leap upwards in 1974 to over £4,500 million. It was expected to remain over £4,000 million in 1975. During the same time the nominal annual per capita income of the population rose from less than £10 to over £4,000, the highest in the world after the smaller Gulf oil states of Qatar and Abu Dhabi. In 1974, oil provided 78 per cent of the country's G.D.P.

In 1975 the Kuwait Government achieved full ownership and financial control of its own oil industry. In 1974 it negotiated a 60 per cent share in the Kuwait Oil Company, leaving BP and Gulf with 20 per cent each. In the spring of the following year the government began negotiating the take over of the remaining BP and Gulf holdings. It already had a majority control of Aminoil (the American Independent Oil Company) which was operating Kuwait's half of the Neutral Zone on land and also of the Arabian Oil Company, the Japanese concern which operates in the offshore area of the Neutral

Zone. Overall control of the oil industry now rests with a
Supreme Oil Council and the Kuwait Oil, Gas and Energy
Corporation (KOGEC) a new state organisation with a capital
of KD 150 million (£225 million) of which KD 50 million (£75
million) is paid up. The founding elements of KOGEC were the
already existing state-controlled organisations dealing with oil,
natural gas, electricity, oil transport and petro-chemicals. In
making its 60 per cent participation agreement with the concessionary oil companies Kuwait set a pattern which was quickly
followed by Saudi Arabia, Iraq (with the Basra Petroleum
Company), Qatar and Abu Dhabi, rather than the slower
take-over during a period of five years that had been originally
envisaged by the Gulf oil states.

The Kuwait state's assumption of control of the oil industry
coincided with the huge increase in oil revenues from the price
rises in· 1973-74. In the decade between 1962-72, Kuwait
earned £3,100 million (KD2,635 million) from oil. In 1972-74,
she earned another estimated £4,800 million, bringing the total
for 1962-74 to £7,900 million. During the next five years until
1980 she may earn another £20,000 million.

Where do these huge amounts of money go? The money all
passes in the first place through the hands of the Kuwait
Government. In the decade up to 1972, before the oil price
increases changed the whole scale of the state's financial
resources, the government spent most of the oil money at home
on the current annual budgets, on capital development or on
land-purchase schemes – government expenditure for 1971-72
was KD405 million (£476 million); and it saved part of it. By
1972 about KD700 million (£823 million) was held in reserves
and public investments abroad. The remainder, over £500
million, was given or lent abroad during the decade in various
forms of aid to other Arab countries. Much of the large sums
which subsequently passed into private hands through such
transactions as land purchase was also invested
abroad – Kuwait was then saving 40 to 50 per cent of her GNP
and investing 40 per cent of this abroad. There are no reliable
figures for Kuwaiti private holdings abroad, but foreign assets
held by commercial banks in 1972 totalled £350 million.

The vast increase in oil revenues since 1972-73 brought an
expansion of all these four elements of government expenditure, public and private savings and investment, and foreign

aid. But the proportions changed. Domestic government expenditure, including development investment, although it rose in the budgets from KD310 million in 1972-73 to KD959 million in 1974-75, could no longer absorb more than a quarter to a third of the oil revenues.

In 1974 oil revenue was estimated to be between £2,700 million and £3,000 million in excess of domestic needs. More than £450 million of this surplus was committed in aid to Arab and African countries and in subscriptions to international multilateral aid institutions such as the International Monetary Fund and IDA. Probably a similar amount was committed in military support for Egypt, Syria and Jordan, the Arab 'confrontation' states facing Israel.

According to the Kuwait Minister of Finance, Mr Abdurrahman al Attiqi, the government intended that in 1975 half of Kuwait's revenue should be invested in local projects, one quarter given in grants or loans to other Arab countries and most of the rest made available as aid to other developing countries. By 1980 all the state income would be needed for investment in Kuwait and in other developing countries. But during 1975-80 it looked as though Kuwait might still have more than £10,000 million surplus to her domestic requirements, part of which would go in foreign aid and part would be invested or held in reserves abroad. By March 1974 declared foreign assets under the control of the Ministry of Finance and Oil were about £1,700 million and at the end of the same year Kuwait's foreign exchange reserves stood at £770 million. Kuwaiti private holdings abroad are believed also to have risen to a figure equal to that of the state's. By 1975 Kuwait's total foreign monetary holdings were estimated at between £4,500 and £5,000 million.

The main purpose of this book is to describe Kuwait's aid operations and particularly one important aspect of them. In the last resort they will depend on the development of Kuwait itself, so let us look first at the effect the sudden torrent of oil money has had on the Kuwaitis. For good or ill it has brought enormous material and moral changes to Kuwait, transforming it in little more than a decade from a quiet traditional desert town into a kind of Arab Los Angeles, spreading its highways and suburbs over the surrounding desert to take the daily flow of its scores of thousands of big American cars. It created a state and a society in which public and private enterprise, modern welfare socialism and the ancient patriarchal authority of the desert are curiously blended.

Some rough indices of Kuwait's social and economic growth during that decade may be cited here. Between 1963 and 1971: electricity consumption increased from 508 megawatts to 2,636 megawatts; 1,000 kilometres of new paved roads were built; the number of schools rose from 140 to 245; pupils from 59,551 to 150,679; teachers from 2,941 to 10,413. In 1966 Kuwait University was opened. Between 1965 and 1971, the government built 10,352 houses for Kuwaiti low-income groups. Between 1962 and 1971 the government health services almost doubled in size: the number of doctors and dentists rose from 341 to 666 and other medical staff from 1,999 to 3,557. The number of hospitals was reduced from twelve to ten but clinics and health centres increased from 184 to 302.

In weathering these changes and absorbing the sudden tremendous impact from the outside world, not only in the shape of goods and ideas, but also in the form of over 450,000 foreign immigrants, the tolerant, outward-looking and practical attitudes acquired by the Kuwaitis through their past history of trading and seafaring stood them in good stead.

The beginning of the oil boom coincided with the accession to power in 1950 of the late Sheikh Abdullah As-Salim As-Sabah, who was a more democratically-minded ruler than his predecessor. The coincidence marked the first steps towards a gradual devolution of political power, a resharing of the new wealth and the planning of Kuwait's economic and social development.

For the first time Kuwait city had an elected municipal council with some say in the spending of the oil revenues and the future organisation of the city. Twelve years later, soon after the British treaty was ended and Kuwait became fully independent, and a member of the Arab League and the United Nations, a constituent assembly was formed to draft a new state constitution. A fifteen-man cabinet was appointed and elections to a 50-seat National Assembly were held in 1963 and again in 1967, 1971 and 1975. The powers of the Assembly are limited since only the Ruler and the Council of Ministers or cabinet can initiate legislation. But any minister can be forced to resign by a no-confidence vote in the Assembly. The Assembly can also complain to the Ruler about the premier, and the Ruler can then either dismiss the premier or dissolve the Assembly. The Ruler's control over the oil revenues is limited by the annual budget which must be approved by the Assembly.

The elections to the Assembly in 1971 and 1975 appear to have been less subject to government influence than the two previous ones, though there were again accusations of the gerrymandering of constituencies. Bedouin from the desert were said to have been brought in and if necessary given Kuwaiti citizenship to vote in areas where the opposition was strong.

The reins of power are still held by an oligarchy formed by the ruling family, headed by the Ruler, to which some members of the merchant and new technical class have been coopted. But this power is to a certain extent tempered and balanced by a more vociferous opposition in the Assembly, by the growth of an educated class and by a press which is freer than in many Arab countries.

In the cabinet formed after the 1971 elections, most of the key posts were held by members of the two branches of the ruling family, the Jabirs and the Salims. The present Ruler, Sheikh Sabah-As-Salim, took over in 1965 on the death of Sheikh Abdullah As-Salim As-Sabah. His cousin from the other branch of the family, Sheikh Jabir, is Crown Prince and became Premier. The latter's brother, Sheikh Sabah Al Ahmad, was Minister of Foreign Affairs and Information. The Ruler's nephew, Sheikh Saad, was Minister of Defence and Interior and another nephew was commander of the National Guard. But the important posts of Minister of Finance and Oil, of Minister of State for Cabinet Affairs and Minister of Education went to representatives of the new educated class from outside the family ranks and two other technical ministries were given to businessmen.

There were about a dozen university graduates and professional men in the Assembly in 1971-5, compared with only two in the previous Assembly, among a pro-Government majority of merchants and tribal leaders. Several of the graduates were to be found in the opposition groups which formed about a fifth of the Assembly and stretched from Left to Islamic Right. The most radical and influential element in the opposition – unofficial, since officially there are no political parties – were the six members sympathetic with the left-wing, pan-Arab Nationalist Movement, whose leader is a well-known local physician, Dr Ahmed Khatib. Opposition themes, apart from echoing the radical nationalist political currents of the Arab world, were broadly concerned with greater political liberalisation, such as permission for political parties and votes for women, with attacks on bureaucratic inefficiency and corruption, better treatment for non-Kuwaitis, and more careful economic provision for the day when Kuwait's oil supplies begin to run out.

It was pressure from the Assembly opposition which forced the government to impose a ceiling on oil production in 1972 and to drop its proposed 25 per cent participation agreement with the oil companies in favour of a 60 per cent share leading to eventual full control.

In the 1975 elections a similar pattern was repeated in both the new Assembly and cabinet. In the sixteen-man cabinet, members of the ruling family still held five key portfolios with the Crown Prince as premier. More than half of the 48 Assembly members who stood for re-election lost their seats, including one of the radical group. The trend towards younger and better educated members was maintained among government supporters, independents and the opposition. The trend was accepted by the government but it could also count on the loyalty of some twenty mainly Bedouin constituencies to maintain its majority.

The pressure for a freer and more efficient society seemed likely to grow as the new University of Kuwait began to pour out its graduates in increasing numbers to join the stream of the thousands of young Kuwaitis returning from studies abroad. Though easy money has shown signs of sapping the energies and ambitions of some Kuwaiti youth, educated Kuwaitis are aware that if they do not keep up in the race for modernisation they will find themselves increasingly dependent on the foreign residents and workers who already form a majority of the population.

At present these foreigners, even those who have been long resident or who were born in Kuwait, are politically and in some respects economically second-class citizens. The electorate is limited to literate, native-born Kuwaiti males over 21. This means that in 1972 out of a population of some 750,000 (since increased to nearly a million) only 40,000 had the vote.

Most of the more than 450,000 foreigners are from other Arab countries, over a third of them Palestinians, but there are also a considerable number of Iranians as well as some Indians and Pakistanis.

Theoretically foreigners can acquire Kuwaiti citizenship after 15 years' residence, though this provision has been suspended in practice since the 1967 Arab-Israeli war brought a new wave of Palestinian refugee immigrants. But even when naturalised they cannot vote or occupy the most senior government posts. Without citizenship they not only have no vote but cannot own landed property or run their own business except with a Kuwaiti partner, though this provision is frequently got round. Except for the free health service and primary education, foreign workers have less priority than Kuwaitis in access to social benefits. They usually earn less than Kuwaitis in similar jobs but they come to Kuwait nevertheless for jobs and money and in some cases because they enjoy greater freedom and business opportunities there than in their own country.

Kuwait citizens earning less than £2,000 a year are entitled to receive special government aid, but many Iranian immigrants who, until the oil boom in Iran, provided most of the unskilled labour, earn less than £300 a year and get no subsidy. Working for the Government – which employs two-thirds of the Kuwaiti labour force – is an additional form of social security since many of the jobs appear to demand only symbolic effort or perfunctory attendance.

Kuwaitis also enjoy completely free medical and hospital care, free education up to university level with grants for students, housing subsidies, a free local telephone system and free school meals dispatched from a fantastic central kitchen which can provide more than 50,000 meals a day.

An obvious danger of political instability arises from too sharp differences between the two halves of the population. This was one of the reasons that led the Kuwait Government to ask its Planning Board to work out a new population policy which would deal with problems of citizenship. Other reasons were its recognition of Kuwait's need to retain skilled foreign labour and the fact that, without certain basic decisions or assumptions about the future size and character of the population, economic or urban planning was almost impossible.

If the aim was a high rate of economic growth, this could only be sustained with the help of foreign labour; indeed, if the· population growth were to be slowed down or stabilised, it might involve reducing oil production. Of Kuwait's average population increase of seven per cent over the past decade, three per cent has been from natural increase and four per cent from immigration. If this growth were to continue it would affect the physical as well as economic planning of the state – implying more houses and social services, more roads, water, electricity and so on. It would also have obvious political repercussions in making the Kuwaitis even more of a minority in their own country.

The Population Commission set up by the Planning Board recommended a new system of permanent residency as a method of acquiring a form of citizenship giving all rights except political rights. The selection of such citizens would be based not only on length of residence but also on age, education, language and skills. The Commission forecast an increase in the foreign labour force. Its report has not yet been adopted by the Planning Board or officially published.

Planning of a kind has existed in Kuwait since the early fifties when the municipal council, on British advice, commissioned a development plan for Kuwait City.

It was a plan for the physical reconstruction of the city, not for the country's economic development, but, whether consciously or not, it also had important social and economic repercussions.

The first part of the plan was for the extension of the city beyond the old wall with a series of ring roads and new residential areas. But the crucial decision was whether to leave the old city as it was or to rebuild it as a new government and business centre. After a hot debate it was decided to demolish and rebuild the old city centre. The government purchase of privately-owned land for this purpose fulfilled two aims: it assured government control of development and at the same time it was a simple and rapid method – before other social welfare and social security schemes or the expansion of government jobs – of sharing out some of the oil revenues instead of leaving them entirely in the hands of the ruling family. The biggest share-out took place between 1964 and 1968 when the Government spent over £300 million in land-purchase. Between 1964 and 1972 it spent altogether £422 million (KD360.6 million) for this purpose and now owns 95 per cent of the land in Kuwait.

Although there was little historic sentiment or architectural merit attached to the old city, its destruction and replacement by a new motorised city covering twenty times the former area meant also a blow at the traditional way of life of a close-knit community which had been like that of a medieval town. This intimacy had helped to maintain traditional social values, loyalty to the family, tribe, community and religion, the personal frugality and thrift born of poverty, and a conservative attitude towards the status of women. Neither the sense of intimacy nor the connected values have been entirely destroyed, but they have been overlaid by the fragmentation, dispersal, anonymity and thirst for change characteristic of modern urban life, and by the opportunities for material self-indulgence opened up in a suddenly wealthy consumer society.

In 1953 the Kuwait Government established a development board, and a development programme was drawn up. The programme consisted mostly of the provision of physical infrastructure, such as roads, schools, hospitals, electric power and water, including the world's biggest plant for the distillation of fresh water from the sea. There was also some encouragement of local industry: in 1961 the government began to take part directly with private enterprise in financing new industrial ventures.

In 1962 the present Planning Board was set up. It is under the chairmanship of the prime minister, and includes other ministers and some non-official members. It was supposed to take over the role of the cabinet in dealing with economic and social affairs. But it was not until 1967 that the first comprehensive five-year plan was submitted to the National Assembly. It was then shelved by the Assembly with the tacit connivance of the Government. This was partly for domestic political reasons and partly because the 1967 war and Kuwait's subsidies to Egypt and Jordan led to a reduction in home development spending. In 1968 the planning board ceased to hold regular meetings.

But in 1971 it was revived with a new composition – ten members instead of four representing private business – following the election of the new Assembly and the appointment of a less conservative cabinet.

Meanwhile economic development continued on a piecemeal basis and faced problems special to Kuwait and other Gulf oil states. Agriculture is virtually non-existent in Kuwait because of the desert terrain, scanty rainfall and lack of economic sources of water for irrigation. Farming and fishing between them employ less than 2,000 people. The oil industry, the mainspring of wealth and almost the only local source of raw material, itself employs only 7,000 workers.

The government is the biggest employer, especially of Kuwaiti labour. It employs 38 per cent of the total available man-power and 75 per cent of the Kuwaiti labour force. Wages and salaries are also the main item in government expenditure. These increased from KD63.9 million in 1964-65 to an estimated KD184.3 million for 1972-73. Together with the land purchase schemes, this high level of government employment is the main means of achieving a social distribution of the state's oil wealth. Its direct beneficiaries are in the first place Kuwaiti citizens. But much of this expenditure has a social and political rather than an economically productive purpose.

For the creation of genuinely productive jobs and for the diversification of the economy to reduce future reliance on oil, hopes have necessarily been pinned on industrialisation and on making Kuwait a commerical, financial and technological centre. The idea has been to use for these purposes the by-products of oil, the cheap power from natural gas available in the oilfields, the large amounts of surplus capital from oil earnings and the brains and skills that money can buy.

In 1963 a British firm of consultants produced a report for the Kuwait Government on diversification. It recommended the development of petro-chemicals, especially fertilisers, of cement, plastics, silicon glass and tyres, aluminium smelting and steel making, and manufacture of refrigeration equipment.

But Kuwaiti private investors were at first reluctant to put their money into local industries, partly because of the traditional preference for investment in land and property or commercial transactions with a high and fast rate of profit. Another reason was the not ill-founded fear that industries in Kuwait face such obstacles that they cannot be competitive without government support. The local market is small and all raw materials except oil have to be imported. Skilled labour is in short supply and also mostly comes from abroad. The infrastructure and investment facilities on which industry could rely in more developed countries were missing.

The Government tried to overcome some of these obstacles by itself sharing in financing industrial projects, by providing credit and infrastructure facilities and by tariff protection of the home market.

The Kuwait National Petroleum Company, the Petro-Chemical Industries and Fertiliser Company and the big Shuaiba oil refinery were among the new industrial projects financed partly by the Government during the sixties. The oil refinery opened in 1965 was the centrepiece of a new industrial complex at Shuaiba, one of two new industrial satellite towns outside Kuwait city, the other being the oil town of Ahmadi. At Shuaiba the Government offered industrialists gas, power and water supplies and docking facilities. It also in 1965 passed the National Industries law to grant industry tariff protection and tax concessions.

Later industrial developments included a new 4.5 million tons a year natural gas liquification plant due to be completed in 1978 at an estimated cost of nearly £400 million. Four liquid gas tankers being built in France will be added to Kuwait's existing tanker fleet of eleven vessels totalling over two million tons. The Kuwait Shipping Company also has 23 ships operating and fifteen more on order. In 1975 the 300,000 tons a year cement plant at Shuaiba was expected to be complemented by a second plant with a capacity of 750,000 tons.

A World Bank report on Kuwait's industries suggested the creation of an industrial development organisation which might match the supply of credit with careful supervision of projects and management, rather as the Kuwait Fund for Arab Economic Development does when it lends money in other Arab countries. In 1974 the Government set up the Kuwait Industrial Bank to meet at least part of this purpose.

The performance of Kuwaiti industry, including the state-financed petro-chemicals and fertiliser companies, has been erratic. In 1971-2 manufacturing still supplied only three per cent of GDP, and construction 2.8 per cent compared with 63 per cent for oil and gas. But the general trend in the main industries – chemical fertilisers, building materials and flour mills – over the past few years has been upward. By 1971-2 non-oil industrial production totalled KD41 million in value and had increased by three per cent over the preceding five years. In chemical fertilisers, production of urea rose from 44,500 metric tons in 1967 to 182,200 metric tons in 1971 and over two million tons in 1974, and ammonium sulphate from 62,500 to 65,400 metric tons to 658,000 tons in 1974. Ammonia production also increased to nearly 1,900,000 tons in 1974. Chemical fertilisers were the main factor in the substantial rise in non-oil exports of Kuwaiti origin and were the second biggest export after oil.

In addition to its participation in and support for local industry, the Government has also financed or shared in numerous Kuwaiti financial institutions, banks and investment companies engaged in both domestic and foreign operations. But Kuwait has still a long way to go before it rivals Beirut's former status as a financial and commercial centre. One obstacle to this aspiration has been the Government prohibition on foreign ownership of banks and finance companies. But, especially since 1973, there has been a big increase in the number of joint ventures between Kuwaiti public and private investors and foreign concerns, especially in other Arab countries.

The abandoned first five-year plan envisaged government capital expenditure of KD507 million (£591 million) between 1967-72. The amount actually spent in the public sector was KD260 million (£303 million) and the next three or four years were seen as an interim period of catching up on postponed public works projects. A second five-year development plan was being prepared in 1971-2 which was intended to be based partly on a new physical plan prepared by the British town planner, Professor Colin Buchanan, and on the population policy studies undertaken by the Planning Board.

The new plan was also expected to place more emphasis on Kuwait's role in the Arab region and on the Arab Common Market. Although the prospects for an effective Arab Common Market did not look bright, the then Director General of the Kuwait Planning Board, Mr Ahmed Duaij, believed that the Arabs had no choice but to try and develop a Common Market in the face of the other big regional groupings, the European Community, the African Common Market and the Asian group centred on India. The Gulf area, with only 1.5 million people – if one leaves out Iran – is not big enough for meaningful industrial development, he says, whereas the Arab countries could form a market of 100 million people. Moreover, the foreign investments Kuwait needs to place to help ensure a future income apart from oil will, he feels, be as sound and secure in the Arab World as in the West.

But the plan preparation seems to have been overtaken by events, by the big changes of 1973, the impact of the Middle East war and the increases in oil prices and revenues. Development has instead continued on a year-to-year basis. Development budget allocations rose from KD88.5 million (£132 million) in 1973-4 to KD145 million (£217 million) in 1974-5 (out of a total budget expenditure of KD959 million – £1,400 million) and a similar sum was anticipated for 1975-6 (out of a total budget of KD910 million – £1,365 million).

The development allocations were mostly for electricity and water projects and other public works, including an extension of Shuwaikh port. Contracts were awarded for two new power stations with a capacity of 800 megawatts and KD30.3 million (£45 million) was allocated to extend the telephone network. Other projects include a television centre, thirty schools, five hospitals, a new airport runway and a KD46 million (£69 million) sports complex.

All these were in addition to the major projects already mentioned such as the new liquid gas plant, and oil and gas transport. But oil remains the key to both the development of Kuwait itself and to the help it can give to other Arab and Third World countries.

Even with a restricted production and a slackening in the increase in world consumption, the European demand for Middle East oil is likely to remain high enough to ensure Kuwait of an income of some £4,000 million a year over the rest of the decade and perhaps more thereafter. But what about Kuwait's ability to satisfy that demand? How long will Kuwait's oil last? Orthodox expert opinion is that Kuwait's reserves are enormous and will last between sixty and seventy years at the present (1975) rate of output. Kuwait's 'published proved' reserves were estimated in 1973 as 9,300 million tons (11,000 millions tons if one includes Kuwait's share of the Neutral Zone). This compares with 7,900 million tons for the whole of North America, 17,500 million for Saudi Arabia (the biggest in the Middle East, with Kuwait second), and 84,100 million tons for the world as a whole.

But some critics in Kuwait feared that her reserves might be exhausted in 25 years or less if production were not restricted. The question became a matter of controversy in the National Assembly, both among the radical group and those pressing for a more vigorous development of the Kuwaiti economy and for a reduction of Kuwait's spending in other Arab countries. It led in 1972 to the Kuwait government imposing a ceiling on increases in oil production. Output was restricted to three million barrels a day. The Assembly finance committee pressed for a ceiling of only 1.5 million barrels a day but it was feared that this would reduce the supplies of natural gas on which industrial development plans were based. Actual production in 1974 was the equivalent of 2,275,000 barrels a day or 2,755,000 barrels a day including the Neutral Zone.

In her first decade as an independent state, before the great leap in oil revenues in 1973, Kuwait, as already noted, provided over £500 million in public grants, loans and other forms of assistance to other Arab countries. Between the 1967 war and 1973 the bulk of this money was taken up by annual direct grants which still continue to Egypt and Jordan of KD50 million (£58 million) to compensate them for war losses.

Before 1967 Kuwait had made numerous Government loans and gifts from its state reserves to Arab governments for budgetary support or balance of payments assistance, including an early £25 million long-term loan to Iraq which helped to smooth the path for Baghdad's relinquishment of its territorial claim to Kuwait. By 1968 these loans to nine Arab countries totalled £145 million. Kuwait also then allocated 0.5 per cent of her national income – some KD2 million a year – to the provision of schools, hospitals and other services to the then Trucial States and the Yemens through the General Authority for the Arabian Gulf and the South Arabian States.

Finally, there was the Kuwait Fund for Arab Economic Development which in the first eleven years of its operations lent KD106.4 million (£123.4 million) to finance more than thirty projects in a dozen Arab countries.

Since the last Middle East war and the oil price increases in 1973 the scale of Kuwait's aid effort has vastly increased. It has been extended in scope to include not only the Arab countries but also other Muslim states and the developing countries of the Third World as a whole.

As already noted, Kuwait is estimated to have commited more than £450 million in 1974 to external economic aid and probably about a similar sum in 1973-4 to military support for the Arab 'confrontation states'. This aid was in three different forms: to multilateral development institutions, to regional organisations, and to direct bilateral assistance.

The first heading included 55 million dollars (£25.5 million) to the International Development Association; a contribution of 480 million dollars (£220 million) to the special oil facility of the International Monetary Fund; purchases of World Bank bonds totalling over 400 million dollars (£182 million); and 36 million dollars (£16.3 million) for various United Nations aid agencies.

Under the second heading of aid to regional development organisations there were: Kuwait's share of KD30 million (£45 million) in the Arab Fund for Economic and Social Development which the Kuwait Government was considering increasing to KD75 million in 1975 when the member governments passed a resolution to increase the Arab Fund's capital from KD102 million to KD400 million (£600 million); a 20 million dollar share in the Arab Bank for Economic Development in Africa; 30 million dollars to the Special Arab Fund for Africa (to help meet the increased oil costs for African countries); 17 million dollars to the Special Fund for Arab non-oil producers; over 100 million dollars to the Islamic Development Bank, and a 17 million dollar loan to the Asian Development Bank.

Under the third heading of bilateral aid came a large variety of government to government grants and loans; assistance from the General Authority for the Gulf and South Arabia, the budget of which was raised to KD10 million (£15 million) in 1975-6; and, finally, the operations of the Kuwait Fund for Arab Economic Development. The Fund's loans had risen to a total of some KD259 million (£384 million) by 1975.

This impressive aid effort has been inspired partly by genuine altruism and partly by a political purchase of good will on the part of a weak state with more powerful neighbours.

Within a few months of achieving independence in 1961 Kuwait had to fend off a threat to her sovereignty from General Qassim in Iraq. As her ability or willingness to rely on British protection was reduced and eventually ended, so her need increased to rely on recognition and support of her status by the rest of the Arab world. The first essential of her foreign policy was to help maintain political stability in the Gulf area. As part of this purpose she aimed to establish credentials as a progressive state in harmony with the predominant currents of Arab nationalist sentiment, though as far as possible without taking sides in Arab quarrels.

But behind this policy was not merely prudence but a certain positive vision of the interdependence of the Arab world and more recently of its place and that of the developing countries as a whole in the world economy and world community, a vision which has been most clearly manifest in the work of the Kuwait Fund which the Kuwait Government was considering increasing to KD75 million.

3 The Kuwait Fund

The history of the Kuwait Fund for Arab Economic Development has two main phases. The first covers the first twelve years of its existence when its concern was with only the Arab world, and its funds were relatively limited. The second phase runs from July 1974 when with the new flow of oil money, its capital was quintupled to KD1,000 million (£1,500 million), and its responsibilities extended in a new charter to helping all developing states. This broadening of its concern has not basically changed the nature of its work or of its role in the Arab world of which the foundations were laid in the first phase. Such change as there has been is in the new framework created by the big increase in Arab oil revenues and the sudden proliferation of other Arab development funds and institutions. These bodies have been in many cases modelled on the Kuwait Fund or have been helped into existence by the Fund and are able to supplement its development work in different but parallel fields.

The Kuwait Fund originally was established in December 1961, on the last day of Kuwait's first year of national independence. The Fund thus had its origins in a time when Kuwait was looking for recognition of its new status and for international support against a threat from Iraq. At the same time criticism was increasingly being heard in the Arab world, especially among the radically-minded, about the 'Bedouin nouveaux-riches' of the Arabian oil states. Saudi Arabia was perhaps the main target for such criticism, but Kuwait seemed more vulnerable, and Iraq's threat had brought her new wealth further into the limelight.

Nevertheless the original inspiration of the fund was not entirely defensive; it also had a positive element. There was behind it a local tradition of mutual help springing from Kuwait's history as an internationally-minded, seafaring mercantile community. The tradition of help for a neighbour in distress which led ship-owners or merchants to rally round the family of one whose ship was lost led Kuwaitis to recognise more readily that the whole Arab area needed aid.

The Iraqi crisis and Kuwait's application for membership of the United Nations led to the dispatch around the world, especially to Africa, Asia, Latin America and the Arab world, of official missions to explain Kuwait's point of view. The aim was to secure support for Kuwait's case against Iraq at the United Nations and to propagate an image of Kuwait different from that of an extravagant newly-rich Bedouin sheikhdom. On their return the missions recommended setting up an international aid fund to show the world and the Arab countries in particular that Kuwait was a responsible member of the international community and ready to use its new wealth to help those in need.

A somewhat similar process led to the expansion of the Fund's scale and scope in 1974. After the 1973 Middle East war and the quadrupling of oil prices, another Kuwaiti mission, this time staffed by the Fund, was sent to African and Asian countries to show them that the Arabs as a whole were aware of their needs, were ready to help them and were anxious to retain their political sympathy in the Arab conflict with Israel.

There are many claimants to be the father of the Kuwait Fund. It is impossible to pinpoint one person but some of the credit for the eventual decision to create it must go to the then Ruler of Kuwait, a man of international outlook, the present Ruler who was then Minister of Foreign Affairs and the present Prime Minister who was then Minister of Finance. It was in the Ministry of Finance that the original basic concepts were worked out and that the first brief law of seven articles setting up the Fund was drafted. But from this beginning the Fund might have developed quite differently from the way it has. The evolution of its present operational philosophy and its remarkable degree of independence from political manipulation, comparable with that of the BBC in Britain, are the result largely of the special nature of Kuwait's political society and of the efforts of the present Director-General, Abdulatif Youssef Al Hamad, who has run the Fund almost from its beginning.

The Fund's character, purposes and organisation were set out in more elaborate and more workable terms in its second Charter, dated 14 April 1963, which governed its operations until its new charter was granted in 1974.

The new Charter repeats most of the provisions of the first one, except as regards the Fund's capital and geographical scope, and the appointment of the Prime Minister instead of the Minister of Finance to be chairman of the governing board.

The Fund is an agency of the Kuwait Government but is an autonomous public corporation with its own legal personality. It has two remarkable characteristics as an aid institution: it was the first, and for many years the only, national agency – as opposed to an inter-governmental agency – set up for the specific purpose of regional development; and until recently it was a rare example of a national agency giving aid to developing countries which was itself financed by a non-industrial country.

The Fund's purpose as outlined in the original law was 'to assist the Arab states in developing their economy and to provide them with loans for the execution of their development programme.' In the first Charter this was redefined as being 'to contribute to Arab projects by granting loans to the Arab states and countries or by providing guarantees or by any other means that may be deemed fit by the Board of Directors.' In the 1974 Charter, Article Two defines the purpose of the Fund as 'to assist Arab and other developing states in developing their economies and, in particular, to provide such States with loans for the implementation of their development programmes . . .'

Article 13 of the new Charter says that the Fund may carry out this purpose by making loans to such states or to corporate entities which they control or which are controlled by joint ventures between these states, provided that the objectives of such corporate entities are not purely limited to the making of profit'. The Fund may also provide assistance by giving guarantees to states or corporate entities, 'or through any other means which the Board of Directors may consider appropriate.'

In practice most of the aid so far given by the Fund has been in the form of development loans – but the Fund is clearly not excluded from giving other forms of assistance. In recent years it has given an increasing number of direct grants for economic surveys and technical assistance programmes, and has begun to give loans for the general operations of local industrial banks, which themselves use the money to help finance specific projects.

Nor does the Fund in its dealings with the Arab world see its role as purely that of a lending institution or as a source of 'hand-outs' to the needy. It sees its function rather as that of a development agency, actively studying and promoting economic development in a business-like manner and providing a catalyst for a collective regional effort. This role has become more, not less, important with the great expansion of Arab capital available from oil and the growth of more Arab development institutions with big funds but little experience.

In its approach to the non-Arab developing countries, the Fund has not the same imperative of promoting regional development as in the case of the Arabs for whom regional integration has a political as well as economic motivation. And the non-Arab countries, like the Arab states, vary widely in their ability to organise their own development and use aid effectively.

The Kuwait Fund's governing body is a Board of Directors composed of eight Kuwaitis 'of recognised competence' appointed by the Prime Minister who is himself ex-officio chairman of the Board. The Prime Minister can delegate the Minister of Finance to act as chairman in his place. The Director-General, appointed by the Chairman on the recommendation of the Board, is in charge of administrative, financial and technical matters and is responsible for the day to day operation of the Fund.

The Board decides general policy and gives final approval to loans, and to the Fund's own accounts. In practice, however, the Director-General plays a very influential, indeed decisive, part, in both the formulation and the execution of policy. This has certainly been true of the present Director-General, Abdulatif Youssef Al Hamad, who has occupied this post since 1963. He has left the unmistakable imprint of his personality, quiet but tenacious, idealistic but practical, on the organisation, methods and above all the human style of the Fund's operations.

I first met Al Hamad in London in 1971 at the headquarters of the United Bank of Kuwait, discreetly and influentially established in a City alleyway in the shadow of the Bank of England. I saw a young-looking man in his middle thirties with a lean, alert face, shortish-cropped black hair, black-rimmed spectacles and a mild, slightly pedantic manner. He was wearing a dark chalk-striped suit and could at first sight have been any modestly prosperous City businessman. But behind the gentle appearance one quickly became aware of a buoyant character and a sensitive intelligence. A few weeks later I visited him again at the Fund headquarters in Kuwait, then an unassuming building looking like a small block of flats, in one of the sandy suburbs of the city. The Fund was then building its present handsome new headquarters in the centre of city. (It was doing so with some misgivings for fear that it might lose something of the compact intimate atmosphere of its old offices. In fact, through imaginative architectural design and the determination of the staff, much of this atmosphere has been preserved in the new building while gaining in space, comfort and modern equipment. In 1975, however, the old worry was renewed because the expansion of the Fund's activities seemed bound to involve a big increase in staff and the need for an additional office building.)

At my second meeting with him, Al Hamad was no longer in his City suit but in Kuwaiti national dress – the flowing white robe called the *dishdasha*, and the Arab headdress of *kefieh* and *agal*. Apart from being well suited for the hot summer climate, this costume seems to be usual for Kuwaitis in high official positions who try in all the rush of modernisation not to lose touch with their traditional Kuwaiti background, and may also thereby like to distinguish themselves from the many non-Kuwaiti Arabs who surround them.

Like many Kuwaiti institutions, the Fund has a very cosmopolitan, or rather inter-Arab staff. Of a total of about eighty in 1975, its score or so senior specialists came from half a dozen different Arab countries. They included distinguished academics, former senior civil servants, engineers and financial administrators. Among those I met in Kuwait or working in other Arab countries were a Palestinian professor of economics who had studied and taught in the United States, an Oxford-trained economist from Iraq, two other economics professors from Syria and Egypt, an Egyptian professor of international law, a Sudanese engineer who used to run the Sudan railways, another Sudanese who was governor of his country's Central Bank before joining the fund as financial adviser, and a young agronomist from the Yemen.

More young Kuwaiti graduates are now being recruited and

trained by the Fund. Some stay with the Fund, while others go on to leading positions in other Kuwaiti institutions. The aim is to train more Kuwaitis for technical as well as administrative jobs. Al Hamad is a Kuwaiti, as are also his deputy, Dr. Nasser Al-Sayer and the directors of all departments.

In an anticipated expansion of the staff to about 100 or 150, the proportion of Kuwaitis was expected to increase, but the Fund planned to retain a predominantly inter-Arab staff, as an integral part of its character. The expansion of the Fund's activities to non-Arab countries posed the question of recruiting some non-Arab staff, a difficult problem partly because of the common working language of Arabic, though the Fund's specialists are also fluent in English and sometimes also in French. So far there is only one non-Arab on the technical staff, a Ugandan African in the legal department.

Abdulatif Al Hamad himself studied in the United States, graduating from a small college near Los Angeles and then taking a course in international relations at Harvard. In 1961 when Kuwait was trying to get into the United Nations against a Soviet veto, he was coopted onto the Kuwaiti government mission in New York. Once Kuwait had got its UN membership, he was offered a career in the Foreign Ministry on his return to Kuwait. But he decided that the diplomatic service was too frustrating and too full of cocktail parties – not creative enough. So, although he knew nothing then about finance and economics, he joined the Fund, thinking he could be more useful there.

At that time, in September 1962, the Fund organisation still existed only on paper, though it had already granted its first loans. There was a Board of Directors and a Director-General, Abdul Aziz Al Bahr. Al Hamad was appointed assistant to the Director-General and succeeded him in the post a few months later. There was then only one other employee apart from himself. They worked from one or two rooms without even a clerk, and did everything from arranging loans to moving the office furniture around.

When Al Hamad became Director-General his first tasks were to build up a suitable organisation and to establish a proper method and philosophy of work. By that time the first loans – to Jordan and the Sudan – had already been made by the Fund without any serious prior investigation. Al

Hamad early sought the help and advice of the World Bank. An expert from the Bank came to Kuwait for two years to advise on loan procedures. Although the Fund took the Bank as its model, it adapted the Bank methods to its own circumstances. Al Hamad, while gratefully recognising the Bank's help, emphasises that the Fund is not just a smaller carbon copy of the Bank but has a philosophy of its own.

The Fund's philosophy and method of operation have had several distinguishing features. The first, compared with the World Bank, is its Arab character, using the word Arab in the widest sense of applying to all the Arabic-speaking countries. This, with its Arab staff, has given the Fund an intimate knowledge and an entrée in its operations in the Arab countries which are not possible for an international organisation coming from outside. In relations between the Fund and Arab governments, institutions and individuals, there is a high degree of dedicated involvement: there is no feeling of 'them' and 'us', the problems are 'ours'. For although the Fund was set up and is controlled by the Kuwait state, it was an Arab institution intended primarily for the development of all the Arabs by the Arabs themselves. It was rather as if the British Government, in its pan-European enthusiasm, had set up a fund for the development of Western Europe, with British money and a British Board of Directors and Director-General and a staff drawn from all over the European Common Market.

With the expansion of its activities to the Third World as a whole, the Fund did not intend to lose sight of this primary task of Arab self-development. Nor did it expect to be able to enjoy the same intimate relations in aid operations with non-Arab states as with its Arab partners. But it believed its path in non-Arab countries was smoothed by the fact that Kuwait was itself a developing country and the Arab countries as a whole are an integral part of the Third World and share its needs and aspirations.

Aid to the Third World was seen, like that to the Arab countries, as part of a broad pattern of self-help by the developing countries and a planned international redistribution of resources within the world economy.

Two other principles of the Fund philosophy are its political and ideological neutrality in dealing with other countries and its own autonomy and resistance to political pressures in

Kuwait itself. The Fund, claims Al Hamad, does not exert the kind of 'leverage' or pressure on governments to adopt particular kinds of economic policies or ideological attitudes that other aid institutions are sometimes accused of using. It is aware of the social and political factors affecting economic growth but believes it must work within the existing social and political situation in each Arab or developing country. It is reluctant to challenge priorities in the development programme of a potential borrower: its only requirement for aid is that the project under consideration for a loan should have a high priority in the development programme, that it should be intrinsically sound and that there should be evidence that it would have a significant impact on the economic development of the recipient country.

The basic element in economic development, Al Hamad believes, is the human being, the human mind. Development is essentially a mental process; the attitude of mind is basic. The success of development has to be measured not only by the number of projects or programmes successfully executed but by the degree to which this brings the 'take-off' point nearer. And in thus transforming the structure of production, the inner psychological drive and determination to suceed are of crucial importance.

This is one reason why the Fund itself has attached so much importance to the human factor in its operation, in its choice of staff and the way they operate both at headquarters and in the field. At home the 'spirit' of the Fund is informal, hardworking, cooperative and egalitarian: abroad it aims at a close working relationship of trust, and an unobtrusive frankness based on sympathy with and realistic knowledge of the countries and personalities involved. The 'feel' of a country or economic situation born of first hand experience, is considered as important in forming a judgement on aid projects as paper data or mere technological ability.

This 'feel', already existing or acquired over the years in the case of the Arab world, will need time to achieve in the new field of operations in non-Arab countries. One problem already encountered is that of language, especially in dealing with some French-speaking African countries.

The Fund staff have been carefully recruited for their ability, experience and character, because of the importance Al

Hamad attaches to the personal influence and example of the Fund officials in dealing with client governments. The tone is set by their own relaxed relations with each other. When they are at headquarters they reduce formal meetings to a minimum. Instead they often talk things over during the morning coffee-break when they gather informally in an atmosphere like that of a university senior common room. They work as a team of equals, with the Director-General only the *primus inter pares*. They feel their way to a consensus which is achieved usually because of the common approach created by years of working together.

But their standards are high. In a reaction against the casual slapdash methods often found in Arab bureaucracies they are scornful of inefficiency or slackness. 'We sniff if someone is two minutes late for an appointment', said one of them, 'but at our staff meetings Abdulatif warns us against being too arrogant.'

Al Hamad is aware that, especially in view of the intense competition for talent in the Arab world, the Fund will be hard put to maintain these high standards and methods in a rapid staff expansion, but he has been making every effort to do so.

Staff from all the departments of the Fund take part in appraising and discussing a loan application before it is approved and sent to the Board of Directors for final confirmation.

In most cases the real point of decision about a project comes earlier than the formal approval and it is sometimes difficult to identify exactly when it occurs. For by the time a project has crystallised in a form suitable for a Fund loan, the Fund staff have often already been intimately involved in its evolution and in helping the government concerned to iron out attendant problems or to give more practical shape to the original concept.

Indeed, this kind of economic midwifery has become almost as important a function of the Fund, especially in the less-developed Arab countries, as the money it lends. In Bahrain, for example, the Fund's most important contribution to the setting up of a multi-million pound aluminium smelter was not the small share of the capital it provided but the advice and know-how it supplied in developing the project from an idea to a detailed proposal able to attract outside investment. In other cases, the Fund's involvement is so close that it is itself looking for opportunities for development which it can help governments to investigate. In the Sudan, for example, the Fund prompted the government to undertake pre-investment studies of a coordinated national transport system, which the Fund is helping to finance.

The original object of the Kuwait Fund, says Al Hamad, was to promote the welfare of the Arab individual, and this attitude transcends all boundaries or ideologies. It has now been extended to include all developing peoples but how far the same degree of political non-discrimination will apply in the case of non-Arab states remains to be seen.

Because of its Arab character, its 'political neutrality' and general flexibility of approach, the Fund has sometimes been able to do things in Arab countries that non-Arab institutions could not do. It may find that its role as an instrument of a developing country will sometimes give it a similar advantage in dealing with other non-Arab developing countries as compared with international aid institutions which are largely controlled and staffed by the developed Western states.

This difference in approach made possible in the Arab world was demonstrated in the first operation which the Fund undertook in Tunisia, a loan for an electric power station granted in 1963. The World Bank had originally agreed to support the project but had been obliged to draw back because of still unsettled political problems of compensation by the Tunisian Government to the former French electricity companies which had been nationalised. Another project in Tunisia, this time for agricultural development, had been rejected by the World Bank because the expected economic return was too low. The Fund was not deterred from granting a loan by the low return – though the economic viability of any project is essential – because it considered that other social benefits from the project, in raising living standards and changing agricultural attitudes and social habits, were also important. More recently, Al Hamad points out, the World Bank itself, under Robert McNamara, has also begun to be more concerned with social change.

The Fund now enjoys a degree of political independence in its lending operations which is unrivalled by most other national aid agencies.

The Fund is, of course, under the control of the Kuwait

Government both through having the Prime Minister as the chairman of its governing board, and because the Government provides all its capital. It also has to submit its budget to the National Assembly for approval but this is only its small administrative budget, which in 1975-76 was KD3.7 million (£5.5 million); the Assembly has no direct control over the Fund's lending operations.

In fact, so far the Fund has usually succeeded in avoiding the two main kinds of political pressures – apart from a reduction of total funds – to which aid operations are most often subject in other countries: the allocation or reduction of aid according to political priorities or ideological preferences, and 'tied aid', the linking of aid to the supply of goods from the donor country.

This independence has not been achieved without a struggle. At first the Fund Director-General had to fight hard to establish the new concept that loans should be based on serious economic criteria, independently evaluated, and should not be simply political hand-outs ordered by Kuwait government ministers. One of the first tests occurred in 1963 when a mission from the newly-independent Algerian government, then the heroes of the Arab world, came to Kuwait in search of funds. Al Hamad was summoned back post-haste from an international conference by the Minister of Foreign Affairs and was told that the Fund must sign an aid agreement with the Algerians before the mission left. The Government wanted an immediate public agreement to show Kuwait's generosity and Arab fraternal feelings and thus enhance its prestige. It had not yet fully understood that there had to be an examination of the projects on which aid was to be spent.

To have followed the Minister's wishes would have killed the Fund's chances of developing into a serious independent body with objective economic criteria. But if the then newly-fledged Fund refused it would have built up powerful political resentment against itself. So Al Hamad compromised. He proposed that Kuwait agree at once to give Algeria a loan of £10 million, subject to agreement on the projects for which it was to be used. This satisfied the desire of the Kuwaiti and Algerian politicians for an immediate prestige agreement, while leaving control of how the money was to be spent in the hands of the Fund. Agreement was completed in a few days on the principle of financing projects but without commitment to any specific project until it had been fully appraised. It took another four years to negotiate all the projects.

The Fund's autonomy has been helped by the skill with which it concentrates on getting the right decisions taken while leaving the public glory to the ministers and politicians. Over the years it has also strengthened its position at home because the good international reputation it has built for itself has begun to reflect back on Kuwait itself. Kuwaiti politicians find this enhances the international prestige of the state and of themselves. The Fund's autonomy has become a valuable part of its reputation which the politicians now accept. Although up to 1973 the Fund had given in project loans less than half the amount given by the Kuwait government in 'political' loans, there was growing recognition that the Fund's money had been more effectively spent, even from the point of view of political prestige.

This success brought problems as well as opportunities. Faced with the new international responsibilities created by the 1973-4 increases in oil prices and revenues, the Kuwait Government made greater use of the Fund and its Director-General as a spokesman for its politico-economic policies towards the oil consumers, the industrial countries, and the Third World. The Director-General thus became more closely involved publicly with the conduct of the Kuwait Government's international policies. At the same time, the Fund's standing with the government enabled it quickly to seize the new opportunity to enlarge and broaden its aid operations.

This increased political involvement was perhaps inevitable because, in effect, after 1973 the theme of Arab oil money and development, which had been quietly pursued by the Fund for more than a decade, suddenly emerged as one of the most urgent and dominant themes of world politics.

'Political insurance' was of course one of the original motives for setting up the Kuwait Fund. Aid is clearly part of the process by which the state of Kuwait has sought the goodwill of other Arab countries and now seeks that of other developing countries, in order to strengthen its own independence and the international influence of the Arabs as a whole. As has been already pointed out, when the Fund was launched that independence was not only newly acquired but also directly threatened by the claims of Iraq. But political protection was not the only motive for creating the Fund, for such protection could probably have been achieved more simply by direct grants or by government-to-government loans.

Behind the conception of the Fund and its subsequent development there was undoubtedly a genuine vision; not only a real desire to use Kuwait's sudden great wealth to help other Arab countries, but also a belief in a common Arab destiny and in the need for all Arabs to cooperate in the revival of their once great civilisation. Similarly, retaining the political goodwill of the Afro-Asian countries and their votes for Arab causes at the United Nations was undoubtedly an important motive for extending the operations of the Fund to all developing countries, but there was also a genuine vision of a new world economic process. This vision was outlined in several speeches by Abdulatif Al Hamad at international meetings and was shared by other Arab spokesmen. It envisaged a triangular cooperation between the technologically advanced oil-consuming countries, the oil producers with surplus funds, and the developing countries seeking to industrialise and modernise themselves. Oil money and Western technology would together transform the economies and societies of the Third World, including the Arab countries. The oil price increases, if their results were properly managed, could bring about a more rapid and spectacular reallocation of international resources than anything priviously achieved through the aid programmes of the industrial states.

The working out of this process has begun but is still mostly for the future. In its more immediate concerns in the Arab world, Kuwait has tried to maintain a foreign policy which, while moving sympathetically with the main stream of Arab nationalism, avoids being forced to take sides in inter-Arab disputes. In the broader international scene Kuwait is officially non-aligned but leans towards the West and towards Muslim countries; this has not however prevented the Fund from giving loans to non-Muslim countries in Africa and Asia or to countries like Sri Lanka which are not only non-Muslim but have leftward-leaning regimes. Although many Arab states have republican regimes and at least partly socialist economies ideologically different from those of Kuwait, it has not barred them from Fund aid. By 1975 the Fund had granted loans or given other assistance to fourteen Arab countries including two new members of the Arab League – Mauritania and Somalia, and was considering aid to another new member, Oman. The four other members of the League – Saudi Arabia, Libya, Qatar and the Union of Arab Emirates in the Gulf, have oil revenues of their own. Some members of the UAE have already received substantial Kuwaiti aid, not from the Fund, but from the special fund for the Gulf and South Arabia, in the form of hospitals, schools and other social welfare benefits.

In recent years, the Fund has granted loans for projects in Syria and Iraq, where the Baathist regimes were for long critical of the rulers of the Arabian oil states, though usually, in the case of Kuwait, the criticism was expressed in more guarded, general ideological terms. If, as appears, there was a political brake put on Kuwait aid to Iraq as a result of their current border dispute this was probably the result of a straight state-to-state conflict in which incidents led to Kuwaiti blood being shed, rather than because of the ideological character of the Baghdad regime. The Fund was also approached by the revolutionary socialist regime of South Yemen for help when it was in desperate financial straits after achieving independence. An agreement was signed with South Yemen on the very day that the Kuwait regime was being denounced as being an 'imperialist stooge' in demonstrations in the streets of Aden.

A more recent demonstration of the Fund's autonomy – and, it might be said, of the flexibility in foreign policy that its existence gives to the Kuwait government – occurred in Jordan. After the civil war in 1970-71, in which King Hussein's army crushed the Palestinian guerrilla forces, the Kuwait Government suspended the subsidy it had been paying to the Jordan Government since the 1967 Khartoum agreement. But the Kuwait Fund continued its operations in Jordan and helped the Jordan Government to work out a new project to be jointly financed by the Fund and the World Bank. The Kuwait Government subsidy was later resumed.

When the Fund was first set up it had an authorised capital of KD50 million (£58 million). This was increased to KD100 million (£116 million) in 1963 and KD200 million (£232 million) in 1966. Then, in 1974, following the big increase in oil revenues, it was raised spectacularly to KD1,000 million (£1,500 million). But the actual amount of money available for loans has depended on the capital paid in each year by the

Kuwait Government. This in turn has depended on the condition of the state budget and reserves, on the government's other commitments and on the prevailing political climate. Up to 1966 the amount of capital paid in was KD68 million and in that year an attempt was made to systematise the annual increases of capital. It was agreed by the Government and National Assembly that up to the first KD100 million would come from the Government's reserves, while the next KD100 million would be provided from fixed annual budget appropriations. These appropriations would be kept in a special credit account and handed over to the Fund in the year following the year in which the Fund's commitments equalled half its capital – in other words when its loans and grants totalled KD100 million. But the situation was drastically changed by the 1967 war and the commitment then taken on by the Kuwait Government to pay KD50 million a year to Egypt and Jordan to compensate them for war losses. Between 1967 and 1971 the Fund received virtually no fresh capital from the Kuwait Government. The Fund had to rely on its own resources but this also brought the advantage of greater independence. In 1971 and 1972 the Fund received altogether another KD10.25 million following the big increase in Kuwait's oil revenues from the Teheran agreements between OPEC and the oil states in 1971. The Fund continued meanwhile to expand its lending within cautious limits: between 1968 and 1974 it increased its loan and grant commitments from KD56.65 million to KD134 million.

By early 1974, on the eve of its big expansion, the Fund's authorised capital was KD200 million, of which KD113 million had been paid in. When its authorised capital was increased to KD1,000 million the previous system of obtaining paid-in capital partly from government reserves and partly from budget appropriations was maintained. The new law laid down that up to KD400 million (£600 million) should be paid out of government reserves in transfers from time to time according to the needs of the Fund. The remaining KD600 million (£900 million) would be paid from a proportion of the budget revenues to be fixed annually. By 1975 the paid-in capital totalled KD328 million (£492 million).

The new situation created by this expansion of funds and of role will be discussed more fully later in this chapter. Meanwhile let us look again at the operations of the Fund during the preceding twelve years. I said earlier that during the leaner years, after the 1967 war, the Fund had managed to achieve a cautious expansion of its lending. Some might say that it was too cautious. For there are two aspects of the Fund's Charter which would have given it opportunities even then for lending on a far larger scale, indeed on a scale then proportionately far greater than that available to many bigger international aid institutions. First, all of the Fund's authorised capital can be regarded as investible and so available for loans; unlike most similar institutions, it does not have to set aside part of its capital as a guarantee of its own indebtedness.

Secondly, the Fund is entitled to borrow or issue bonds for up to twice its capital plus reserves. Since reserves are intended to be twenty per cent of capital, this means that before 1974 the Fund could eventually have borrowed up to KD480 million (£550 million). This would have given it a legal limit of KD680 million for lending, or over five times the amount it lent during its first twelve years of operation. Since 1974 this limit has been raised to KD3,400 million (£5,100 million).

But so far the Fund has not made use of its borrowing powers and now probably no longer would need to do so. It has been operating within the limits of its paid-in capital, together with money from repayments and interest and its own investment earnings. The Director-General of the Fund defends the application of this policy during the Fund's first decade on the grounds that during that period the Fund was still learning and consolidating. While gaining experience and establishing sound relationships with its client countries and other international agencies, it gave priority to 'caution, prudence and sufficient preparation'. The course of events has justified this policy in that when the big flood of oil money arrived from 1974 onwards the Fund found itself uniquely well-equipped among Arab institutions to deal with the new situation.

Another reason may have been political prudence. When the Fund was cut off temporarily from fresh injections of Government capital owing to the consequences of the 1967 war, there was growing domestic pressure to reduce Kuwait's foreign financial commitments in favour of home development. It may have seemed wiser for the Fund to 'maintain a low profile' until circumstances changed. Some of the pressure was eased by the increase in oil revenues from the Teheran agreements, which more than offset the subsidies to Egypt and Jordan.

Meanwhile the Fund authorities hoped to disarm potentially hostile critics by showing that the Fund was able to pay its way and continue operations with the good management of its existing resources. This may also have appeared a necessary extra defence of the Fund's political autonomy. Kuwait Fund loans are made in Kuwaiti dinars which are freely convertible and they can be used to buy goods from anywhere (except Israel, because of the Arab boycott). There was a clause in the Fund's first Charter (dropped from the 1974 charter), which said that projects for which loans are given 'should not be in conflict with the economic interest of Kuwait or any other Arab country'. At a pinch this could have been invoked by a domestic lobbyist to try, for example, to block a loan for an enterprise directly competitive with a similar one in Kuwait, but this did not happen because of the nature of the projects so far supported by the Fund. Moreover, pressure for 'tied aid' has not been a serious problem because Kuwait has few exports of her own apart from oil and petro-chemicals – though in 1971 the question was raised in the Kuwaiti press of linking aid to one Arab country with purchases of fertilisers from the then languishing Kuwaiti Chemical Fertilisers Company. So far, in any event, the Fund's Board and management have refused to adopt the concept of 'tied' loans. Nor has the Fund ever made it a condition of a loan that a project should be transferred from the public sector to private enterprise, though some of its advisers would undoubtedly like on pragmatic grounds to see a more active role for private enterprise in some Arab countries which have mixed or semi-socialist economies.

While the Fund has no philosophical objection to financing private sector projects, there are several reasons why its loans have, in fact, mostly been for projects in the public sector. First, the loans are made to governments or to government corporations, such as the Suez Canal Authority, and not to private companies. In two cases, small loans went to private companies – both were for tourist hotels in Jordan – and another bigger loan was being considered in 1967 for the Arab Potash Company also in Jordan – but these were made through the intermediary of a government agency.

The Fund is now, however, giving more indirect aid to smaller projects and to private enterprises through the medium of loans to local development banks. Following a Fund survey of industrial banks in the Arab countries, loans have been made to such banks in the Sudan, Morocco, Tunisia and Jordan. Second, the majority of Arab states now have at least partly socialised economies, especially in the field of industry and utilities, and the main impetus for development comes from the governments. Thirdly, the kind of infrastructure projects – in transport, electric power and irrigation – that the Fund has so far chiefly financed are by their nature nearly all under public ownership or control.

The Fund's conditions and procedures for granting loans are closely modelled on those of the World Bank, but they have some special features of their own. On controversial issues, such as whether aid should be tied to projects or given for general development; whether it should cover local currency costs or only foreign exchange; whether it should be only for materially productive projects or also for activities such as education which may indirectly stimulate production, the Fund until recently took the more orthodox conservative line then predominant in aid institutions.

So far (at the end of 1975) its loans have all been for specific projects or institutions and not for filling gaps in budgets or in balance of payments. (Aid for these latter purposes has been given by the Kuwait Government but not through the Fund.) The loans are paid against detailed bills for goods or services. The Director-General of the Fund believed that planning and the evaluation of needs in the Arab economies were still too vague and embryonic for 'programme aid' to be fully effective. However, in the new phase after 1974, the greater funds at his disposal may make him feel more able to experiment with programme aid and with other new forms of aid operation, as some of his staff would like to see happen.

The loans are given for part or whole of the foreign currency costs of 'productive' projects. They are not usually given for local currency costs, but exceptions can be authorised by the Fund's board; one such exception was a loan in 1973 to the North Yemen to cover the local costs of an agricultural project for which the foreign exchange element was being provided by the International Development Association. In the light of its own experience, the Fund management does not share the view of some critics that financing only the import element of a project encourages recipient countries to produce 'prestige' projects with a high import content.

The Fund finances 'productive' rather than 'social welfare' projects such as education, health and housing. It believes that building up the Arab countries' productive capacities should have top priority, since it is eventually on these that a higher level of social welfare expenditure will depend. Moreover, there are other agencies active in the social welfare field, including the Kuwait Government's aid agency for the Gulf and South Arabia and, in intention, the new Arab Fund for Economic and Social Development. But the trend at the World Bank towards support for 'non-materially productive' projects, such as education, has not gone unnoticed at the Fund headquarters.

The projects chosen for loans must be of high quality and with a high priority rating in the development programme of the receiving country. They must usually be technically and economically sound and financially self-liquidating, that is, capable of paying off the loan and becoming self supporting. For all loan applications, the Fund staff carries out a careful technical and financial study of the project itself and of its relation to the general economy of the country concerned, including on-the-spot visits from Fund missions. Apart from examining how far the project is 'bankable', its value and priority are judged according to four main criteria: its contribution to expanding the country's productive capacity; how far it will help to increase foreign exchange earnings (most aid-receiving countries have serious foreign exchange problems); how far the receiving country can itself finance the local currency element in the costs without undue strain; and its effect on employment. Since most of the schemes financed by the Fund are capital-intensive and bring little direct increase in employment, the first three considerations are usually more important. But in some cases, such as an irrigation project in Central Morocco, the increase of jobs in a depressed area was a stronger argument in favour of aid than the more marginal profitability of the investment.

However, while the Fund assessment tries to take into account various benefits, including social and secondary ones, it gives its main attention to the level of direct returns which would make a project acceptable on conventional banking standards. The Fund's Director-General does not accept the

argument that international institutions should finance more
shaky ventures because the better projects would be able to find
commercial financing anyway.

But the Fund does not exact full commercial terms for its
loans. Neither are the terms as 'soft' as those recommended by
various international bodies, such as the United Nations Conference on Trade and Development, and the Development
Assistance Committee. The Fund's loans are usually for from
ten to 25 years, with a grace period before repayment of up to
three years; interest rates vary between 3 and 4 per cent (of
which ½ per cent is a service charge.) But some loans have
been for fifty years with no interest but only ½ per cent service
charge. Al Hamad estimates that the 'aid component' (measured as the 'grant element' in Fund loans due to reduced
interest rates) varies from 25 per cent to 85 per cent. It averages
50 per cent for loans for agriculture, 35 per cent for transport,
and 30 per cent for industrial and power projects.

There are certain statutory limits on the amounts the Fund
can lend. The first Charter laid down that the financing of any
single project should not exceed ten per cent of the Fund's
authorised capital. This ceiling appears to have been removed
in the 1974 Charter which, however, repeats the added proviso
of the first Charter that the financing of any project in the form
of direct loans should not exceed 50 per cent of the total needs of
the project. This limit may be exceeded, however, in excep-
tional cases where capital for a vital project cannot be raised on
reasonable terms. But such action has to be approved by a
two-thirds majority of the Fund Board of Directors.

The Fund standard loan agreement (which is broadly based
on that used by the World Bank) calls for certain assurances
and guarantees from the receiving country. The borrower has
to provide necessary information, allow inspection of the project by the Fund staff and to guarantee the Fund's assets and
income from nationalisation or seizure. There is a clause con-
cerning the efficient administration of the project. The borrower promises that the project management shall have powers
necessary for 'the diligent and efficient carrying out and operation of the project' and undertakes to consult with the Fund on
any changes in management. Apart from its preliminary 'project appraisal', the Fund staff keeps in close touch with the
carrying out of the schemes. It is sometimes able discreetly to

help in maintaining the impetus of progress where it is threatened with delay by bureaucratic inertia or other obstacles. In some cases it has advised and secured changes in management.

Another clause in the Fund Charter and loan agreements provides that no other external debt shall have priority over a Fund loan. This was a point which, it was feared, might raise certain problems in the event of joint aid operations by the Fund with other donors who might claim a similar priority. It seems to have been taken care of by a phrase in the new Charter which says that this proviso applies 'except within such limits as the Fund may accept'. Until 1973 most of the Fund's loans were made through bilateral agreements without any other lenders taking part. An exception was a loan to the Yemen in 1968 which was part of a joint operation with two United Nations agencies. Since then the Fund has taken part in an increasing number of joint operations with other Arab donors and with international agencies. They include loans to Bahrain for an aluminium smelter; for the reopening of the Suez Canal, and for a fertiliser plant in Egypt; irrigation in the Sudan and North Yemen, road building in South Yemen, and a power project in Jordan.

The Fund also embarked on a joint technical assistance operation with the World Bank in establishing and training an economic development office in the North Yemen, which was the first such joint operation between the Bank and a national aid agency. The Fund would undoubtedly like to see such cooperation extended. Its Director-General sees a possible future role for the Fund in making its goodwill, experience and skills, and special advantages of language and contacts available to advise on and supervise aid from other international agencies to Arab countries.

The Fund is, however, aware that one of the present advantages it has enjoyed compared with bigger or more international aid agencies is the comparative simplicity of its operation. It deals with only one government to get its funds. It has a small but highly efficient staff who are from many different Arab countries. They have therefore been able, through a common language and background and the absence of any special political axe to grind, to build up influential relations of confidence, intimacy and professional respect with responsible officials and experts in the Arab governments. At the same time the Fund staff have established close working relations with the World Bank and other international aid organisations. The role of the Fund in bringing these organisations and the Arab governments closer together and in encouraging the Arab states to work out their development plans in a more realistic and internationally acceptable fashion and to create new Arab development institutions has been almost as important as the money it has itself lent.

Over the past thirteen years the different Arab countries have shown varying degrees of skill and care in making the best use of the Fund's services, depending partly on the outlook of the Governments concerned or the ability and experience of their officials. Some have been notable for their active cultivation of the Fund and the careful working out of their projects. Others were slow in offering reliable projects or had several projects under study but not many fully worked out. In one or two countries where the economic administration is particularly weak, the Fund itself has had to help to identify and work out projects for which loans might be asked.

Sometimes the Fund itself has had to work patiently to overcome the suspicions of some Arab governments of its loan conditions or their mistaken belief that Fund loans can be obtained by political pressure. In most Arab countries there was usually a false start with the governments trying to put pressure on the Fund through the Kuwait Government. The aid recipients always had to be convinced that the Fund does not work through political channels, but once the Arab Governments have accepted the non-political character of their relations with the Fund they jealously protect it.

In Iraq, for example, relations with the Fund have mostly been very smooth. But a problem arose over loan terms on one occasion when the Iraqis wanted the Fund to finance a project that the Fund did not much like. The Fund preferred another project. The Iraqis then said that the Fund should either finance both projects or neither. So the Fund replied that it would drop both projects. Eventually the Iraqis came round to the Fund's point of view.

There was also a conflict with the Syrians who wanted financial help for an oil pipeline. The Fund sent a Norwegian engineer then on its staff to investigate the project. The Syrians kept changing their ideas and the Syrian prime minister then made a speech publicly criticising Kuwait for holding up the money. So the Fund withdrew its operations from Syria until the Syrians accepted its conditions of working – at the same time it indicated that the Kuwait government could do what it liked about giving a direct state loan to Syria.

Subsequently relations with Syria were resumed and four years hard work by the Fund helped the Syrians to put through a very important project for building grain silos which had been hanging fire for years.

This growing Arab acceptance of 'the rules of the game' for international lending is one of three main intangible achievements of the Fund, in the view of one of its senior staff. The second is the Fund's following up of projects and its insistence on efficient management being employed. And the third is the help given by the Fund in introducing Arab countries to international institutions, such as the World Bank. This help is provided in two ways, in familiarising Arab Governments with the procedures required by international aid institutions, and in the authority which is given to a project in the eyes of such institutions if the Fund decides to throw its weight behind it. The Fund's endorsement of a project and its moral support are often as important as the money it provides, since it encourages aid or investment from other sources. One example already mentioned is the Bahrain smelter. The Fund's backing also helped to arouse the World Bank's interest in the Jordan potash scheme, sadly halted by the 1967 war, and its earlier help for the Algerian oil pipeline had encouraged other international interest in Algeria. The Fund was also able to stimulate international aid agencies to help North Yemen which otherwise might have remained isolated and neglected after the Yemen war ended. But the Fund's staff do not like to talk too much about this aspect of their work, as they fear it might diminish its usefulness. They prefer working quietly and discreetly behind the scenes.

In the years immediately before the big flood of oil money began, the Fund was turning its attention increasingly to general development problems of the Arab world as well as to specific projects. In the post-1973 situation some of its conclusions are even more – rather than less – apposite. Some have already begun to be applied. It considered that during the coming decade remedying the structural weaknesses of the Arab national economies and societies would be more important than the provision of capital. There would be a growing need to create new Arab development institutions, strengthen the operational organs of development in Arab countries and improve the quality of their personnel, and encourage better planning organisations, more efficient administration of agriculture, and management of public utilities. This would require more emphasis on 'technical assistance' and on the mobilisation of Arab resources of skilled and educated people, especially in the scientific and technological field.

More coordination would be needed between various Arab aid programmes and development institutions. The scale of development thinking could also be extended in several directions: the regional approach which might for certain projects transcend country-by-country planning; multi-year programming by the Fund itself; greater promotion of private investment; and decentralisation of the handling of aid, so that small projects in private industry or tourism can be financed through local development institutions.

The Fund, as noted earlier, has already begun to give loans to industrial development banks in the Arab world and has begun to increase its technical assistance grants for pre-investment studies. It helped to set up a new Inter-Arab Investment Guarantee Corporation and hopes to see established a 'Law and Development Centre'.

But probably the most significant extension of the Fund's responsibilities and potential field of action, before its 1974 expansion, occurred with the establishment of the Arab Fund for Economic and Social Development. This is a new inter-governmental aid body for the Arab world of which all twenty states of the Arab League are members but which is itself outside the administrative framework of the Arab League. The purposes of the Arab Fund, as defined in Article Two of its Charter, are three-fold. First, to finance investment projects 'by means of loans granted on easy terms to Governments, and to public or private organisations and institutions, giving preference to economic projects that are vital to the Arab entity, and to join Arab projects.' Second, to encourage, directly or indirectly, the investment of public and private capital in such a manner as to ensure the development and growth of the Arab economy. Third, to provide echnical expertise and assistance. The intention, as indicated above, was that the new fund should give special encouragement to regional, multi-national projects and should give aid for social development, such as health, education and housing, as well as to directly productive economic projects.

The headquarters of the Arab Fund is in Kuwait. The Director-General of the Kuwait Fund is on the board of directors of the Arab Fund and is in charge of Kuwait's contribution of 30 per cent of the new agency's subscribed capital. When the Arab Fund began lending operations in April 1973, its working capital was KD102 million (£153 million): in 1975, as already mentioned, there was an agreement in principle to raise it to KD400 million (£600 million). (Like the Kuwait Fund it is authorised to borrow up to twice its capital, so that its total lending resources could eventually be KD1,200 million (£1,800 million). The Director-General of the Kuwait Fund is a member of the new organisation's four-man executive board of directors and the first Director-General of the Arab Fund is a former senior official of the Kuwait Fund and subsequently Lebanon's Minister for National Economy, Saeb Jaroudi. The ultimate governing body of the Arab Fund is a Board of Governors composed of the Ministers of Finance from the twenty Arab states or their representatives, which meets at least once a year. It elects the Board of Directors and appoints the Director-General.

The idea of the Arab Fund goes back at least to the mid-fifties when the Economic Council of the Arab League agreed to establish an Arab regional financial corporation in 1957. This agreement was never implemented. In its present form the Arab Fund originated in a proposal for a regional development organisation drafted by the Kuwait Fund and put forward by the Kuwait Government at the Khartoum Arab summit meeting in September 1967. It could be interpreted as a move by Kuwait to encourage a bigger sharing of the aid burden among the other Arab oil states, since she had herself during the Khartoum conference shouldered the heavy new responsibility of paying KD50 million a year in direct subsidy to Egypt and Jordan. The Kuwait Fund was asked to draft a new convention and tried to improve the 1957 document. At a meeting of Arab economic experts in Algiers in October 1967 the draft convention was remodelled nearer to the 1957 agreement and later approved by the Arab Economic Council, the economic organ of the Arab League. The Kuwait Fund was asked by the Arab League governments to organise the first meeting of the new Fund's Board of Governors in February 1972 at which the Director-General was appointed as the first step towards setting up the necessary organisation and starting operations. the Arab Fund signed agreements for loans for eleven projects. Three more were approved by June 1975. This brought the Fund's commitments up to about 200 million dollars (£91 million) for projects whose total cost was 800 million dollars (£364 million). According to the Director-General, Saeb Jaroudi, whom I saw in Kuwait at that time, there were thirty more projects then in the pipeline and more expected to mature by 1976.

Saeb Jaroudi said that simultaneously with individual projects the Fund considered it very important to tackle broader programmes. These were of three types. One was concerned with reducing the Arab world's dependence on food imports. The Arab Fund had found that the Sudan had great potential for food production – upwards of 200 million acres suitable for agriculture and livestock (see Chapter 8 on the Sudan).

A pledging group of Arab Ministers of Finance would be asked to authorise a ten-year inter-Arab programme costing several billion dollars to develop Sudanese agriculture. After the pledging, the Fund would set up a special authority to manage the programme and its projects. Some of the projects would be suitable for joint Arab ventures which would open up avenues for direct investment in Arab countries. The programme also envisaged close cooperation with international institutions and with the industrial countries in the fields of technology and management.

The second type of programme concerned hitherto neglected regional projects in the Arab world. Soon after its inception, the Arab Fund began to study a programme for an inter-Arab telecommunications network, together with the United Nations Development Programme and the International Telecommunications Union. By 1975 the first study of telephones, satellite and coaxial cables had been completed, and Arab ministers had already agreed on the satellite component. The Arab Fund was also helping with a project in Algeria and Morocco which would provide automatic telephone connection with the whole of the Maghreb. A first study had also been made of a major inter-Arab highway network, beginning with the road from Beirut to Damascus and thence to Amman, Baghdad and the Gulf areas. Discussions were also in progress with the UNDP for a five-year programme for regional development projects with the Arab Fund acting as agent.

A third type of programme would deal with agriculture and with industries which were important to more than one country in the area, such as textiles and mechanical engineering. It was necessary to avoid duplication and prevent too many small projects where a big one was better. There were possibilities of pooling raw materials, manpower and marketing. Some projects might be commercially viable if they had infrastructure support from the Arab Fund.

Of the social aspects of the Fund's operations, Jaroudi said that in its first two years the Fund had supported mostly economic projects, but several of them had social aspects, such as water supply and sewage. The Fund was, for example, studying a five-year programme to improve the water and sewage systems of Cairo to meet the needs of the Egyptian capital's expanding population. But the Fund would go more into social areas with the regional programme already mentioned which would include the financing of technical training, schools and other institutions. One project already under way was for the training of merchant marine officers at Alexandria. The Fund also emphasised the training of man-power in dealing with the least developed countries. In the increasing funds earmarked for technical assistance the stress would be on helping the least developed countries, such as the Yemen, Somalia and Mauritania, with a nucleus of planning units specialising in community development.

Saeb Jaroudi added that the operations of the Arab Fund were being coordinated with other regional funds and development programmes, such as the Kuwait Fund and the United Nations West Asian Development Programme.

The role played by the Kuwait Fund in initiating the Arab Fund, the preponderant share of Kuwait in its capital (Saudi Arabia with 18.8 per cent and Libya with 12 per cent are the next biggest subscribers), and the availability of the expertise and experience of the Kuwait Fund staff are all factors likely to ensure useful support to the management and operations of the new Arab body now that it is under way. This backing, and the fortunate timing of the Fund's establishment, just as huge new oil funds were about to become available and feelings of Arab solidarity were at their peak, have given this inter-Arab venture a good chance of avoiding the fate of most of the previous attempts at regional economic cooperation launched by the Arab League which have survived only as dusty documents on foreign ministry shelves or in the titles of officials with jobs but no work.

The Kuwait Fund's role in helping to launch the Arab Fund to a promising start, despite the problems of dealing with many different governments, could very well rank as one of its most remarkable achievements to date.

Another of the Kuwait Fund's initiatives to encourage a bigger flow of Arab funds for development was the scheme, already mentioned, for guaranteeing private Arab investment in Arab countries. At least until 1974, the private funds available from the oil countries for investment abroad were far greater than anything offered in the way of official aid.

During 1965-70 Kuwait alone saved an average of 50 per cent of her GNP – down to 45 per cent in 1970-72. But it is estimated that 40 per cent of these savings were invested or spent outside Kuwait. Of this some 13 per cent went to various Arab countries in the form of official aid.

But the remaining 27 per cent of savings or 13.5 per cent of GNP went abroad in government or private investment, much of it in private funds. With the increases in oil revenue, savings and foreign investments have also expanded.

A substantial part of these private investments from Kuwait as well as from other oil countries in the Gulf and the Arabian Peninsula has gone to other Arab countries, chiefly Egypt, Iraq, Syria, Jordan and Lebanon, in the form of loans, direct investments, property deals and bank deposits. The total might, however, have been far greater but for the political risks faced by investors in some of these countries – risks of nationalisation or expropriation or of stringent exchange control blocking the recovery of profits. If Arab private investors were to put more of their money into Arab countries rather than into Europe or the

United States, pan-Arab patriotism was clearly not enough. They needed assurances against non-commercial risks and for this purpose assurances only from the receiving country were not convincing enough.

With this picture in mind, the Kuwait Fund submitted a proposal for an inter-Arab investment guarantee scheme to the conference on Arab Industrial Development held in Kuwait in 1966 under United Nations auspices. After having been adopted unanimously by the conference, the proposal was discussed at two meetings of Arab financial experts in Kuwait in November 1967 and March 1970. A convention drafted by the Kuwait Fund was adopted by the Council of the Arab Economic Union at its 15th session in Damascus in August 1970. By January 1975 it had been signed by fifteen of the Arab League states and ratified by fourteen, all of whom had subscribed their share of the initial working capital of KD10 million (£15 million). Those League states which had not yet signed but were considering doing so were Saudi Arabia, South Yemen, Bahrain and Somalia.

The Inter-Arab Investment Guarantee Corporation officially began operations in mid-1974 after the appointment of its first Director-General, Dr Abdul-Aziz Mathari, a Tunisian who had formerly worked for international investment institutions.

The Corporation gives insurance against non-commercial risks, such as expropriation, confiscation and nationalisation; against unreasonably prolonged moratoriums on debt repayments; against newly introduced restrictions on the transfer of money; and against riot, revolution or war. Priority is given under the convention to investments which promote economic cooperation among the member countries, and in particular joint Arab ventures and other projects which promote Arab economic integration; to investments which develop productive capacity; and to investments which, without the Corporation's guarantee, might not be otherwise made.

The projects to be guaranteed can be private, public or semi-public and in any economic sector. The guarantee system is only for the Arab world, not for Arab investment outside the Arab world. An individual investor must be a national of an Arab country; a corporation must have its seat in an Arab country and its funds must be under the 'substantial control' of an Arab country. This does not rule out joint ventures by Arab and non-Arab investors in an Arab country.

At the Corporation's headquarters in Kuwait, Dr Mathari pointed out to me the difference between its operations and those of the export guarantee systems of European countries. The European system is to guarantee exports of goods, while the Arab system is a guarantee of investments. The Arab scheme was also the first to be built on an inter-governmental and multilateral rather than bilateral basis.

Dr Mathari stressed that although the Corporation was not a financial institution, it would not be simply a passive insurance institution guaranteeing only investments already decided upon, it also intended actively to encourage investment in Arab countries and help to identify opportunities for it.

Parallel with the setting up of the Corporation, there was discussion of the adoption of an inter-Arab Investment Code. A preliminary draft of the code, worked out by Kuwait Fund experts, was adopted with only slight alterations by the Council of the Arab Economic Union at Damascus in August 1970.

The Investment Code would apply only to Arab investors in Arab countries. But special investment laws to encourage all foreign investment have been passed in several Arab countries in the last few years. In the outline so far agreed the code accepts the right of Arab governments to control the conditions of ownership and operation of foreign investments and the employment of foreign nationals. At the same time it lays down six principles: Arab investors should enjoy adequate security and protection with treatment at least as good as local nationals and no less favourable than other foreign investors. They should have the right to transfer profits, debts and compensation out of the country and repatriate their principal 'within the limits compatible with the economic situation of the country'. They should also have the right to reside in the host country to administer their investment but should not interfere in the country's domestic affairs.

Another aim of the Fund, worked on by its research and legal departments, was to set up a Law and Development Centre. The idea was to train Arab lawyers in the external aspects of economic development, so that when, for example, an Arab country enters into economic negotiations with a foreign party it should not be handicapped, as often happens now, by lack of expertise.

One question which seemed to be a good deal in the thoughts of the Fund staff before its 1974 expansion was how far the Fund could and should lay greater stress on the encouragement of Arab regional economic integration, whether through the harmonisation of several national development plans or through encouraging joint multinational projects. The Fund was clearly sensitive to criticism that it had not done enough in this direction.

But the consensus at the Fund headquarters seemed then to be that while greater regional integration was undoubtedly desirable in some respects and might eventually need greater attention, the economic and especially the political obstacles in the way were still too great to hold out much hope of early progress. There were very wide differences between the Arab states in resources and degree of development, such as between Egypt and the Yemen, or between Lebanon and Morocco. There was still also very little real development planning in the Arab world despite the proliferation of five-year or seven-year plans: in many cases there were no seriously-based priorities. Even where there were obvious economic advantages in joint projects, such as the agricultural development of Northern Syria and Iraq, or the exploitation of the Jordan waters, political obstacles stood in the way.

Talking of Arab integration after the Fund's first decade Abdulatif Al Hamad said: 'How can you expect to achieve much in ten years in countries so different – it is much more difficult than the European Common Market. The Fund has so far been selling the idea of itself and working in twelve different Arab countries. We found much scepticism at first which has gradually worn off. Now we feel we have crossed a major boundary because the Fund is now dealing with every potential Arab borrower.'

With the increased Arab wealth and greater inter-Arab cooperation since 1973, as well as the Fund's own expanded capital, Al Hamad and his colleagues have been giving more intensive thought to the Fund's role in regional planning and integration.

Al Hamad's earlier positive but cautious attitude to regionalism was set out in a speech made in 1972 when he spoke of 'the need to transcend, in a growing portion of our operations, the country by country approach to project assistance.

Although the Fund has always looked upon itself as a *regional* development institution, and while we hardly need to be convinced of the virtues of Arab economic cooperation, it should be pointed out that no serious propositions of a regional character have yet been submitted to the Fund. In fact, joint ventures amoung Arab states for the common exploitation of their resources would always receive special consideration by the Fund, provided the sponsors themselves take the initiative and present really viable and well thought out propositions. Here also, perhaps, it may be suggested that we should adopt a more active – or should I say activist – attitude, and that we should attempt to identify and promote regional ventures. We have, in fact, taken such an initiative in helping to promote the creation of the Arab Fund for Social and Economic Development and the Inter-Arab Investment Guarantee Corporation . . . I can only express the hope that the economic and political situation in the Arab world will allow further advance along this road.'

Although Al Hamad has remained sceptical of too extensive or rigid regional plans, he stressed in a number of lectures and speeches in 1975 the importance the Fund attached to the development of a regional outlook not only among the Arab states but in the Middle East region including also non-Arab states such as Turkey.

The new situation which began to develop at the end of 1973 for the Kuwait Fund and the Arab world was, as described in the opening chapter, the result of the double impact of the October war and the accompanying oil crisis. The Arabs suddenly had enormously increased financial resources at their disposal and greater self-confidence in their ability to manage their own affairs, including those operations involving advanced technology. But at the same time the war and its diplomatic aftermath, together with the big oil price increases and the use of oil supplies as a political weapon, made it vital for them to avoid losing friends or making new enemies. At the United Nations and in other bodies such as the Organisation for African Unity and the conferences of non-aligned countries, the Arabs had been able to secure increasing support from Third World countries in their conflict with Israel. But it was precisely most of these developing countries, not themselves oil-producers, which had felt themselves proportionately hardest hit by the increase in oil prices. Moreover their plight was apt to be neglected in the international discussions on recycling oil surpluses which usually centred on the problems of the big oil-importing countries of the industrial world – Europe, the United States and Japan. Various measures were initiated multilaterally and bilaterally to help the Third World oil importers. These included a special IMF fund to which the Arab oil states and Iran subscribed a large share, and two special Arab funds, one of 200 million dollars to help African states, and a second of 80 million dollars a year from OAPEC for the least-developed Arab countries. But there was some resentful criticism, especially in Africa, of what was regarded by some as the slowness and limited scale of international and Arab help.

At the beginning of 1974 the Kuwait Government decided to send a goodwill mission to visit the African and Asian countries to report on their problems and advise on what Kuwait might itself do to help. The Kuwait Government's main purpose was no doubt to win friends and influence people for the general Arab cause in the Middle East conflict. But in the minds of Abdulatif Al Hamad and the Kuwait Fund, who were entrusted with the mission, there was also evolving a broader idea of the role the oil states could now play in bridging the gap between the industrial and developing countries and achieving smoothly a 'reallocation of real resources'. As one of Al Hamad's chief advisers, Dr Zacharia Nasr, put it: 'For the first time we could see light at the end of the development tunnel' and not only for the Arab world, though its prospects were brightest and still the Fund's chief concern, but also for other developing countries.

The Kuwait Fund mission, headed by Al Hamad, went first to six African countries. On its return it recommended to the Kuwait Government the creation of a fund of a billion Kuwaiti dinars – either by creating a new fund or by expanding the capital of the existing Fund, to provide loans on the same lines as the Kuwait Fund not only to Arab countries but also to developing countries universally. This meant expanding the scope of the Fund's operation from fifteen Arab countries to fifty or sixty countries all over the world.

In Al Hamad's words: 'The Minister of Finance got the point in less than twenty minutes. It was agreed to add KD800 million to the existing Fund capital of KD200 million, and that the Fund would run the operation. It took only from January to March to reach this decision. So then we went to another fourteen countries in Africa and told them of the Kuwait Government's intention.

'On 17 July 1974, our capital was extended to one billion dinars and the prime minister became chairman of the board. The Fund management was asked to write its own statutes for a new charter (issued in December 1974) – in itself remarkable.

'The Fund took on a new shape. We faced a new challenge and new tasks. It was almost like starting again – with more self-confidence and experience but at the same time with a record of quality and standards which we could not afford to fall short of.'

When the change in the Fund was officially announced, the Director General and the Director of Operations, Faisal Khaled, undertook a further tour of ten Asian countries to introduce the Fund to governments there. A mission was also sent to five countries in Africa and four in Asia to begin the appraisal of possible projects, or, where this was not possible, to recommend studies which could be financed to prepare projects. At the same time the Fund contacted other developing countries in Asia and Africa to exchange information.

Between July 1974 and June 1975, loans and grants totalling KD46 million (£69 million) were made for projects and studies in ten developing countries outside the Arab world, five African and five Asian.

Two loans went to Bangladesh, one of KD6.4 million (£9.6 million) for the use of electric power in an irrigation project, and another of KD2.3 million (£3.45 million) for the Manu River project. The latter scheme is to develop an agricultural area of 56,000 acres in the north-east of the country and includes flood protection, drainage and irrigation measures.

A loan of KD7.6 million (£11.4 million) went to Malaysia for land settlement in Palong. This project aims to clear a large forest area for rubber plantations on which 5,500 families of poor landholders will be settled. The total costs of the project are estimated at KD39.4 million (nearly £60 million).

Sri Lanka received a loan of KD7.5 million (£11.25 million) for an urea fertiliser plant to be built near Colombo, intended eventually to meet all the country's fertiliser requirements and provide a surplus for export. The total cost is expected to be

KD42.3 million (£63.4 million). The foreign exchange element of KD29.6 million (£59.4 million) is being provided jointly by the Kuwait Fund, the Asian Development Bank and the governments of Western Germany and India.

A loan of KD5.75 million (£8.65 million) was given to Uganda for the second phase of a government programme to expand livestock production involving the creation of 140 cattle farms averaging 3,000 acres each. Uganda also received a technical assistance grant of KD230,000 (£342,500) for studies of the sugar and electricity industries.

Tanzania was granted a loan of KD4.5 million (£6.75 million) for a project to expand the production of the cotton textile factory at Mwanza; Rwanda received a loan of KD1 million (£1.5 million) for a tea growing and processing project.

In addition there were several technical assistance grants to non-Arab countries. Afghanistan received a grant of KD400,000 (£600,000) for the study of two projects, one for the development of the sugar industry and the other for an irrigation scheme. The first project is to renovate and expand Afghanistan's only existing sugar plant and build a new one in the city of Herat. The second is to use the waters of the Farah-Rud River to irrigate an area of 40,000 to 60,000 hectares in a region of the country which is one of the least developed and most neglected but which has good farming potential.

Grants of KD200,000 (£300,000) went to Mali for studies of an irrigation project and a cement plant; and KD90,000 (£135,000) to Nepal for a study of dairy products. Guinea received KD150,000 (£225,000) for a study of road construction and Guinea-Bissau KD200,000 (£300,000) for a study of port and airport construction.

The Kuwait Fund also earmarked KD10 million (£15 million) as a loan for one of the most ambitious schemes in Africa which involves the African states of Mali and Senegal together with neighbouring Mauritania which recently became a member of the Arab League. This is the programme agreed between the three countries for the joint exploitation of the Senegal River Basin for purposes of agriculture, mining, hydro-electric power and navigation. The programme is intended to be implemented in stages over a period of 40 years at an estimated cost of 3,400 million dollars (£1,600 million). The first stage, to be completed by 1982, is expected to cost about 200 million dollars (£90 million pounds). It involves the construction of a dam and a port in Mali, a barrage in Senegal and nine other ports along the Senegal River, two of them in Mauritania.

The Kuwait Fund took part in a conference held in July 1974 at Nouakchott, the capital of Mauritania, attended by 13 states and 12 international institutions to discuss ways of financing the programme.

In November 1974 the Fund Board approved the allocation of KD10 million (£15 million) for this programme, subject to the submission of individual projects to the Fund for appraisal. But no loan agreement has yet been made.

Another forty or so projects were under consideration by the Fund by mid-1975. In its widened field of operations the Fund continues to concentrate on basic development needs, that is, the infrastructure projects which are needed by all developing countries. The task of identifying worthwhile projects is easier in Asia than in Africa. In Asian countries such as India and Malaysia there are plenty of well-prepared and studied projects to be financed, though in the case of India some of them are on such a huge scale that it is difficult for any one aid organisation alone to provide all the required financial backing and partners have to be found. In Africa, many countries which are greatly in need of help have few properly studied projects ready.

Its expansion faces the Fund with some new working problems, in addition to that already mentioned of retaining its informal team methods and high standards despite the inevitable increase in numbers of staff. In dealing with non-Arab countries the legal department, for example, had, for the first time, to prepare the texts of loan agreements in foreign languages, usually English or French, as well as in Arabic, although the Arabic text remains the authoritative one. The new aided countries are treated on exactly the same legal basis as Arab countries but their local laws have to be studied to see how they affect the loan agreements. One other new legal aspect has arisen. This is the question of the Arab economic boycott of Israel. Kuwait Fund aid is not normally tied to purchases from particular countries or from Kuwait itself, but in order not to violate Kuwait's own laws, the Fund has to have an understanding with non-Arab recipient countries that Kuwaiti money is not used to purchase goods from Israel for projects the Fund is helping to finance. The question is more difficult when the Fund is sharing in joint financing with other institutions. It does not arise in the case of Arab countries; for they are all committed to the boycott in any case.

The extension of operations to so many more countries means a much heavier burden of work in research and apprais-al. Consideration is being given to some of the research being contracted out to other international development research institutions, such as the Ford Foundation and the Institute for Development Studies at Sussex University. There are also an increasing number of joint appraisals with the World Bank and with Arab and other development institutions, and a decen-tralising of appraisal work by increasing loans to national development institutions for projects of their own choice.

But the staff of the Fund believe that in the new phase, when more new development institutions are also springing up to deal with the Arab world and the developing countries, the importance of the Kuwait Fund lies more than ever in the quality rather than the quantity of its operations. It can still serve best by providing an example of high standards of effi-ciency and probity in a field in which it was a pioneer.

Expansion to non-Arab countries also poses new questions of politics and priorities. The choice of non-Arab countries to be helped first was not, according to senior Fund officials, a result of deliberate priorities so much as a reflection of the pressures of the time, particularly those of limitations of staff. First to be dealt with were the countries neighbouring on the Arab world, in Africa and then in Asia. But the Fund also had in mind the poorest and most in need. It had begun with Uganda, Rwanda and Tanzania in Africa, which were considered the most needy of the African states. In Asia it began with Bangladesh and Sri Lanka, and then Nepal and Malaysia. By the end of 1975 the Fund was about to sign a KD15 million (£22.5 million) loan agreement with India for a hydro-electric and irrigation scheme and hoped soon to be operating also in Pakistan and possibly Indonesia.

Whether by chance or design, the choice of non-Arab loan recipients so far seems also to indicate a balance between Muslim and non-Muslim countries, while total loans and grants to all non-Arab countries are about half the total value of new loans and grants to Arab States. Perhaps this was a shrewd – or instinctive – compromise between the political sentiments of the Kuwait Government and public and the economic and social perceptions of the Kuwait Fund.

Whatever the reason, Abdulatif Al Hamad is also certainly anxious that the Fund's help to other developing countries should not be in any way detrimental to its work in the Arab world.

At the same time as the first loans and grants were being given to ten non-Arab African and Asian countries, as already listed, the Fund granted twelve loans and four grants to Arab countries, totalling over KD85 million (£127 million). They included assistance to two new states of the Arab League, Mauritania and Somalia, which had previously not received help. In Mauretania the Fund granted two loans for road maintenance and construction: at present only 460 kilometres of Mauritania's 7,000 kilometres are asphalted, the rest being earth tracks. The first loan was of KD1.15 million (£1.7 million) for twenty years at nil interest for a road programme financed jointly with IDA and the Canadian International Development Agency. The second, also interest free, was of KD5.8 million (£8.7 million) to help finance the building of the 600 km long Nouakchott-Kiffa highway. The Fund also gave Mauritania a grant of KD175,000 (£262,500) for the study of a long-term plan to exploit the country's mineral resources and of new industries that might be based on them.

In Somalia, the Fund granted a loan of KD6.2 million (£9.3 million) (for twenty-five years at 1 per cent) to expand the electricity supply of Mogadishu, the country's capital. It also gave Somalia a grant of KD200,000 (£300,000) for studies of irrigation and livestock which is the mainstay of three-quarters of the population.

The 1974-75 commitment brought the total of funds committed to loans and grants during the Kuwait Fund's first thirteen years of operation from 1962-75 to KD259 million (£385 million) of which about KD230 million (£345 million) went to fourteen Arab countries. An additional KD70 million (£105 million) was expected to be committed in the year ended July 1976.

In addition to those already detailed, the loan projects have included an oil pipeline system in Algeria; an aluminium smelter, flour mill, electric power and water plant, and a causeway and bridge in Bahrain; expansion and reopening of the Suez Canal, shipbuilding, natural gas, fertiliser and electric power plants in Egypt; a hydro-electric project and cement factory in Iraq; irrigation and electric power, phosphate mining, tourist hotels and an industrial bank in Jordan; a hydro-electric plant and grain silos in Lebanon; irrigation schemes, a sugar factory, an industrial bank, electric power and a phosphates project in Morocco; modernising the railways, building two sugar plants, roads and agricultural schemes in the Sudan; grain silos, an oil refinery and a power station in Syria; electric power plants, agricultural development, the fishing industry, a gas pipeline, phosphate mining and airport improvement in Tunisia; road building and irrigation in South Yemen; and agriculture and salt mining in North Yemen.

In addition, the Fund has given grants for technical assistance and other purposes, totalling nearly KD3 million (£4.5 million). To Arab countries these include grants (in addition to those already noted to Somalia and Mauritania) to North and South Yemen, Jordan and the Sudan for economic surveys of transport, agriculture, livestock development and the textile industry; and to North Yemen for technical assistance in setting up an economic administration, jointly with the World Bank. (For details of loans and grants see charts in the Appendix.)

The following chapters describe in greater detail some of these projects and the countries in which they are operating.

4 Morocco

Morocco is the Arab country closest to Europe, separated from Spain only by the twelve miles of the Gibraltar Straits. (The name 'Gibraltar' itself comes from the Arabic 'Jebel Tariq', the mountain of Tariq.) It is also the country from which the Arabs in the seventh century launched themselves into Europe as far as the Loire and subsequently established control of southern Spain for eight centuries. Yet it remained for long one of the least accessible to modern European influence and retained longer than most other Arab states its independent Arab character. It was the only part of the Arab world – except for the more remote areas of the Arabian Peninsula at the other extremity – which was not overrun by the Turks. When the Turkish empire in Africa and Asia was gradually taken over by the European imperial powers, Morocco eventually fell under French and partly Spanish rule. But under the French protectorate and the small Spanish enclaves much of the traditional Arab society and the structure of the Sherifian empire, which had changed little from the Middle Ages, was preserved side by side with twentieth century economic and social innovations.

Educated Moroccans today are intensely aware both of their Arab past and of their modern links with Europe. In hopeful moments they see Morocco as profiting from the ability to draw on the best of Arab and European cultures and providing a link between the two sides of the Mediterranean whose history has often been so closely intertwined – an idea shared by the people of other Mediterranean Arab countries. In darker moods they see only muddle as the result and they despair of bridging the gap created by the ambiguous legacy of colonialism.

In my first impression of the Moroccan capital of Rabat, in September 1971, the past and the present blended harmoniously. The bus from the airport passed by the long, fortified walls enclosing the old city, with a glimpse through arched gateways of narrow lively streets, before reaching the modern business centre. From there a taxi took me through handsome, almost deserted tree-lined suburbs of European-style villas to a remote but elegant modern hotel, a glass tower set among fine formal gardens in the Andalusian style, where fountains played among subtly aromatic shrubs.

But under the harmonious exterior there were obviously deep strains. Marrying two cultures and adapting to the modern world a state large in area and with a population of some 15 million – which until only sixty-five years ago was a secluded medieval empire, is a harsh test of statesmanship. It is full of pitfalls and temptations for the individual as well as for the state. Sometimes the tensions breed violence.

Along Morocco's Atlantic coast from Rabat to Casablanca, a big European-style industrial city with a population of a million, the road passes by a group of low white buildings just visible behind the dark green of orange groves and cypress hedges. This is the royal summer palace of Skhirat where on Saturday, 10 July 1971, King Hassan II was celebrating his forty-second birthday with a spectacular outdoor party. The amusements included clay pigeon shooting and golf. Music was provided by Egyptian star musicians hired, it was said, at several thousand pounds a day. The 1,200 guests, among them the entire Moroccan cabinet and diplomatic corps, had just begun to sample the sumptuous food when at 1.45 pm the palace grounds were surrounded by heavily-armed soldiers, cadets from an NCO training school. The cadets burst in upon the party, firing in all directions. Nearly a hundred guests were killed and scores more were wounded. Some were picked out in accordance with prepared lists and shot on the spot. King Hassan and his then right-hand man, General Oufkir, Minister of the Interior, hid for two and a half hours in a lavatory beside the swimming pool. The coup at the palace then collapsed after General Medbouh, head of the royal household, who had joined the rebels, was shot by one of the rebels by mistake. Elsewhere the rebels, who had also seized the radio station and broadcast that the king was dead, were quickly crushed by loyal troops.

The whole affair produced a profound shock in Morocco.

The causes of the coup were a matter of dispute. The official version was that a few power-hungry army officers who had already done well out of the regime wanted to do even better. Other non-official interpretations credited the coup leaders with the more altruistic aims of ending corruption in govern-

ment and in the ruling society in the same way as Gamal Abdul
Nasser and the Egyptian 'Free Officers' had overthrown King
Farouk's regime in Cairo.

Whatever the truth – and the official version sounded
unconvincing – it was generally recognised – even by King
Hassan and his ministers – that behind the violence lay the
serious political, social and economic problems with which
Morocco had had to grapple since she became independent in
1956.

The lesson was driven home dramatically only a year later.
King Hassan once more miraculously escaped an attempt on
his life when his plane was attacked by its fighter escort of the
Moroccan air force. This time it was none other than General
Oufkir who was blamed for the plot and who shot himself or
was shot after it failed. Eleven air force officers were later shot
for their part in the plot.

During the following three years the King's absolute rule
survived more challenges. In March 1973 there was a small
attempted uprising in the Atlas mountains blamed by the
government on radical elements of the main opposition party,
the UNFP (National Union of Popular Forces.) Hundreds
were arrested. In a series of trials by military courts, 84 people
were sentenced to death of whom fifteen were executed by firing
squad. Many others received life sentences or long prison
terms. There was continued unrest among students, some of
whom also received heavy prison sentences.

King Hassan sought to buttress his position by a more
popular nationalist foreign policy, by speeding up the pace of
'Moroccanisation' and by a more expansive new five-year
development plan which put greater emphasis on social services and a fairer sharing out of income. He sent Moroccan
troops to help Syria and Egypt against Israel in the Middle
East war of October 1973, and he pressed successfully the
Moroccan claim to the Spanish Sahara, a rich phosphate-
bearing area, in the face of bitter opposition from Algeria.

At home he relaxed some of the repressive measures against
the political opposition but was unsuccessful in seeking their
cooperation in running the government.

It remained clear that, personalities apart, it was by its
ability to deal effectively with Morocco's serious social and
economic problems that any political system in Morocco,

including the thousand-year old Alouite dynasty, would in the end stand or fall.

In Rabat, King Hassan's palace occupies a wide area, a series of graceful white buildings set in spacious gardens and broad avenues and enclosed within a wall. At one corner of the palace proper is the office of the prime minister, a reminder of the close control of the King over the government. The King himself has been prime minister several times and is admitted even by his critics to have been more intelligent and hardworking than many of his ministers. The Moroccan constitution gives the monarch wide powers, including the appointment of ministers, and this role is reinforced by King Hassan's personality.

Shortly after the unsuccessful Skhirat coup, the King appointed a new premier, Mr Mohammed Lamrani, as head of a 'new broom' administration (he was dismissed and replaced after the Oufkir coup). Mr Lamrani is cast in a different mould from most of the Moroccan ministers of his own and previous governments who tended to be highly educated, elegant, youngish men with technological skills rather than political or managerial drive. He is a mainly self-educated former banker and businessman, a large, thick-set man, bushy-eyebrowed, bouncing, bustling and talkative, a hard worker and a bit of a showman. Hearing that I was visiting his office to talk to one of his officials, he called me into his study to sit in on a kind of cabinet meeting at which his economic ministers and chief civil servants were assembled. I was invited to put questions to him and his ministers – a handsome gesture prompted partly by the premier's conviction that the Moroccan regime had received unfairly harsh treatment from the international press at the time of the July coup.

I asked in what way the policy of his government differed from that of his predeccessors which had been criticised for, among other things, allowing the benefits of economic development to go chiefly to the more well-off sections of the population. Mr Lamrani said that his government wanted to bring about a more equal distribution of wealth but needed to reorganise its administration. To expand her economic development Morocco needed and welcomed foreign aid. She was confident of getting more aid from foreign countries and international sources such as the World Bank. She would take aid from anywhere, including Russia, provided it was without political strings.

One of the young officials round the table listed fifteen projects in Morocco then up for the study by the World Bank, including projects in education, industry, tourism, mining and agriculture. A consultative group of ten countries, including representatives of the World Bank and of the Kuwait Fund for Arab Economic Development, meets in Paris once a year to review Morocco's aid needs.

Was not Morocco in danger, I asked, of incurring a heavy foreign debt burden like other developing countries (for 'aid' nowadays usually consists of loans often at the market rate of interest). According to the latest report of the Bank of Morocco, Morocco's foreign debt had risen to 700 million dollars. Of this 'aid', 40 per cent came in 1970 from the United States and 15 per cent from France.

Mr Lamrani claimed that Morocco was among the least indebted of the developing countries. Her payments to service foreign debts amounted to only eight per cent of her foreign payments, whereas the danger limit set by the International Monetary Fund was twenty-five per cent.

(In 1972 foreign debt was 24.4 per cent of GDP and debt servicing rose to 9.4 per cent of the value of Morocco's exports of goods and services. But between 1968 and 1973 Morocco's foreign assets tripled and continued to increase. Expanded earnings from tourism, phosphates and emigrant workers' remittances more than covered an increased trade deficit and provided a growing balance of payments surplus.)

But was not Morocco's economic development affected by its political structure? Were any changes intended there?

The premier declared bluntly but rather defensively that the system of government was not an obstacle to the economic development programme. In a context like Morocco's the political label on the system – such as monarchy – was not important. The monarchy in Morocco was a good deal more liberal than the fascist kind of regimes in some republics in some other neighbouring countries – and he didn't, he said, necessarily mean Arab, but European too.

This view is not shared by the Moroccan opposition political parties. Two days before seeing the prime minister I had visited the leader of the moderately left-wing UNFP, Maître Abdurrahman Bouabid, a tall thin lawyer with a brown leonine face and longish grey hair. We met in his flat full of books and paintings. He gave an impression of intelligence, vitality and anxious moderation. He was almost the only one of the top leadership of the UNFP in Rabat to escape arrest after the Atlas rising in March 1973, and he was the leading defence counsel in the subsequent trials. It was essential, M. Bouabid told me, for Morocco to have a more representative system of government, not entirely subservient to the King, with more popular contact and responsible to an elected Assembly as well as to the King. But neither the UNFP nor its more conservative ally, the nationalist Istiqlal, wanted to abolish the monarchy, which was generally recognised as having an important unifying role in the country.

The young generation in Morocco wanted change, said Maître Bouabid, but were subject to mixed influences – the leftism of Europe and the nationalist radicalism of the Arab Middle East. Young army officers tended to think of the model of Algeria – of military rule, efficiency and socialism with an Islamic overtone.

The planned promotion of economic development in Morocco dates from the beginning of the French protectorate in 1912 with the building of roads, railways, ports and power stations. Between the Second World War and its achievement of independence, Morocco's public investment programmes were coordinated with France's own ten-year modernisation plan. Morocco had two four-year plans for 1949-53 and 1954-7 in which expenditure totalled the equivalent of £500 million. Nearly half of Morocco's public expenditure was financed by the French government in Paris. Altogether some £700 million of French capital, public and private, was invested in Morocco between 1946-56, much of it in long-term, low-interest official loans.

After independence, the Planning Office, which had begun in 1949 with one French civil servant and a staff of two clerks, became part of the Ministry of National Economy and Finance. A Higher Planning Council, under the chairmanship of the prime minister, was set up in 1957, and given the task of producing a five-year plan for 1960-5. In the meantime there was a two-year interim plan which envisaged spending £76 million, though less was actually spent. The working out of projects was delayed because French administrators and technical specialists were leaving the country and were having to be replaced by inexperienced or untrained Moroccans. This lack of trained specialists was a serious handicap to plans for spreading modern methods among the farmers, such as 'Operation Plough', an ambitious scheme intended to bring small farmers together in cooperatives and teach them to use tractors, better seed, fertilisers and subsidised credits.

After some delay caused by King Mohammed the Fifth's dismissal of the Government and his personal assumption of the premiership, the first five-year plan was approved in November 1960. It provided for investment totalling just over £600 million and aimed at an annual increase of seven per cent of GNP – reduced to 6.2 per cent when the plan was revised in 1962. Its other two main aims were to lessen the country's dependence on foreign technicians, capital and markets and to integrate the traditional and modernised sectors of the economy. It gave top priority to the reform and modernisation of agriculture. Moroccanisation of the civil service and administrative reforms were to be accompanied by intensive training and education to increase the number of qualified Moroccans. The state would help to set up basic steel and chemical industries, while encouraging private industrial investment.

In the event, the amount actually invested during the first five-year plan was only £375 million and the growth rate achieved was only 14 per cent instead of the 35 per cent originally hoped for. The following three-year-plan for 1964-7 aimed to spend £250 million with the less ambitious target of a 3.7 per cent per annum growth rate. In fact, between 1960 and 1967, GNP increased by an average of less than three per cent a year, mostly in industry, building and public works. Agricultural output increased by only 1.5 per cent a year.

Since population has been growing at the rate of 3.2 per cent a year, living standards either stayed still or declined.

The slow progress was caused partly by the conflict between the two aims of increased production and Moroccanisation. Lack of expertise in government departments meant that projects were not effectively planned and reappeared on paper in one budget after another, the money allocated not being spent.

(In the 1964-7 plan only 68 per cent of credits available were actually allocated). Or, for example, buildings would be constructed without the staffs to operate them. This also hampered Morocco's efforts to get more foreign aid and led to foreign exchange difficulties. Planners were often ignorant of local economic and social conditions and there were not enough trained officials to carry through agricultural schemes. The impetus behind 'Operation Plough' dwindled until the areas it covered dropped by nearly a half.

The Government tried to use up the investment budget and reduce the enormous unemployment by crash programmes of public works. The 'Rural Development Programme' and then the 'National Development' involved afforestation, minor road and water works, clearing fields of stones and cleaning up cities.

The second five-year plan for 1968-72 was a mixed success. It envisaged an investment of nearly £790 million of which £625 million would come from public funds. According to the official figures, public investment was 12 per cent higher than planned, though this was partly accounted for by higher prices. The growth rate averaged six per cent a year compared with the target of 4.3 per cent. Helped by good weather, agricultural production increased by six per cent a year compared with the aim of 2.1 per cent. Industrial output increased by £45 million in value, but many industries were working at only 50 to 70 per cent capacity. Per capita income rose to £150 a year but many peasants and town workers were poorer than the figure indicates. Consumption rose by 2 per cent a year, but the official report on the plan's achievements pointed out that this increase was unevenly divided: the share in consumption of the wealthiest ten per cent of households increased from 25 to 37 per cent while the share of the poorest ten per cent fell from 3.3 to 1.2 per cent. Economic growth did not necessarily help the poorer classes.

As in the previous plans top priority was given to agriculture, together with the training of Moroccan higher grade technicians and administrators. Public investment allocated for agriculture was £208 million of which £62.5 million was for building dams and irrigation works.

Three big dams and some smaller irrigation works were built during the plan period and three other big dams were nearing completion. The three completed dams should have supplied water for the irrigation of 107,000 hectares compared with the plan target of 123,000 hectares. But of this total only an area of 34,000 hectares was equipped for irrigation by the summer of 1973; an even smaller amount was being actually irrigated and brought into production. The plan also lagged behind target in public housing and medical services. The family planning campaign (aimed at reducing the birth rate from 50 to 45 per thousand) was an almost total failure and was virtually abandoned.

Seventy per cent of Moroccans live on the land, mostly engaged in subsistence farming, and agriculture provides a third of GDP. There is heavy rural unemployment or under-employment – over 50 per cent in some areas – and a consequent drift to the towns in search of work. This rural exodus was slightly less than the anticipated half a million people during 1968-72. The plan was subsequently criticised officially for not having paid enough attention to unemployment. It was claimed to have created 485,000 jobs over five years but this still left an increase in the number of unemployed by 115,000 over the same period. By the end of the plan, unemployment was officially estimated at 350,000 with another 700,000 people working for less than half the year.

The third five-year plan for 1973-7 was more ambitious and less austerity-orientated than the second. It based hopes for a rapid expansion partly on the increased revenue from higher-priced phosphate exports (Morocco is the world's biggest exporter of phosphates). The original investment target of the new plan was about £1,300 million but this was more than doubled in 1973 and further raised in 1975 to £4,400 million. The plan aimed at an increase in the growth rate of 7.5 per cent a year – of which 4 per cent was to be for agriculture and 11 per cent for industry. It put more stress on providing jobs and housing, on redistribution of wealth, manpower training, and the encouragement of foreign investment in export-directed industries. For the latter purpose special tax and customs concessions were introduced. The plan also aimed to spend more on bringing existing installations into more productive use. In the first revised version of the plan agriculture was to receive 15.8 per cent of total investments as against 37.2 per cent for industry, and 23.6 per cent for social and cultural equipment. But under the second expansion of the plan more investment was to be made in agriculture. A sum of £46 million was allocated for irrigation works. As the plan period began, six big dams and some smaller works had been completed with a capacity to provide water for 400,000 hectares. The new plan provided for three more big dams but its main emphasis was on developing the existing dams by providing the necessary canalisation and equipment for the new irrigable areas. It was hoped that by 1977 over 670,000 hectares – or two-thirds of the final target of one million hectares of irrigable land – would be under permanent irrigation.

The slow progress in developing and modernising Moroccan agriculture is due not so much to shortage of public funds as to lack of social and technical reforms needed to make the investment fully productive. The second five-year plan recognised that reforms were needed in land ownership and distribution, and in the state services dealing with agriculture. It blamed the lack of progress in introducing new techniques not only on the shortage of trained staff but also on the mistrust and conservatism of the peasants which in turn spring from their need for quick assured returns in a precarious economic environment. Most Moroccan peasants own no land or very little – forty per cent own no land at all. Five to ten per cent of the rural population own over 60 per cent of the land.

The country's five million hectares of cultivable land support 1,150,000 rural households (excluding another 100,000 engaged in stock breeding). This means that even if the land were equally divided there would be only five to seven hectares per household.

But in fact only one fifth of the cultivable land has been available for distribution under the joint agrarian reform fund. It consists of state and other communally-owned lands as well as lands owned by former French colonists. (In 1973 the Moroccanisation of farming was completed with the expropriation of the remaining 2,000 foreign farmers, mostly French, with holdings of 250,000 hectares – a step which led to friction with France.) Most of the rest of the land is owned by big Moroccan landlords. In addition, small landholdings are often made even smaller by the splitting or sharing involved in the Muslim inheritance laws. The second plan recommended redistribution of land to create more viable units, the promotion of cooperatives and the reform of the rental and agricultural taxation systems.

Critics of the regime say that these good intentions have
partly been frustrated in practice because of political
favouritism and corruption which leads to land being redistributed to loyal supporters, and to speculation in land scheduled
for irrigation.

It was in the field of agriculture and irrigation that the
Kuwait Fund at first made its main contribution to Moroccan
development. In 1966 it granted two loans totalling about
KD10 million (£11.6 million) for two important agricultural
and irrigation schemes, the Tessaout and Tadla projects in
central Morocco. In 1972 the Fund granted a loan of
KD860,000 (£951,000) for a sugar factory in north-east Morocco, for which the World Bank also made a loan. This was one of
seven sugar plants being built in a bid to make Morocco
self-sufficient in sugar supplies. Subsequently the Fund made
three further loans totalling KD 11.9 million (£17.8 million) to
Morocco. In 1975 it lent KD 3.5 million (£5.25 million) to help
finance a new 300 mgw thermal power station at Quneitra,
near Rabat, the national capital. The loan was for thirteen
years at 4 per cent interest. The station is expected to be
completed in the summer of 1979.

Also in 1975 the Fund made a loan of KD6 million (£9
million) to the Moroccan National Bank for Economic
Development (BNDE). This was part of the new Fund policy of
lending to local development institutions and industrial banks
for them to re-lend for smaller projects at their discretion. The
BNDE has responsibility for providing part of the finance for
the five-year plan, especially for the promotion of labour-
intensive and export-directed industries, including encouragement for foreign investors.

The Fund had earlier made a loan of KD2.4 million (£3.6
million) through the same bank for a phosphoric acid and
mono-ammonium phosphate plant to be built near the town of
Safi. Phosphoric acid is a key product for the manufacture of
high-grade chemical fertilisers and the project is intended to
develop Morocco's share in the international trade in phosphate products. The total cost is estimated at KD46.6 million
(£70 million). Other sources providing the foreign exchange
element besides the Kuwait Fund include the World Bank and
the West German Kreditanstalt für Wiederaufbau.

The second and smaller of the two earlier agricultural schemes supported by the Fund was to extend irrigation over an additional 23,000 hectares of the Tadla plain, where 67,000 hectares were already under modern irrigation. The scheme which began in 1965 and took longer than the expected five years to complete, included irrigation and drainage facilities, farm development, local farm development centres, roads and flood protection works. It was to cost just under KD8 million (£9.28 million) of which KD2,700,000 (£3.13 million) was provided by a Kuwait Fund loan for 15 years at 3 per cent.

Among the 23,000 people living in the Tadla project area, the improvements would, it was hoped, mean many more jobs as well as increased production. Instead of three-quarters of the local workers being unemployed there would be full employment. The expanded production would match the increase in population over the next 20 years while at the same time raising the wage rate by 80 per cent.

Reducing unemployment and raising local living standards were also the main motives for the Fund's grant of a loan of KD7,350,000 to the bigger Tessaout project. The total cost of the project, involving the building of a large dam, a hydro-electric power station and irrigation canals and technical services for an area of 27,200 hectares, was expected to be KD16,750,000 (£19,430,000).

After a Fund mission went to Morocco to investigate the project in 1964 and 1965, it reported that on purely economic criteria the project could not be considered favourably despite an expected substantial increase in value of production. In the first fifteen years of operation it would have an adverse effect on Morocco's balance of payments and the government would not get back the money it put into construction in under 140 years unless it substantially raised the price it charged to the farmers for water. These effects would come at a time when the Moroccan government's finances were already heavily strained and the foreign reserves position weak.

But the Fund nevertheless decided to grant a loan on easy terms – 3½ per cent interest and twenty years to repay beginning five years after the loan was granted. It considered that the social benefits in an area whicn has high unemployment, a low living standard, wide-spread starvation, illiteracy and disease, were more important than the effects on the national finances.

The area, the population of which is mostly of Berber stock, had lagged far behind the rest of Morocco, so that the government had strong political as well as economic motives for investing in development there.

It was estimated that the project would triple the number of employed workers (though the numbers involved are a tiny proportion of Morocco's unemployed). Over a period of 25 years it would raise the employment rate in the area from 20 per cent to 31 per cent despite a doubling of the population. Wages would rise by over 150 per cent though the pressure of unemployment would probably keep labourers' wage rates down.

The Tessaout project area lies about 37 miles from Marrakesh, the great city of central Morocco, the gateway to the southern Atlas and the Sahara. Along the road from Rabat to Marrakesh the landscape is alternately dreary and exciting. The road goes by Casablanca, the second biggest industrial city in the Arab world after Cairo. That day it was a city of white and grey rocked by a grey wind and white sea. As we turned inland through the Settat area where, apart from Casablanca, the remaining French 'colonists' were concentrated, (there are 90,000 French people still in Morocco), rain came in heavy bursts out of a lowering sky. Great plains of salmon-pink earth were broken by occasional forests of eucalyptus and pine. The road crossed a deep wild ravine with a torrent foaming at the bottom of it, climbed through hills to a plateau and then rolled on undeviatingly for fifty miles across a bare gravelly steppe to Marrakesh.

The romantic reputation of Marrakesh does not prepare one for the fact that, like other ancient Moroccan cities, it has a large modern section which is the part most arriving visitors see first. My hotel, ultra-new with its glass, black leather furnishings, dim lights and air conditioning, was set almost surrealistically among palm groves on the edge of the modern town. Above the palm leaves rose the square stone tower of the Koutoubia mosque among its quiet gardens near the entrance to the old city.

The next day my guide to the Tessaout project was the local regional director for the Agricultural Development Office (Office de la Mise en Valeur Agricole), M. Belfouzi. He was in charge of the Haouz region which includes most of Marrakesh province and a great part of his work was concerned with the

Tessaout project. M. Belfouzi was a tall, thin, dark young man in his early thirties or late twenties, trained in agronomy and engineering in France. The son of an army officer, he said that he had felt a vocation for agriculture from childhood. He thought it was the best way of serving his country. He was quiet and efficient, though one could see that he was often exasperated by the difficulties of his job, particularly dealing with less educated people.

We went first to his office in Marrakesh to look at maps and reports on the general lay-out and progress of the project.

The area covered by the project is 52,000 hectares (130,000 acres) of which just over half was to be irrigated from the dam. The population involved is 43,600 in 166 villages. Sixty per cent of the area is privately owned land, mostly in very small holdings with a few big properties. A detailed survey carried out of 7,000 hectares showed that nearly half the holdings were of half a hectare (1.25 acres) or less, totalling less than five per cent of the total area, while over thirty per cent of the land was held by one per cent of owners with average holdings of 200 hectares.

The project area had already been partly irrigated by a very old and elaborate water-system of 'seguias' or unlined earth canals, most of them several miles long. The total length of the seguias was nearly 200 miles and their excavation is estimated to have taken half a million man-days, a remarkable piece of ancient engineering. As the Kuwait Fund report on the project pointed out, the seguias could only have been built and maintained within the framework of a strong collective organisation and the distribution of water through them was governed by a refined system of traditionally evolved rules. But they did not include a storage system, were expensive in labour costs to maintain and were only a quarter as efficient as a modern irrigation system.

The planning of the new irrigation system had to take into account the old-established water rights. The new canals had also to be planned so as to create the least upset to the existing pattern of settlement and social organisation that had evolved round the 'seguia' system. An equitable formula was found as the basis for a new system of water rights and the existing seguia irrigation was to be concentrated in a smaller area. At the same time the effective use of modern irrigation involved the regrouping of land holdings and the preparation of land through clearing and levelling to receive the waterflow. The legal and human problems involved were comparable with – only probably far more complex than – those involved in an industrial country in building a new motorway today or a railway in the last century.

It was easier to envisage the problems when we visited the dam and the project on the spot. We drove out from Marrakesh east and then north across sweeping brown plains with villages built of red earth and hazy grey mountains on the horizon.

The road was good but narrow, and made more dangerous by the variety and unpredictability of its users. There was every kind of traffic especially in and around the villages – buses, trucks, motor scooters, cycles, horses and carts, mules and donkeys, people on foot, groups of women in flowing silks of orange, green and pink. Round the village houses were hedges of pale grey-green thorn. Men and donkeys hugged the shade of the high red walls. In the fields or on the bare roadside the peasants stood or squatted, like Murillo paintings in their straw hats and cloaks, graceful and dignified in their poses. Under the bright sun they seemed to create their own shadows in which they sheltered.

We passed by olive groves and large apricot orchards. M. Belfouzi commented disapprovingly on the apricots. They were a bad crop and should not be planted, he said. Eighty-four per cent of all the apricots in Morocco are produced in the Marrakesh area and they all go on the market in a single week. As a result only about a third of them are ever sold and there are not enough canning or jam factories to take care of the rest.

M. Belfouzi explained that the peasants are considered to need a minimum of five hectares of irrigated land to earn a living for their family, reckoning the family as composed of five people of whom three are working. This gives them an income of about ten dirhams or ninety pence a day. (Hired labour gets a daily wage of less than fifty pence). Then there was the problem of the smallest subsistence farmer, the man who has only one hectare or even less. Such a holding cannot really be worked as part of a modern economy and there is pressure on the owner to sell to bigger landowners. But his problem is that if he gives up his small piece of land, to which in any case he clings with great sentiment, he also gives up a way of at least keeping alive in the traditional system. If he is displaced there is no guarantee that there will be a job waiting for him elsewhere in industry. So he might prefer to stay where he is rather than be an unemployed man living in a sordid *bidonville* or shanty town outside Casablanca.

On the edge of the plain, at the foot of some hills – the foot-hills of the High Atlas – we passed Tazert, a red earth village dominated by a small and now partly ruined fortress which was once a palace of the Glaoui, the former Pasha of Marrakesh. Soon a signpost said 13 kilometres to Ait Adel, the site of the dam, and we turned off into the hills. Before long we could see the glittering stream of the Tessaout at the bottom of a gorge. Villages clung to the hills on either side and down in the valley was the intense green of irrigated plots with orchards, gardens and small fields.

Then, a still and massive presence that could almost be felt before one saw it, there was the high grey wall of the dam closing off the valley between the brown hills. White water foamed at the base. Near this outlet at the side of the dam were three tunnels for the projected hydro-electric power installations to be built by the Russians. The dam itself was built and completed in 1970 by German contractors at a cost of £11,250,000 – 45 per cent of the cost, the foreign exchange element, was provided by the Kuwait Fund loan. The dam is 82 metres high and 695 metres long at the crest. It is constructed of earth and rock fill and can store 200 million cubic metres of water.

We drove up to the edge of the dam and walked across it. Behind it a large lake stretched back among an amphitheatre of low mountains. The scene was wild and beautiful. From the top of the dam we looked down over the revetments of grey and pink stones, like enormous rounded seaside pebbles sloping gently, as if it were a giant English seashore, all the way down to the bottom of the valley. It looked less dramatic than one of the more familiar vertical concrete dams, but more solid and reassuring, fitting the landscape more naturally.

Leaving the dam we drove down along the river to look at one of the diversion canals which take water to the project. We passed through miles of olive groves, full of luxuriant big trees. Too big, said the ever-vigilant M. Belfouzi, because it encourages the peasants to use the bad old method harvesting the olives by beating the tree and letting the fruit fall to the ground.

A rough stony track led down from the road past flickering olive trees and silent staring villagers: a boy with a big hat was driving a few thin cows, men with round heads and hard noses jolted along on donkeys. The sun sparkled on two small girls in long cloth-of-gold dresses, and a woman with a headscarf striped with silver. The diversion dam was at a place called Agadir Bou Ashiba. There was a long, low weir with dark water pouring slowly and smoothly over it and next to it a sluice system. The water tumbled away through a tunnel under the hill which led down to the main irrigation channels further downstream on either side of the Tessaout river valley.

Here was an illustration of the difficulty of ensuring that anything works efficiently in Morocco, because of the lack of trained people. There had been no water going through the diversion channel for a month because, it was thought, the sluice gate machinery had broken down. What had really happened was that the man living on the spot who was supposed to regulate the gates did not know how to work the machinery properly, how to turn if off and on. He was an unskilled man like a night watchman. He had to be replaced by someone better trained and better paid.

Apart from the dam and diversion, the building of primary canals in the area, a total of 50 kilometres (32 miles), was almost all finished, as well as half of the secondary canals. Work was in progress on the regrouping and preparation of land in the four sectors into which the project area had been divided. In the first sector seven thousand hectares were nearly finished and the peasants were due to be settled on new lands. On.7,500 hectares in the second sector settlement was to take place during 1972-3. In the other two sectors a legal basis for the regrouping was still being established.

In one of the sectors where the building of canals was just being completed, we stopped where a secondary irrigation canal – a raised semi-circular concrete channel – crossed the road and a third-size channel, smaller in diameter, led off from it between the road and the fields. A fourth level channel, only of unlined earth, carried the water to the fields. A peasant was using some of the water on his small plot which was flooded and dotted with heaps of manure. He was cultivating lucerne. M. Belfouzi stopped to reprimand him for not using the proper water technique. Instead of making several syphons from the channel on to the field, he had made a breach in the earth bank of the channel in the traditional way so that the water poured through unevenly. The flow of water through the first, second and third canals is controlled by officials of the OMVA, while groups of farmers appoint two representatives each to regulate the fourth channel flow according to a timetable agreed with the OMVA. The OMVA also decides the planting programme.

M. Belfouzi pointed with pride to the fields where thick golden stubble still showed the density of the wheat crop in the first year of the new irrigation. He said they had had a yield of 25 to 28 quintals of wheat from the irrigated lands, instead of the eight quintals they had expected. This was partly because in addition to the irrigation they had had good rains. He talked of the marketing problem, a big one for the peasants, especially the internal market. Very high profits were made by the big merchants and middlemen. There was sometimes as much as 1,000 per cent difference between the price for produce received by the peasant and the retail price in the market.

'The peasants won't sow new crops they are not sure of selling. It's no use my telling them to sow sugar beet, for example. They say, "Yes, we know it's a paying crop but who is going to buy it?" Nor will they spend money on improvements such as fertilisers, which they haven't got. They say, "We know ten dirhams' worth of fertilisers will do wonders but we haven't got ten dirhams".'

Nearby, past some fields of water melon, was an Agricultural Development Centre, and advisory, supervisory and demonstration centre run by the Ministry of Agriculture. There are four such centres in the project area and nine in the whole Marrakesh region. Eventually each centre will deal with about 3,000 hectares and 800 households. The staff consisted of eight men – four demonstrators or teachers, three specialists in cooperatives and one for programming. Alongside the demonstration farm and the office buildings were neat, pink-plastered bungalows in a well-kept garden for the staff. A young man with a stubbly chin was in charge. Another young man ran the farm school where about twenty-five young farmers' sons, aged eighteen to twenty-four, come for two years to learn modern methods. They also learn something about administration and how to deal with government departments.

Near the road towards the outer edge of the project area a

crane was unloading from a truck the big concrete pipes and half-pipes for a secondary canal. The canal followed the line of an old seguia which was still flowing and would continue to do so until the new channel was ready. Donkeys passed slowly with huge loads of straw in long, plaited bundles balanced in a curve across their backs like gleaming golden bows. Fields were being crumbled up and levelled by a huge yellow-painted machine with wheels taller than a man and a leveller like a big bulldozer. They broke up and flattened the pink earth into a smooth dust like old-fashioned face-powder. Two young Frenchmen, bronzed and naked to the waist, watched from a small pick-up truck by the road-side. Levelling is a vital part of preparing for irrigation on the principle that 'water must flow everywhere and remain nowhere'. The gradient has to be calculated to a matter of centimetres.

Then came the Tessaout river, the primary canals on either bank, and roads shaded by eucalyptus trees. In this area 900 hectares of state land was given to the people whose land was flooded by the building of the dam. They have a new village with modern pink-washed buildings and a graceful water-tower, new houses financed by the World Food Programme, a dispensary, a school and a Development Centre.

So far cooperatives have been organised only on collectively-owned lands. But on private land there were groups of farmers sharing machinery.

I asked M. Belfouzi whether, politics apart, he thought a more collectivised agriculture would be the right thing in this area. He said – and it was his personal, not official opinion – that there was no doubt about it. There was already an old tradition of collective action and of self-help in time of trouble among the tribes. It was better for the peasants to work together. Rather than each having his tiny bit of land and dealing with merchants separately, they could put their lands together and hire a truck to take their produce to market to be sold at auction.

There should, he thought, not be state farms but state help and state supervision and more cooperatives. But the big land owners were influential.

On my return to Rabat, some of the problems of development in Morocco were outlined to me with realistic frankness by a senior official in the Government planning secretariat. I conclude this chapter by giving his comments in some detail because they still seem applicable not only to Morocco but also to many other Arab countries.

In his view the chief problems were as follows:

1 The lack of qualified 'cadres' or trained people at all levels. This includes secretaries who can be relied upon to organise a meeting of officials, messengers who can read the names on a file, plumbers who can really mend taps, gardeners who don't kill trees when they prune them, drivers who can even read the car manuals, let alone repair the car. The inability to rely on such trained people reduces the efficiency of even the most able administrator by perhaps fifty per cent. Add to this a general lack of education, training and experience and at lower levels the mass of illiterates.

2 The problem of the *système foncière* or structure of property ownership. The fact that land is often owned in tiny holdings, for example, of one hectare or less, makes it difficult to develop. Yet the collectivisation of land raises many other problems.

3 Social habits: a new Moroccan bourgeoisie has emerged to replace the departed French colonists. But it is not a dynamic bourgeoisie of entrepreneurs: it prefers to use its money for speculation or investment in buildings or land. The difference between rich and poor is perpetuated in new forms.

4 The psychological problem of the 'patriarchal relationship'. People wait to be told what to do next. They don't take initiatives and there is no continuity of effort.

5 The problem of mixed cultures. Moroccans are caught between European and traditional Arab cultures. The trend towards 'Arabisation', the use of Arabic in public life – an issue peculiar to North Africa – raises problems of education and the supply of teachers. The culture conflict has a special effect on the position of women. Sometimes women regress towards their traditional status when they get married: they give up the mini skirt for the djellaba, even resume the veil; they turn themselves away from jobs and outside interests to devote themselves to babies and cooking.

6 Population: there is no real progress yet in limiting its growth. It will reach 25 million by 1980. Morocco has a population control programme on paper but it has little effect. Its success depends on the cultural level of the women. Many

women fear contraception will bring them sterility or disease.
But if a woman is working she doesn't wish to have – and can't
have – lots of babies.

7 Population growth is one of several classic problems of
developing countries that also exist in Morocco. Others include
unemployment, the growth of cities with slums, shanty towns,
inadequate transport and social services, lack of health and
education services and too heavy foreign debt – aid is now
nearly all in loans and is either very expensive in interest or tied
closely to difficult conditions.

But, despite the lack of cadres, if more aid were available it
would be used, my informant said.

5 Algeria

No other Arab people, except perhaps the Palestinians, has suffered as much from foreign colonisation as the Algerians or made such heroic sacrifices for its national independence. Nor has any faced such enormous problems after independence in material reconstruction and the recovery of its submerged national culture. The Algerians themselves say they had a million casualties in the eight-year war of independence out of a population of ten to twelve million. Two million people were forcibly displaced during the war, driven from their villages into camps. Hundreds of villages and farms were destroyed.

The abrupt departure of the French settlers after independence suddenly stripped the country of most of its administrative, technical and economic skills, for very few Algerians had been given the chance to acquire such skills and experience in their own country.

It is not surprising if, as a result of these experiences and the continued sacrifices required during the first ten years of independence, Algeria, when I first revisited it in October 1971, seemed at first a dour place after the leisurely charm of Morocco. But the dourness is partly an aspect of the seriousness and vigour with which the Algerians tackle their problems and also perhaps an expression of the down-to-earth character of their society. For, unlike most other national and social movements in the Arab world, the Algerian revolution and independence movement was not led by the middle class – the French presence had prevented the emergence of an effective Algerian bourgeoisie in place of the former traditional leadership – but sprang from the workers and peasants, who were directly involved in the struggle.

This involvement created a heritage of self-reliance and a readiness to accept sacrifices in a wider common cause. Consequently nowhere in the Arab world – not even in Egypt – has the aim of national independence been more closely linked with that of economic and social development, or more passionately pursued than in Algeria. It has also inspired the militant attitude of Algeria in seeking a fairer share of the world's goods for the developing countries as a whole through the creation of a 'new international economic order'. From the beginning of their independence the Algerians were determined to pull themselves up by their own bootstraps and, in the words of a foreign observer in Algiers, 'you could already hear the bootstraps creaking'. This did not mean that the Algerians rejected all foreign financial or technical help, but they were careful to accept it only on a scale and on such terms as would not limit their control of their own resources and economy. In their development effort they took a calculated gamble. They gambled on being able to use their oil and natural gas resources and the foreign exchange they earned from them to create rapidly a new industrial structure which within a decade would give the country the basis of a modern economy. Their chances of success were greatly increased by the large expansion in oil revenues after the quadrupling of oil prices in 1973-4.

In the argument among development economists about whether it is better to invest first in agriculture and so create industrial demand indirectly, or in industry first, the Algerians firmly chose industry. In the other big argument about whether to go first for more jobs or for higher productivity (Algeria's unemployment rate is believed to be as high as 40 per cent, especially bad in the countryside), the Algerian regime chose productivity. It has invested heavily in highly capitalised industry which employs relatively few people.

By comparison agriculture was at first left to look after itself. It was only after the launching of the officially styled 'agrarian revolution' in 1971 that more serious attention was paid to farming. Since the increase in oil revenues in 1973 the allocation for investment in agriculture has trebled but it is still proportionately a good deal less than investment in industry.

The supply of consumer goods as well as of jobs had a low priority. The resulting austerity led to grumbles from both peasants and townspeople. But the policy was maintained by the discipline of the national revolutionary party, the FLN (*Front de Libération Nationale*) and the authority of the military socialist regime which emerged from the national liberation movement. It was backed by popular pride in national achievement and an acceptance of the need for present sacrifice in order to build a better future.

Algeria was not only bolder than many other Arab or Third World countries in launching on a crash programme of industrialisation. It also led the way among the Arab oil states in seeking to share in and eventually control, the production and marketing of oil and gas, with the aim of strengthening its independence and ensuring control of its major economic resources. Since 1974, it has been overtaken in this respect by the Gulf states which have obtained in some cases full financial ownership or a bigger share in the operations of the former concessionary companies. But except for Iraq they do not yet play such an active part in the actual conduct of technical operations as do the Algerians. In 1975 the Algerian Government agreed to renew for another five years the arrangements by which it has a 51 per cent share in joint Algerian-French oil companies, but altogether it controlled 75 per cent of oil production in the country, as well as all the natural gas.

Under Algerian socialism most of the other important industrial and commericial enterprises and services have been nationalised or brought under government control. In agriculture, much of the subsistence farming on privately-owned land continues as before, though with limitations on land ownership and with official pressure to form cooperatives. But in its agricultural revolution, the regime does not seem to be encouraging a spread of the system of self-management which resulted from the spontaneous take-over of former French colonist-owned lands by farm workers after independence.

The ideologists of the FLN claim that Algeria's socialism and one-party system go back not to Karl Marx but to the traditional collectivism which persisted even under the French in the large areas of the country which the French controlled militarily but did not effectively administer.

Apart from industrialisation, the other foundation the Algerians count on for their future development is education. And here they have a double problem which is unique in the Arab world. They have not only to build a new educational system but also to recover the use of their own national language, Arabic. When Algeria became independent ninety per cent of the Muslim population were illiterate. But most of what education there was took place in French not Arabic; French was the official language of public life. A similar problem existed in Morocco and Tunisia but on a smaller scale. Algeria is still the second biggest French-speaking country in the world. It employs over 8,000 French 'cooperants', or specialists, mostly teachers, out of a total of some 12,000 foreign 'specialists'. But a programme of gradual 'Arabisation' has been introduced in education and in society as a whole. All Algerian officials are now required to know some Arabic, and parts of the administration, such as the judiciàry, as well as some university faculties in the humanities, are now Arabised. But much public business is still conducted in French and there are enormous problems involved in complete Arabisation of the administration, because so many files and documents, such as past registers of land and of births and deaths are in French with gallicised versions of Arab names. In education, Arabisation is being carried out in gradual stages because of lack of trained teachers. The Algerians are also trying to avoid the kind of confusion that occurred in Morocco where total Arabisation of the first stages of education left pupils unable to deal with later stages which were still in French.

Since 1964 Algeria has spent a quarter of its state budget on education – in 1974 it was 30 per cent. By 1972 two million out of three million children between the ages of six and eighteen were at school compared with 300,000 before independence, and the number of university students had increased from one thousand to seventeen thousand. A hundred doctors were being produced a year instead of two or three, and eighty engineers where there were none before. Efforts are being made to expand technical schools and train middle-grade technicians, but the numbers of all technical specialists, managers and skilled workers being produced are still well behind the scores of thousands that will be needed to carry through the national development plan.

Under the second four-year plan for 1974-7, the number of universities is to be increased from three to seven and the number of engineer graduates is to rise to 600 or 700 by the end of the plan period.

Algeria's first four-year plan for 1970-3 declared its aim to be 'to lay the bases of a modern and independent industrial economy, to transform rural life and to create an educational system and a renovated cultural heritage'. It was the first stage towards achieving long-term targets. The ultimate aim was to have created, before the end of the century, an industrialised economy from which the country could live, by which time the estimated oil reserves would have been used up. But before then, by 1980, the hope was to achieve among other things: lasting employment for all the active male population; education guaranteeing a minimum cultural level and producing 100,000 university students; new housing at the rate of 100,000 dwellings a year; water, electricity and gas supplies in all towns and villages.

Three priorities in productive investment were set out in the first plan and continued in the second plan for 1974-7. The first was to exploit the country's mineral wealth, especially oil and natural gas, so as to increase the internal financial resources. The main purpose of oil production is to earn foreign exchange, but gas is seen as the basis of cheap industrial and domestic fuel and of home economic development.

The second priority is to consolidate the basic industrial production needed for modernising agriculture and to develop industries such as steel, engineering, fertilisers, electric power and building materials. The third stage is to develop production to satisfy primary needs and a wider demand for consumer goods.

Some of the basic principles of the first plan were explained to me in Algiers by the Secretary of State for the Plan, Mr Bel Khodja, a cool young man in a small cool office on the sixth floor of the Palais du Gouvernement, the massive white administration block built by the French and still housing most Algerian ministries. Pigeons strut on the window-ledges, as in Whitehall, and there are magnificent views across the city to the harbour and the sea. The day I called (in October 1971) the lifts weren't working. Nor was the water working at my hotel, and the telephone was erratic. Algiers, a city of a million and a half people, was bursting at the seams with ever-increasing numbers of children, young men and cars. There was not enough of anything – buses, water, electricity, houses. But compared with the Algiers I had first seen at the height of the independence war, a city of hate, cruelty, arrogance and fear, it seemed a civilised and human place.

Mr Khodja said that Algeria had rejected the advice given to many developing countries to give priority to agricultural development. The Algerians saw industrial expansion as the motor force of economic expansion. The policy of investing in industry had already multiplied demand in many sectors. It was true that heavy capital industry, such as oil, chemicals and steel, did not provide many jobs but they were the basis for industrial advance on which future resources and jobs depended. Employment was a long-term problem which could only be solved through rapid development: this was was more important than the short-term provision of jobs.

Algeria was not neglecting agriculture, he claimed, but did not see the solution for its problems there. The main function of agriculture was subsistence, to feed the country. Algeria was still importing food, so production had to be increased. In the agrarian revolution, whose doctrinal texts were then being prepared by the Government, there were three essential purposes. The first was to end exploitation and limit land ownership so that paid labour in agriculture was limited or eliminated. The second was to organise production on a larger scale by careful doses of collectivisation, with the aim of ending micro-ownership of land, which was uneconomic. The third purpose was to provide the peasants with the production resources they needed – credits, seeds, fertilisers and technical services.

The plan counted on some foreign help but chiefly in the form of credits for the capital goods imports provided for in the plan. Essentially Algeria did not want 'aid' which, claimed Mr Khodja, was often not really aid at all but loans with strings attached or with high interest rates. But help from friendly governments in backing export credits was welcome. For the next ten years at least oil would remain the most important element in Algerian development but the aim was to use it so as to build other industries and reduce dependence on oil.

One of the men then chiefly responsible for the execution of the industrial programme was an enthusiastic young Frenchman, who had become an Algerian citizen, M. Castelle, Director of the Ministry of Industry and Power.

He scribbled some figures rapidly on a blackboard to illustrate for me the growth of Algerian industry since 1967 (before that year there was very little industry). Investments in industry had risen from 750 million dinars (£62 million) in 1967 to an anticipated 4,500 million dinars (£370 million) in 1973. Industrial production, especially in steel, electricity, food products and textiles, had trebled between 1967 and 1971 and would almost double again by 1973.

Electric power would be doubled by 1973 with new generators at Oran, Algiers, Skigda and Annaba, and high tension lines between them. A gas liquification plant was being built at Skigda and work would be completed during 1972 on new steel, fertiliser, cement and mercury plants. 5,000 million dinars (£416 million) worth of plant would create 13,000 jobs.

There were many problems, especially in coordinating the different sectors of the industrialisation programme. Sometimes there were delays in supplies of electric power and gas, or transport, or cement. But in going full steam ahead one must expect trouble, said M. Castelle. Perhaps, he speculated, it was in any case cheaper to go fast and make mistakes than to go slowly, because during the interval international prices of capital goods rise fast.

'The Boeing is taking off with a learner pilot at the controls' was M. Castelle's colourful metaphor for Algeria's development situation. 'Everything depends on the next few years. We have our backs to the wall. By 1980 we must establish an industrial base or sink.'

During the first plan, described by M. Castelle, actual public investment was 34,000 million dinars (£2,850 million) compared with the original target figure of 26,400 million dinars (£2,200 million). About 45 per cent of investment went into industry; 15 per cent to agriculture and 40 per cent to social and economic infrastructure. The plan was officially claimed to have fulfilled its aim of a nine per cent growth rate and to have created 300,000 new jobs.

The original version of the second four-year plan for 1974-7 aimed at a big increase in investment up to 54,000 million dinars. But with the big rise in oil revenues after 1973 the target figure was almost doubled again to 100,000 million dinars (£10,000 million). It was hoped to achieve a growth rate of ten per cent a year, and to create 450,000 new jobs outside agriculture. The second plan still stresses industry, especially heavy industry, which gets 46 per cent of investment. But the big increase in available funds means that more can be allocated to housing (nearly 200,000 new dwellings), health (50 new hospitals), manpower training, as well as job-creating, smaller industries and more efficient farming. Agriculture is allocated 16,600 million dinars, (£1,600 million) or three times the amount spent on it under the first plan. The agrarian reform programme is intended to reverse the decline in productivity which set in after the French left and to reduce the rural exodus to the towns estimated at 100,000 people a year. The first stage of the reform was the distribution of a million hectares of public land to 54,000 landless peasant families and their grouping into cooperatives. The second stage, begun in 1973, was the break-up of the remaining big Algerian-owned private estates and the redistribution of another million hectares to 60,000 more land-less families. The plan was eventually to settle the whole farm population in 1,000 model villages. The third stage, opening in 1975, was to increase livestock production on twenty million hectares of steppe land in southern Algeria where the nomadic population was to be settled in new towns and villages. But a major part of the agricultural programme was to be devoted to improving productivity through more irrigation, fertilisers and machinery. New dams, wells and irrigation works were to be allocated 1,717 million dinars (£170 million) with the aim of bringing another 110,000 hectares under irrigation.

The expanded industrialisation programme under the second four-year plan covers 900 major projects at a cost of 63,350 million dinars (£6,300 million) of which 48,000 million dinars (£4800 million) is to be invested by the end of 1977. Once again oil and gas development takes the lion's share with a plan allocation of 19,500 million dinars (£1,950 million) and heavy investment in refineries, pipelines, liquification plants and liquid gas tankers. Other projects include two new steel conver-ters which will boost steel output to 1.5 million tons a year, a big petrochemical complex and an expansion in cooperation with foreign firms of the building and assembly of cars, trucks and farm machinery.

Not more than 25 per cent of the money needed for the second plan was to come from foreign borrowing. In 1973 Algeria borrowed about 1,500 million dollars on the Eurodollar market and obtained a 200 million dollar loan from an interna-tional banking consortium for the purchase of three gas tank-ers. But in the following year the government decided not to borrow any more from private sources. In 1973 it was granted a 24.5 million dollar loan from the World Bank, the first from that institution since 1964, and a year later it received another three long-term loans totalling 157.5 million dollars from the Bank. In 1974 the Arab Fund for Economic and Social Development and the Kuwait Investment Corporation jointly contributed 70 million dollars to an international 150 million dollar soft loan for the development of a gas tanker port.

By 1975 Algeria's foreign indebtedness totalled 11,000 million dinars (£1,100 million) and its servicing represented about eight per cent of the country's exports.

Whether the Algerians will succeed in their attempted break-through to an industrial economy without more massive outside aid depends not only on their own energy, determination and readiness to accept an austerity existence in the meantime, but also on their oil and gas resources. Algerian oil first came on the world market in 1958. Since then exports have risen from half a million to over 50 million tons a year with an expected rise to 65 million tons by 1977 – though the fall in world demand after 1973 meant that this last figure was less likely to be achieved.

The Algerian Government's share of oil export earnings rose, with the help of the big price increases, from £250 million in 1971-2 to about £1,350 million in 1975. Ninety per cent of Algerian oil goes to Western Europe and two-thirds to France. For the European market Algeria enjoys a transport advantage over Middle East producers, for it is only four to five hundred miles from the Algerian ports to Marseilles compared with nearly 5,000 miles from the Arabian (Persian) Gulf, and 1,600 miles from the oil terminal at Tripoli in the Lebanon.

Among the Arab oil producers Algeria is in a middle position. She is not a really big producer on the scale of Saudi Arabia or Kuwait. Her exploitable oil reserves have been estimated at 1,000 million tons. On the other hand she has vast natural gas reserves estimated at 3,000 billion cubic metres, or six per cent of world gas reserves. Neither is she solely dependent on oil, like some of the Gulf states, without other resources to develop. She could survive if necessary without the oil but the oil money and power from the natural gas can be put to good use for domestic development.

The discovery of oil in the Sahara in the fifties prolonged the Algerian war of independence and so cost scores of thousands more Algerian lives. For this reason, if for no other, the Algerians' determination to ensure that their oil is under adequate national control and used for the country's benefit is fully understandable. For the French tried at first to separate the Sahara from the rest of Algeria and the Algerians were obliged to reject a peace settlement which would have left the Sahara oil-fields under French political as well as economic control. The Algerians already foresaw the future importance of the oil and gas for the economic foundations of their new state.

Algeria's first move to share in the operations of the oil business came not through production but through the building of a pipeline, a project in which the Kuwait Fund played a part.

At first, eighty-five per cent of Algerian oil was produced by three French companies at two main oil fields of Hassi Messaoud and Edjeleh, but American and other foreign firms then began to produce a growing share. French companies also owned the two first main pipelines, one to Bougie and the other to La Skhira on the Tunisian coast. Both pipelines were built in 1960 with a combined capacity of 26 million tons. There was also a gas pipeline running 312 miles from the main gasfield of Hassi R'mel to the port of Arzew where a £24 million plant liquified some 1,500 million cubic metres of natural gas a year for export to Britain and France.

In 1963 it was foreseen that oil output would begin to outstrip the existing pipeline capacity. Some of the smaller oil producers who were then coming into production formed a company, TRAPAL, and asked the Algerian Government for authority to build a third pipeline from Haoud el Hamra to Arzew. Despite protests from TRAPAL that it had the exclusive right under the companies' concessions to transport its own oil, the Algerian government decided to build and operate a pipeline – a bigger one – itself.

To build and operate the new line, the government created SONATRACH (*Société Nationale de Transport et de Commercialisation des Hydrocarbons*). This was SONATRACH's sole original purpose but its operations were extended to other aspects of the oil business after the 1965 Algiers agreement. This agreement replaced the one made at the time of the Evian peace settlement which had left the French with a ninety per cent control of a joint French-Algerian partnership in Saharan oil. The Algiers agreement gave Algeria a fifty per cent share in future exploration and exploitation in four main concession areas, with SONATRACH becoming the Algerian partner. It also increased the Algerian share in existing operations and improved the government's oil revenues. At the same time France promised to contribute 1,000 million francs (£80 million) over five years for natural gas and industrial development in Algeria, eighty per cent in cheap long term loans and the rest in the form of grants.

In 1970 a number of the smaller oil companies operating in Algeria, affiiliates of American, German, Italian and Anglo-Dutch concerns, were nationalised on the grounds that they had not been sufficiently active in prospecting. Their production capacity was taken over by SONATRACH.

This was soon followed by a new step towards a more complete Algerian control of the oil industry. In February 1971 after a deadlock in a dispute over increased oil prices, President Boumédienne announced that the Algerian state would take over a 51 per cent share in seven French oil companies and would fully nationalise all natural gas deposits and pipelines. After a period of conflict during which the French government and companies tried ineffectually to organise an international boycott of Algerian oil and gas and Algerian exports to France were stopped, a settlement was reached on compensation, future sharing and prices.

The pattern was set when in June 1971 SONATRACH signed a ten-year agreement with the biggest French company, the partly government-owned CFP (*Compagnie Française des Pétroles*). The CFP became a 49 per cent shareholder in a new Franco-Algerian company, ALREP, with an option to sell out to SONATRACH after five years. Compensation was fixed at £25 million to be paid over seven years. Agreements with other French companies soon followed.

Algeria thus consolidated its position as the first Arab oil producing country to share directly both the profits and the risks of a major oil operation, an activity hitherto controlled by a few powerful industrial countries.

Since then there has been a massive shift in control to the governments of the oil-producing states. But when in 1963 the Algerian Government decided to build and operate its own pipeline it was a bold experiment. It was to be the first pipeline to be owned and operated by Arabs themselves, and there were then scarcely any Algerians with training or experience in the oil business. Because it was a new departure, it was not at first easy to get foreign financial backing. According to the Algerian Minister of Finance, Mr Ibrahim Mashroog, the intervention of the Kuwait Fund in support of the pipeline venture was especially important as a demonstration of confidence in Algeria's ability to carry it through and as a catalyst which helped to bring in other foreign aid and investment.

The pipeline project was completed in three stages at a total cost of £75.7 million, of which the Kuwait Fund provided KD10 millions (£11.6 million) in two loans.

The first stage was the building of a pipeline of 28-inch diameter and 500 miles long from Haoud el Hamra in the Sahara to Arzew on the Mediterranean, some 200 miles west of Algiers. It included the construction of three pumping stations, two crude oil tank farms at the receiving and shipping terminals, and shipping facilities, including two offshore floating berths and two submarine loading lines. The total cost of this stage was £34.5 million. The Kuwait Fund provided a loan of KD 7.5 million (£8.3 million) to meet part of the foreign exchange costs.

The second and third stages were to expand the capacity of the pipeline and terminal facilities up to 22 million tons of oil a year, at a cost of £13.4 million. For this the Fund gave a further loan of KD2.5 million (£2.76 million).

The oilfields served by the SONATRACH pipeline have 'proven' reserves of 780 million tons. The pipeline, completed in 1966 by a British firm, follows the track of two already existing pipelines. It starts five hundred feet above sea level at Haoud el Hamra and, after running through 125 miles of flat desert, climbs through the mountains rising to 4,000 feet over the Atlas, before crossing the coastal plain to Arzew.

Arzew is one of three industrial ports being developed under the four-year plans. It lies about 25 miles from Oran, a handsome town of half a million people, which was once the commercial capital of French Algiers. Oran was one of the places hardest hit by the French exodus when Algeria became independent. Sixty-five per cent of the city's population and 85 per cent of its trained workers and administrators left.

The road out to Arzew crosses the red earth of the coastal plain past neat white villages, often with a church tower (but no minaret) and former settler farms, reminiscent of Italy. Then above a green curve of vineyards rose a great tangled mass of metal, like the internal organs of some huge metallic animal, the tubes, grids, cylinders and chimneys of a new oil refinery under construction. It was being built by a Japanese company together with SONATRACH. A signpost said 'Arzew' and pointed towards more chimneys, tanks and industrial debris, topped with a pennant of flame from a tall pipe burning off waste gas. Beyond gleamed the blue line of the sea.

Arzew was once a quiet little fishing village and summer resort. It still has a charming square, a palm-lined avenue and a few blue-shuttered houses straggling down to a small harbour with fishing boats. Then it was chosen as a pipeline terminal, and became the first site for the creation of an industrial complex based on oil and gas. The other two ports chosen as centres of industrial development are Annaba, the centre of the steel industry, and Skigda, which is to have a bigger gas and petrochemical development.

Arzew's first industrial installation, built among the vineyards and the sand-dunes in 1963, only a year after Algerian independence, was a gas liquification plant. It was an Anglo-French enterprise pioneering a new technique of liquifying natural gas so that it could be shipped for export instead of moving it through a pipeline in what was previously the usual way. Its operations are based on long-term contracts to supply the British and French national gas companies. Britain takes two-thirds of the plant's output – about 909 million cubic metres a year – and forty per cent of the company's capital is British. French *Gaz de France* lent a third of the cost of building the plant and takes a third of the production in repayment. SONATRACH has 20 per cent of the capital, while in all the other gas installations it has at least a half-share.

In a subsequent big gas export project, which includes a liquification plant at Skigda three times the size of that at Arzew, SONATRACH shares fifty-fifty with the US El Paso company. In 1975 the first of two contracts with the El Paso company accounted for half of existing exports and contracts totalling 20,000 million cubic metres a year. A second El Paso contract for 10,000 million cubic metres a year was still under negotiation, as was a deal with a consortium of European gas companies for the export of 15,500 million cubic metres a year. Two new pipelines have been completed to Skigda and eventually there will be three liquificátion plants each at Skigda and

Arzew. The second El Paso deal involves 600 million dollars investment in pipelines, a liquification plant at Arzew and nine gas tankers.

A completely Algerian staff of 600, including fifteen maintenance engineers, now runs the ammonia and fertiliser plant which has been operating at Arzew since 1969. The plant, built by a French firm under American licence, normally produces about 1,000 tons of liquid ammonia a day, but, when I visited it, it was temporarily out of action. The nitric acid and fertiliser section was running at just over half capacity.

On top of a hill overlooking Arzew is a square white building with big windows. This is the control room of the oil pipe-line and terminal. The young Algerian in charge of the automated control system explained that the terminal could load the biggest tanker at the rate of 5,000 tons an hours.

Almost all the skilled people running the pipeline and terminal are now Algerians. They have been trained either in Britain or France or in a special school on the spot. But there are still a few British specialists there.

Many of the Algerians in responsible positions in industry and government administration are very young. They are educational products of the post-independence era, like the British-trained engineer who showed me round the construction site of Arzew's new oil refinery. Construction had begun in February 1970 and the aim was to have the refinery operating by June 1972 with an eventual capacity of 2.5 million tons a year. (The work was completed by 1973). Seven hundred men, including 450 Japanese specialists and skilled workers, were building the plant, together with 1,200 Algerian workers employed by sub-contractors. It was a scene of intense activity with Algerians and lithe young Japanese with long, smooth, black hair under their white plastic crash helmets, working side by side.

The manager of the plant project was an Algerian in his early thirties. He had a doctorate in engineering from Paris but had never built a refinery before. But he could call on help, where necessary, from foreign specialists in different fields. Under him he had twenty Algerian engineers who had studied at French, British and Algerian universities and had also learned their job on the spot. 'Most of us', said the manager, 'came straight from university into immediate contact with reality, so we had to digest this reality and establish scientific methods of work. Our Algerian cadres work thirteen hours a day, seven days a week.'

They had a heavy responsibility, for the plant was costing 70 million dollars (£28 million) of Algeria's precious foreign exchange. SONATRACH was ultimately responsible for the whole project, with the help of foreign credits.

Meanwhile, if the Algerian people have had to pay with tightened belts for these hopes of an industrial future, they have also been able to get some fun out of the process. A million of them including busloads of peasants from the country, went to visit the 1971 industrial fair just outside Algiers. The road out to the fair, when I went there, was jammed with cars. The fair site is superb, right next to the sea. The main permanent exhibition building, housing the products of Algerian nationalised industries, was built by the Chinese. It has a huge roof span, but, brilliantly lit, gives a feeling of lightness and gaiety.

There was an atmosphere of festival, with flags flying, lights blazing, music blaring. Crowds, many in family groups, wandered admiringly round the international pavilions or stood to watch a demonstration of German machine tools, a new French truck, a film of the Chinese revolution or an American Western with equal absorption. They were enjoying the fair as a spectacle, but in the Algerian pavilion as they inspected the home-made goods, the textiles and furniture, the books and the cosmetics, as well as the displays of the oil and gas industries, car assembly and railways, they could also feel they were sharing in something achieved by themselves.

6 Tunisia

Tunisia is the smallest of the Maghreb countries and has the fewest resources. But it is in some respects culturally and politically the most advanced.

Tunis, with its French-speaking educated society and its political élite, dominated before and after independence by the benevolently autocratic father of the nation, President Habib Bourguiba, bears a stronger imprint of European influence than any other Arab capital except perhaps Beirut in the Lebanon. (And curiously the Lebanon is the homeland of the Tunisians' reputed original ancestors, the Phoenicians who founded Carthage, now a suburb of Tunis where a few meagre classical ruins lie scattered among the white villas of the commuters).

But the sophistication of Tunis – as well as the natural dignity and intelligence of most Tunisians – is apt to obscure the hard facts of poverty and backwardness in much of the rest of the country, which are as forbidding as in Morocco and Algeria.

Tunisia has made a no less determined attempt than Algeria to develop its economy and to establish its economic as well as political independence after a long period of colonial rule. Decolonisation was a less formidable task in Tunisia than in Algeria because the European settlement there was on a smaller scale and more of Tunisia's own culture and political and social structure was allowed to survive. The Tunisians were also able to secure their independence without a devastating war. On the other hand, Tunisia lacked Algeria's oil riches and so had to rely more heavily on foreign aid.

Independent Tunisia also chose a different development path. Where the Algerians put their money on a rapid industrialisation, the Tunisians put agriculture first. And in their development of agriculture they often attached more importance to the provision of jobs than to the increase of production. They tried to combine the human advantages of small-scale farm ownership with the efficiency of larger-scale farming operations through a system of production cooperatives. But the system had to be modified and almost abandoned after its attempted comprehensive enforcement led to the country's biggest domestic political crisis since independence.

Tunisia's efforts at development and decolonisation have been interlinked and have reacted one on the other. In two key sectors where the link was close – in agriculture and in electric power supply – the Kuwait Fund was able to help the Tunisians in a way that would have been more difficult for any other foreign aid agency.

Tunisia is still basically an agricultural country. It has few industrial raw materials or sources of power, except a modest amount of oil and natural gas, some phosphates and iron ore. Two-thirds of its people live on the land and mostly carry on traditional subsistence farming. But they produce less than one-fifth of the Gross Domestic Product, earning a per capita income of about £80 a year and in many cases a good deal less.

The one-third of the population who live in cities or work in the modern economic sector, including a small modern agricultural sector, produce four-fifths of GDP.

For in Tunisia, as throughout North Africa, French and Italian colonisation brought the creation of dual economies and societies, one modern in its modes of production and way of life, and the other traditional. This process also occurred to some extent in the Arab countries of the Middle East. But in North Africa there was a special feature which made 'decolonisation' and development there after independence a more complex affair. This was the encouragement by the colonial power not merely of European investment but also of European physical settlement, and the inclusion in it of an important part of agriculture.

Consequently in the Maghreb countries the development of agriculture after national independence was inseparably linked with the decolonisation process. It involved not only the problem of replacing foreign technical skills and capital, but also decisions about the basic social and economic structures of agriculture and a conscious effort to bring the modern and traditional sectors closer together.

For the first two years after independence Tunisia's main problem was to overcome the dislocation caused by the depar-

ture of the French, and to rebuild the administration of the
Tunisian state and of some sectors of the 'colonial' economy.
One gain in this period was that the number of Muslim
Tunisians employed outside farming – in commerce, industry
and public services – more than doubled, from 210,000 in 1955
to 425,000 in 1960. But the economy as a whole remained more
or less stagnant: the increase in production barely matched the
growth of population. This led to a more positive policy of
government economic intervention.

Tunisia's development efforts have been systematised in a
series of economic plans supervised since 1961 by a National
Planning Council under the chairmanship of the President of
the Republic.

The Ten Year Plan for 1962-71 laid down the broad principles and targets for the country's economic and social
development. Then a series of four-year plans set out investment and projects in greater detail. The ten-year plan attached
great importance to 'decolonisation' and the aim of economic
independence. One of its targets was to achieve a minimum per
capita income the equivalent of £43 or 120 US dollars (in 1961
average per capita income was £60 or 170 dollars), but ninety-
three per cent of the rural population had less than this figure
and 37 per cent had less than £18 or fifty dollars). Other aims
were to achieve a growth rate of six per cent per annum of GDP
and to have full employment by 1971. None of these aims was
achieved.

The Tunisian economy was to be developed with three sectors, public, private and cooperative, running parallel. But
gradually a more socialist emphasis was adopted. In agriculture the stress was to be on cooperatives and in industry on
government investment and participation. The nationalisation
of certain basic industries and public utilities such as electricity
and gas, railways, phosphates and banking was prompted
partly by general economic ideology but in the first place by
decolonisation, since these concerns had been in French hands.

From 1962-72, investment under the plans totalled the equivalent of just over £1,000 million or some 2,500 million dollars,
a quarter of GDP. About 45 per cent of the investment funds
came from foreign aid which totalled around £416 million or
1,000 million dollars.

About half of this investment went to transform the social

and physical infrastructure of the country – education, health, roads, dams, transport, ports. There was a particularly big effort in education, amounting to an investment of 8 per cent of GDP, the highest rate in the world, and bringing schooling to 90 per cent of Tunisian children.

There was also a greater diversification of the economy to make it less dependent on a few exports such as wine, olives and phosphates. But the rate of growth was slower than was hoped for. The Minister for the Plan, M. Mansour Moalla, told me in Tunis (in October 1971) that over ten years the annual growth rate had been four per cent, when five per cent had been expected. (Other, non-official, sources put the growth rate at 3.3 per cent.) This disappointment was partly because of foreign upsets, such as the effect of the Algerian war and the stopping of French aid. But it also reflected over-optimistic forecasting and was connected with internal political and economic difficulties. These difficulties were brought to a head in October 1971 when the Neo-Destour party held its first congress for seven years and endorsed a trend away from the moderately socialist policies previously in force and towards a more liberal, free-enterprise system. Two developments had brought about a slowly gathering crisis leading to the party congress. One was the long illness of President Bourguiba which raised questions about his authority and the presidential succession. The question was at least partially settled by a compromise at the 1974 party congress when Bourguiba accepted the Presidency for life but agreed that he should be succeeded in the first place by the Prime Minister. The other was the attempt in 1969 to force through a drastic and generalised system of production cooperatives in agriculture. This had led to widespread peasant resistance, a virtual rural mutiny, and to the downfall, trial and imprisonment for ten years of M. Ahmed Ben Salah, once Tunisia's most powerful minister and President Bourguiba's right-hand man.

The arrest and trial of Ben Salah (he later escaped from jail and fled abroad) was a political shock almost as profound in Tunisia as the abortive army coup of 1971 was to be in Morocco.

There may have been good arguments on the grounds of economic efficiency, quite apart from ideology, for grouping small farm holdings into bigger, collectively-run production units. But the process appears to have been rushed through

without proper preparation, with little in the way of explana-
tion or persuasion, and the consequent financial losses in the
cooperatives were concealed by State subsidies.

Similar criticisms of bureaucratically imposed policies have
been levelled against other aspects of Tunisia's economic
development plans. The critics also point out that much of the
investment under the plans has been in long-term projects
which are not immediately productive of many jobs. It was
paid for by austerity measures to restrain consumption and by
a chronic balance of payments deficit. This deficit is partly
covered by foreign aid but at the cost of a foreign indebtedness
to service which now takes a quarter of Tunisia's foreign earnings.

After a decade of belt-tightening and high unemployment (in
1970 at least 180,000 men or 15 per cent of the labour force were
unemployed), there was increasing pressure from below for
more jobs and higher living standards. In 1970 on his return
from France, President Bourguiba initiated a new economic
policy which was described to me a year later by the Prime
Minister, M. Hedi Nouira, as one of 'democratisation' rather
than 'liberalisation' of the economy.

M. Nouira, a mild-mannered, middle-aged man with gold-
rimmed spectacles, an economic specialist, said that it was now
intended to rely more on persuasion and incentives than on the
bureaucratic imposition of centralised plans backed by government power. The next development plan was being revised
to give more priority to investment which creates jobs quickly
and to the improvement of housing and supplies of consumer
goods.

This plan, the four-year plan for 1973-6, aimed at a 7.6 per
cent annual growth rate with a total government investment of
T.D. (Tunisian dinars) 1,000 million (£1,000 million). It is
hoped to cut dependence on foreign aid from 40 per cent to 20
per cent of development expenditure. The plan laid stress on
making past investments profitable rather than on big new
projects. It hoped to create 30,000 new jobs a year – it was
estimated that 50,000 a year were needed until 1981. Ten
thousand a year were to come from foreign investment in
export-orientated industry which was encouraged by special
tax and customs concessions. In the first half of the seventies
200,000 Tunisians were working abroad and the Tunisian

Government's aim was to import industry instead of exporting labour. It was claimed that 113,000 new jobs had already been created under the plan by 1975 and that the total would reach 160,000 by the end of 1976.

Under the fourth plan investment in agriculture and agricultural industries during 1974 was TD114.5 million (£114.5 million) or 38.6 per cent of total investment for the year. One of the top priorites in the next and fifth four-year plan for 1977-80 will be the development of water resources, especially to expand the area of irrigated land.

The impact of the Ben Salah affair and of the collapse of the cooperatives policy was felt all the more strongly because of the priority Tunisia has given to agriculture in her development planning. This priority was not only a recognition of the human situation: that two-thirds of the population are on the land. It was also based on economic belief that the demand needed to sustain an eventual industrial expansion must come in the first place from greater agricultural production and employment.

Tunisian planners saw other advantages in putting farming first: it could satisfy local consumption needs which were increasing from the expanding population and changing living standards; it could earn foreign exchange in two ways, as export crops and as food for tourists; and it could create more jobs.

The Ten-Year Plan envisaged investment in agriculture over the decade of 570 million dollars (£247 million) or 26.5 per cent of the total investment under the Plan. The aim was to raise the rate of growth in agriculture from 2.2 to 5.5 per cent per annum. The natural as well as human obstacles were formidable.

The greater part of Tunisia is desert. Only 20 per cent of the total area is arable land. The most important centre of agricultural development is in the north of the country which has the heaviest rainfall and where the main potential for irrigation lies. For there runs the country's most important river, the Medjerda, which rises in Algeria and flows 200 miles to the Mediterranean.

It was also in the north in the lower Medjerda valley and the adjacent Tunis area that the main European colonisation took place. It was there, too, that after independence the Tunisian Government made its main effort to combine decolonisation with the extension of modern farming techniques and an agrarian reform designed to provide more rural employment.

Here too was where the Kuwait Fund was able to make one of its main contributions to Tunisian development. In 1956 when Tunisia obtained her independence and the end of the 94-year-old French protectorate, there were 250,000 Europeans, mostly French and Italian, in her population of some four million. (Ten years later there were 124,000 out of a population of 4.8 million.) Of these eighty-five per cent lived in towns but others owned and worked, either themselves or through hired labour, much of the best land in Tunisia. Some 700,000 hectares (1.7 million acres) had passed into the hands of French settlers or companies.

After independence these 'colonial' lands were taken over by the Tunisian state, at first by agreement with the French Government which paid compensation to the displaced colonists. Then, after the crisis with France in 1960 over the French use of the Bizerta naval base, the take-over was hastened by simple confiscation. The control of the colonial lands was vested in a 'National Office for the Development of State Lands': the farms were to be used as the nuclei of production cooperatives for Tunisian small farmers.

In 1958 an Agrarian Reform Law was passed setting up a Medjerda valley development authority, the OMVVM (*Office de la mise en valeur de la Vallée de la Medjerda*). The OMVVM was responsible for 325,000 hectares (800,000 acres) of land on both sides of the lower reaches of the Medjerda near Tunis and it was within this area that the new agrarian reform law was first to be applied. Under the law, state lands in the Medjerda valley were to be distributed to farmers in plots of not less than four hectares – four to five hectares for market gardening, five to ten hectares for fodder and livestock and four to six for fruit trees. For private land the maximum holding of irrigated land was set at fifty hectares and holdings over that amount were to be expropriated. Some land was to be kept by the OMVVM for direct exploitation.

By 1958 also certain major irrigation facilities begun before independence, including two main dams, a diversion dam and canal system, had been completed. They could supply enough water for 30,000 hectares of land but only 2,000 were being completely irrigated. In 1961 a 'Minimal Plan' for the Valley was drawn up as part of the Ten-Year Plan. Its main aim was to exploit fully the new irrigation structures by putting 44,000 hectares under irrigation. Another 200,000 hectares in the project area was to be developed for dry-farming and 38,000 to be afforested. Eventually an 'Optimum Plan' would aim at irrigating 90,000 hectares but this would require the building of more dams and canals. By more intensive farming it was hoped to settle 40,000 more people in the valley and improve conditions for those already there (previously much of the 'colonial' land was farmed extensively with machinery and employed little Tunisian labour).

In 1963 the Kuwait Fund gave the Tunisian government a loan of KD 2 million (£2.33 million) to cover the foreign exchange element – about a third of the cost – of the first phase of the Minimal Plan. This entailed bringing 8,000 hectares under irrigation and improving the farming of 4,500 hectares of non-irrigated land. In addition to flood protection and soil conservation works the project provided for the building of houses and stables, together with roads, water, electricity and technical services for 1,030 new farms and the improvement of existing farms.

For the next phase of the Medjerda scheme, to develop 12,685 hectares, of which 7,772 hectares were to be put under irrigation, loans were provided by the United States and the African Bank for Development.

A second loan of KD3,200,000 (£3,733,000) for twenty-seven years at three per cent was granted by the Kuwait Fund in 1970 for the final phase of the 'Minimal Plan' for the Medjerda. Work began on this project in 1971 and it was hoped to complete it by 1977-8.

It will add another 13,000 hectares to the irrigated area. It will also create 5,000 more jobs and make it possible for these extra workers to settle permanently in a modern sector of the Tunisian economy. The project includes the provision of irrigation canals and pumping stations, drainage, flood control and wind protection. 3,050 farms are being built with houses, stables, water and electricity. The farmers are supplied with farm machinery and equipment, livestock and seedlings for orchards – part of these are being paid for by long-term credits from the Netherlands, Denmark and West Germany. There will be new rural centres with schools and clinics. Previously new farmers were settled in separate homesteads on their own plots of land. But in the new areas settlement is in villages, a system which has been found to be cheaper and easier for the supply of essential services.

Work on the Medjerda scheme was slowed down, like other aspects of agricultural development, by the upheaval in Tunisian politics and in farm policy caused by the Ben Salah affair.

The Ten-Year Plan had called for the extension of the cooperative system in agriculture – a system which had existed in Tunisia in one form or another since the beginning of the century, although mostly among French settlers. The aim was to consolidate small holdings – further fragmented by the Muslim inheritance laws so that even one olive tree might have several owners – to form 'production units' big enough to make economic use of machinery and modern cultivation methods. The first three-year plan of 1962-4 envisaged the formation of 200 such units but they grew only very slowly. Then in the spring of 1969 came the intensive drive to spread the production cooperatives which led to Ben Salah's downfall and a change of policy.

At the Ministry of Agriculture in Tunis, a handsome marble palace with a courtyard and fountains playing, I asked the Secretary of State, M. Mohammed Gadeerah, in October 1971, about the new policy and how far the Medjerda scheme had been affected. M. Gadeerah, an agricultural engineer by training, was formerly director of the OMVVM. A large, stout man with a small black moustache, he would obviously have driven any project with energy.

He said that the change of policy over cooperatives had been exaggerated. There had been only one change. 'Before, we wanted to force the spread of the production cooperatives. This meant the collective working of the land, common means of production and an end of individual ownership. This trend was pushed too harshly and met with incomprehension and resistance on the part of the peasants.'

The new policy was to create a 'production unit' only on two conditions. The first condition was profitability, an economic criterion: a preliminary agro-economic study must show that the proposed collective working was the most economic method. The second criterion was socio-political: the people affected should be convinced of the value of collective work.

Tunisia was now applying the same cooperative principle as in other countries – free and voluntary membership.

The Medjerda had been spared the full effects of the Ben Salah upheaval, because it had no production units but only service cooperatives. The Medjerda farmers follow the cultivation plan laid down by the OMVVM but they own their land. They benefit from cooperative services – for buying seeds and machinery and tools, for the common use of equipment and for selling their produce.

M. Gadeerah argued that a concentration of land ownership and land working might be necessary and useful after an industrial revolution, but the industrial revolution had not yet begun in Tunisia. At this stage, to concentrate land use and ownership was to increase the use of machinery – which costs foreign exchange – and to reduce employment on the land without having created jobs elsewhere. It was better to keep small farmers going and help them to become more efficient, using the cooperative as a training school.

The Ben Salah crisis, said M. Gadeerah, had dealt the idea of the production unit a mortal blow in the minds of the peasants but they were still open to the idea of the service cooperatives. Since December 1970 the Medjerda system had become the official model for all irrigated areas.

I asked about the main problems he had encountered as director of the Medjerda authority. He said that apart from saline water, salty and poor soil, there was above all the human factor. Tunisian farmers were very specialised and not very adaptable. The change-over from traditional dry farming, olives, corn or sheep-grazing to intensive irrigated farming meant a change in a way of life and in century-long habits.

A hectare growing corn requires, say, ten days' work a year. A hectare growing artichokes with irrigation brings in much more money but needs 250 days' work. Olive groves need ploughing twice a year and then harvesting, but otherwise their owners sit in a café for the rest of the year or keep a grocer's shop. The shepherds are used to grazing nomadically on green where they find it, including other people's land. At first all the people coming into the Medjerda from other areas had only these old habits. They had to get used to working harder, for longer periods and in a more sophisticated and continuous way. Vegetables and other irrigated crops need constant attention. At first the results were disastrous but gradually with the help of the Authority the farmers learned from experience.

I drove out to the headquarters of the OMVVM on the outskirts of Tunis to see the newly-appointed director. He explained what the operation of the scheme meant financially for the individual farmer. The share of land allocated to a farmer must give him an added value of 1,000 dinars, which works out at about five to seven hundred dinars (£420 to £580) a year for a family. Some earn more. The average earnings of the farmers before they came to the Medjerda was only 150 dinars (£125) a year. The national daily wage for hired labour in agriculture was half a dinar a day (42 pence).

The farmer pays a nominal purchase price which covers land, farm buildings and installations and the cost of infrastructure – drainage, water-channels and levelling. The cost is 500 dinars per hectare to be paid over twenty years free of interest. Technical services are supplied free. About 1,700 new farms had been put into operation by 1971.

Escorted by the deputy-director, M. Tarzi, I visited one of the older settlements in the Medjerda scheme, a village called Habibia after President Habib Bourguiba. We turned off the main road along a smaller road lined with trees. On either side stood white concrete farm houses, each on its plot of land. The road ended at a village centre with a large meeting hall, mosque, post office, bank and cooperative centre. A school and dispensary were nearby.

Habibia was established in 1958-9 on 1,500 hectares of former French colonist property which had been nationalised and become state domain. It was given to the new settlers in plots of five to eight hectares. The houses have three rooms, water and electricity. There were now 144 families on the land which was previously farmed extensively with tractors. In addition some of the farmers employ full-time farm labourers to help them.

M. Tarzi explained the crops: artichokes in winter for the European market and tomatoes and peppers in the summer, much of them for canning or making into juice or paste. There were dairy cows, imported from Denmark and Holland, fruit trees and vines, though they were trying to reduce vine-growing.

We stopped at one house beside which a lorry loaded with

peppers was standing. It was on a plot of eight hectares belonging to a robust, youngish man who looked hard-working and successful. He had come from Sfax, 150 miles to the south, twelve years ago and had begun with nothing. He had built up his business partly through the village cooperative and partly independently. Artichokes, he said, brought in 800 dinars (£660) gross or 400 dinars (£330) net. He now paid 170 dinars a year for his house and land – when he took them over in 1959 he had begun paying for them at the rate of 44 dinars a year. He obtained credits for improvements from the agricultural bank at eight per cent.

He employed eight labourers at 600 milliemes (50 pence) a day each. They were making their midday meal outside a mud hut at the entrance to a nearby olive grove. They lived up in the villages in the mountains round about and came down to the Valley to work. They were just *les ouvriers*, men still without land, part of the great number of Tunisians for whom economic development has yet to have a full meaning or to touch more than the fringe of their lives.

From Tunis a delightful little train jolts slowly round the lagoons and the bay to the seaside resort of La Marsa. It passes through a string of suburbs with white-walled, blue-shuttered houses set among palm trees, olive groves and hedges of purple bougainvillea. The stations have echoing romantic names, reminding one of Proust's sea-side railway from Baalbec – Carthage-Byrsa, Carthage-Hamilcar, Carthage-Salambo. Before the white villas and the various parts of Carthage the train skirts a shimmering lagoon on the far edge of which rise the outlines of a less romantic but indispensable structure, the tall chimneys, oil tanks, grids and pylons of the La Goulette electric power stations. Nine years ago La Goulette was the centre of a politico-economic crisis.

Tunisia has few sources of hydro-electric power and at that time she had very little oil or natural gas of her own. She relied heavily for power for industry and domestic use on thermal power stations such as La Goulette, burning imported coal or diesel oil. In 1962 as part of its decolonisation drive, the Tunisian government nationalised the private French companies which had been responsible for electricity generation and supply. It sought foreign aid for an expansion programme to meet the electricity demands growing at the rate of eight to ten per cent a year. This expansion was vital not only because of the increasing population but also for hopes of industrial development and the modernisation of agriculture. The World Bank spent eighteen months studying the possibility of a loan for the expansion of La Goulette but delayed a decision because the Tunisian government had not yet compensated the former shareholders of the nationalised companies. The other main potential source of finance, the French Government, had cut off its aid to Tunisia because of the nationalisation of French-owned farms. So in 1963 the *Société Tunisienne de l'Électricité et du Gaz* (STEG), the state company created to run the nationalised electricity and gas industries, approached the Kuwait Fund which had by then already given Tunisia its first loan for the Medjerda scheme.

The Kuwait Fund was able to dispense with the conditions of compensation laid down by the World Bank. On the basis of the profitability of the expansion scheme it granted a loan of KD3.8 million (£4.20 million) for fifteen years at four per cent to cover the foreign exchange cost of a new steam power station at La Goulette. The project consisted of the installation at La Goulette of two new generating units of 25 megawatts each and of high tension lines to Tunis and Bizerta. It was part of a long-term programme intended to extend the electricity distribution network all over the country, including the supply of two major industries, a steel works near Bizerta and a phosphate plant near Metlaoui in the mining area in the south. When the installation of the new plant was completed in March 1966, La Goulette became the most important source of electric power in Tunisia, supplying about sixty per cent of the total energy consumed in the country. But by that time a second stage in the expansion had already begun. This provided for the expenditure of some £15 million to expand the generating capacity of La Goulette by another forty per cent through the installation of two more power units of 27.5 megawatts each. For this programme the Kuwait Fund gave a further loan of KD 4,600,000 for fifteen years at four per cent. The main work on this project was completed by 1971.

In that year STEG negotiated a third loan for a natural gas pipeline to supply the power station at Gabes. The pipeline was being financed jointly by the Kuwait Fund and the World

Bank, their first joint financing operation. The World Bank lent 7,500,000 U.S. dollars and the Kuwait Fund 2,500,000 dollars (KD 900,000).

Recent discoveries have expanded Tunisia's natural gas reserves to an estimated thirty years supply of her needs. The Kuwait Fund has had under consideration a loan for KD1.5 million (£2.25 million) power station at Ghannouch in southern Tunisia with a capacity of 40 megawatts from two gas turbines. The World Bank has meanwhile lent Tunisia 12 million dollars (£5.5 million) for a 40 megawatt power station, and the Arab Fund in 1973 granted a loan of KD2 million (£3 million) for another gas-fired 40 megawatt station south of Tunis. By 1973 Tunisia had eighteen power stations, mostly thermal, in operation, producing 963 megawatts.

STEG appears to be an example of successful decolonisation in industry. At first the French state organisation *Électricité de France*, which acted as consultant, had supplied specialists to STEG. But by 1971 these were reduced to one engineer and one accountant. All the rest of STEG's staff of 200, including 100 engineers, were Tunisian. Indeed, Tunisia was even in a position to give technical help to neighbouring Libya which has also been decolonizing or 'Libyanising' its economy and public services. A Tunisian team was sent to the power station at Benghazi and Libyans went to Tunis for training.

In 1974-5 the Kuwait Fund granted Tunisia two loans for development in two new sectors – the modernisation of the Tunisian phosphate mines and fishing. It also had under consideration a possible loan of KD3.2 million (£4.8 million) to the Tunisian Bank for Economic Development to finance industry and tourism.

The loan for the phosphate mines was for KD2 million (£3 million) for fifteen years at four per cent. The project includes the mechanisation of three mines, the modernisation of their beneficiation plants, the provision of locomotives and freight cars, and some essential social services, as well as a workers' training programme.

The fishing project for which the Fund granted its loan was part of a wider programme of government encouragement for the Tunisian fishing industry which has expanded substantially in the last few years and now employs nearly 14,000 men centred mainly on Sfax. The programme aims to build 250 coastal fishing vessels in Tunisian shipyards. The International Development Association gave a loan of two million dollars to help replace sailing vessels with motorised boats. The Kuwait Fund loan is for the development of three fishing ports on the east coast at Chabba, Zarzis and Sfax. The total cost of the project is KD6 million (£9 million). The Fund granted a loan of KD2.85 million (£4.2 million) for 19 years at three per cent. Work at Chabba and Zarzis was due to be completed by the end of 1975 and at Sfax two years later. Local employment in fishing was expected to treble to 6,000 crewmen.

The improvement and expansion of the airport at Carthage just outside Tunis is a key element in Tunisia's plans to build up her tourist trade. To help finance this development the Fund granted a loan of KD4 million (£6 million) for twenty years at 3½ per cent for the provision of new airport buildings, workshops and other facilities.

7 Egypt

Of all the Arab states, Egypt has the biggest problems of economic development, both in size and difficulty, and has made the most extensive and impressive effort to overcome them.

With a population of more than 36 million and increasing at a rate of 2.8 per cent per annum, Egypt has a million extra mouths to feed each year and limited natural resources. Most of the country is desert: only four per cent of its area is cultivated, nearly all of it in the long narrow strip of the Nile Valley.

Until recent discoveries of natural gas and bigger oilfields, Egypt had few sources of fuel or basic raw materials for industry, except for the small Sinai oilfields, the hydro-electric power of the Nile and some iron ore and other mineral deposits. She had, it is true, the advantages of a more developed infrastructure and a larger supply of educated and experienced administrators and technicians than many developing countries. But she lacked the source of foreign exchange provided in some other Arab countries by large oil revenues. So she was forced to rely heavily on foreign aid for the foreign currency investment in industrialisation which was needed to provide more jobs and raise the miserably low standard of living of the majority.

Because of her position as the biggest, most powerful, and culturally and politically most influential of the Arab states, Egypt has been able to attract a substantial amount of foreign aid – from both the Western and the Communist Powers and more recently from other Arab countries.

But Egypt's leading position in the Arab world has also brought her extra burdens (apart from increased debt). She has suffered more than most other Arab states – except Jordan, Yemen and Algeria – from the consequences of war and the enormous costs of military expenditure. This double aspect of Egypt's situation was most strikingly illustrated by the Middle East war of October 1973 and the years of 'no peace, no war' between 1973 and Egypt's disastrous defeat in the war of June 1967.

The adverse consequences of Arab leadership had already been felt in Egypt's involvement in the civil war in the Yemen between 1962 and 1968. But more of the benefits of Arab aid were felt after the 1973 war, partly because it coincided with the big increase in oil prices and in the surplus funds of the Arab oil states – though in the first two years after the war it was difficult to disentangle just how much of the promised Arab economic aid was being translated into hard commitments, and even more, how much was actually being disbursed. But certainly it was a good deal more than before 1973, and disbursements were likely to grow as bureacratic and organisational problems were overcome. According to the OECD (Organisation for Economic Cooperation and Development), the oil states of OPEC disbursed about £1,143 million in bilateral overseas development aid in 1974, of which thirty per cent went to Egypt from the Arab oil states and Iran.

Other foreign investors seemed more wary of putting money into Egypt until the uncertainties about war and peace with Israel were resolved. But in time increased Arab investment and the moves towards peace with Israel, including the reopening of the Suez Canal in June 1975, could transform Egypt's economic prospects.

Between 1952-67 Egypt received aid from the United States estimated at a billion dollars. Much of this was in the form of surplus food shipments, especially wheat, paid for by Egypt in local currency, part of which was then made available for local development. Over the same period she obtained probably about the same amount in aid from Russia and the Communist countries, though the figures here are difficult to be sure of because it is not known for certain how Communist arms deliveries to Egypt were paid for. But Russia financed not only the foreign exchange element in the building the High Dam and its giant power station but also much of the Egyptian industrialisation programme, in both cases chiefly through the supply of plant and equipment. More recently, Russia and her East European allies contributed to the ambitious expansion of the Helwan iron and steel complex, expected to cost eventually £E 350 million. (The Egyptian pound is officially worth £1.06 sterling or 2.56 dollars but the free market rate is little more than half those figures.) Egypt also had credits from West Germany and other West European countries and substantial loans from the World Bank and the International Monetary Fund.

Since most of this aid was in the form of loans of various kinds, Egypt's foreign debt had reached some £1,000 million by 1967 – a measure both of the extent of the 'aid' and the burden which the system of aid through loans places on developing countries. In fact, the aid received by Egypt may sound more than it really was, since the total spread over fifteen years averaged only £66.6 million a year, less than four per cent of the Egyptian state budget and a little over £2 per head of population. In 1966-8 official aid to Egypt from Western (OECD) countries averaged 1.4 dollars (50p) a head annually, compared with 30.7 dollars a head to Israel and 6.2 dollars a head to Turkey.

Nevertheless, by comparison, the loans to Egypt by the Kuwait Fund over the same period, totalling KD13.2 million, may appear modest, albeit they were then the biggest total given by the Fund to any Arab country. (By 1975 the total had risen to KD38.3 million [£57.4 million] and was still the biggest). They were applied to two key projects: expanding the Suez Canal and building up Egypt's merchant shipping fleet. But it also has to be remembered that since the 1967 war the Kuwait Government, as distinct from the Fund, has been paying Egypt a direct subsidy, not a loan, of KD40 million (£46.4 million) a year. This is Kuwait's share of the £95 million which Kuwait, Saudi Arabia and Libya agreed at the Khartoum Arab summit conference in August 1967 to pay to Egypt to compensate her for the loss of foreign exchange earnings due to the closure of the Suez Canal.

Since the 1973 war the Kuwait Fund has granted Egypt four more loans totalling KD18 million (£27 million) bringing the total to KD31.2 million (£46.8 million). The loans were KD10 million (£15 million) for the work on clearing and reopening the Suez Canal and two loans of KD4.5 million (£6.75 million) and KD3.5 million (£5.25 million) for the development of the Abu Qir natural gas field. The Fund has also been considering another loan for a fertiliser plant. At the same time Kuwait has increased other forms of assistance to Egypt. In the first week of the 1973 war the Kuwait Government is reported to have given Egypt 250 million dollars (£114 million) out of a total Arab aid of 920 million dollars (£420 million). Kuwait is also a major contributor to the cost of reconstructing the Suez Canal zone towns and to the fund of 1,000 million dollars promised by the oil states to finance arms purchases by Egypt, Syria and Jordan for defence against Israel.

The Kuwait government and Kuwaiti financial institutions were also reported to have made an agreement with Egypt in 1974 for the investment of £612 million in joint ventures of which £529 million would be for projects in Egypt, including pulp and paper manufacturing and a cement plant.

Although oil and its earnings may now be coming to Egypt's economic rescue, it is curious how another element, water – both salt and fresh – has lain at the centre of both Egypt's development efforts and her politico-military troubles. The Nile is her main source of wealth, but her geographical position linking Asia and Africa, the Mediterranean and the Red Sea, has been not only a source of profit but also a cause of danger and loss.

The Aswan High Dam on the Nile and the Suez Canal linking the seas have been two basic factors in the Egyptian development programme. The Dam has provided more irrigation for agriculture and more power for industry, and the Canal until 1967 was the most important single source of the foreign exchange needed for investment in development. It was the withdrawal by the United States, Britain and the World Bank of their offered aid for the High Dam which led to the nationalisation of the Suez Canal Company in 1956 (though it might have happened in any event more peacefully a few years later) and to the Suez-Sinai war. It was Egypt's closure of the Straits of Tiran to Israeli shipping coming from and going to the Red Sea which precipitated the June war of 1967, leading to the Israeli occupation of the Sinai Peninsula and the closure of the Canal.

Egypt's first big planned development effort began in the early sixties with the first five-year plan from 1960-65.

In the early years of the Nasserist revolution, from the coup of 1952 until 1956, there was little basic change in Egypt's free enterprise economic structure, except for a limited land reform. Then, beginning with the nationalisation of the Canal Company, the subsequent sequestration of British and French property and the 'Egyptianisation' of all foreign banks, insurance companies and foreign trade agencies, the economy moved through a phase of 'guided capitalism' to a partly socialist society.

A state 'Economic Organisation' was set up to operate the sequestrated and Egyptianised firms, and in 1957 a National Planning Committee was created to work out a long-term economic and social development plan. Meanwhile an interim five-year plan for industrialisation was launched in 1958.

By 1961 all basic industries, transport, communications and foreign trade operations – and by 1964 virtually all the main firms in the country up to a total of 800 – had been nationalised or brought under public control – though agriculture was still conducted on the basis of private land ownership.

The Nasser regime had moved towards greater government intervention primarily because of the need to mobilise public investment in Egypt. The episode of the High Dam and the Western blockade after the Suez crisis had led President Nasser to believe Egypt could not afford to rely on Western aid for her development. Then the failure of Egyptian private investment to support the hoped-for industrial expansion indicated that if Egypt were to have to rely more on her own resources, then these would have to come in the main from public funds.

In 1960 the Egyptian Government announced the first comprehensive development plan, the first stage of a programme aimed to double the national income over the next decade (per capita income in 1960 was £E50 a year). The first five-year plan called for an investment of £E1,577 million with the aim of increasing the national income by forty per cent or seven per cent a year. The plan got off to a bad start. Half of the 1961 cotton crop was lost from cotton worm. Then came the upheaval caused by the secession of Syria from the union with Egypt in the United Arab Republic. From 1962 onwards the cost of the Yemen war and its effect in reducing and suspending American aid were added to the strain of inflation and to the balance of payments problem which had been created by a rapid expansion. But the plan also produced some impressive achievements. Though less than officially claimed, the growth rate was probably between five and six per cent a year, which is a two to three per cent net increase after taking account of population growth. The first stage of the High Dam – the Dam itself – was completed, the Suez Canal enlarged and several major industrial plants built. Electricity output more than doubled. Of the 1,300,000 more jobs created, 225,000 were in industry but, except for electricity, transport and building, industrial expansion was only about half what had been hoped for. The reasons for this shortfall were the growing shortage of foreign exchange and the priority given to big prestige projects such as the Helwan iron and steel works and the Nasr car factory.

The plan had aimed to dispense with foreign borrowing and achieve a balance of payments surplus, but it ended with a payments deficit of £E76 million in 1964-5 and a total deficit over the five-year plan period of £413 million. Foreign currency earnings from the Suez Canal helped to ease the situation: they rose from £E51 million in 1961 to £E86 million in 1965.

But by 1965-6 Egypt had to cut imports and to impose an austerity programme at home. Lack of imported raw materials and spare parts held up investment and production especially in industry.

At the end of 1966 the austerity policy was changed and a new period of expansion was being prepared when the war with Israel broke out in June 1967. The second five-year plan then being studied was shelved, and after the war development was carried on on a year-to-year basis. A third five-year plan had been expected to start in 1970 but military developments and then the death of President Nasser in 1970 created a new situation and led to further postponement.

The war brought the closure of the Suez Canal, the loss of the Sinai oil fields, and an economic standstill in the Canal Zone from which 700,000 people were evacuated to avoid Israeli shelling and bombing. Russia helped replace Egypt's lost military equipment but the military budget increased to over £E500 million a year. The aid from the Arab oil states helped to cover the loss of the Canal revenue, but in the first year after the war imports and investment had to be cut back even further and the growth rate fell to two per cent. But by mid-1969 there were some signs of recovery, helped by bigger oil finds and by high world prices for cotton and rice.

In 1968 Egypt had her first trade surplus since the nineteen-thirties, though it was achieved partly by a sharp fall in imports.

Some essential development projects went ahead. The High Dam and its power station were completed by the summer of

1970 and the Russians helped in a big expansion of the iron and steel complex. These two projects, together with increased oil output – up from 2,500,000 in 1965 to nearly 20 million tons a year by 1970 – and the prospect of large natural gas supplies were seen as the basis of a future industrial expansion. By mid-1969 Egyptian industry had begun to pay its way in foreign exchange terms, earning more from exports than the cost of its imported materials and spare parts. The growth rate was up to five per cent and industrial growth to 11 per cent a year, including oil.

The 1969-70 budget provided for development investment of £E330 million out of a total of £E2,413 million. (For 1971-2 the figure was £E350 million out of a budget total of £E2,392 million).

When President Sadat took over after the death of President Nasser, Egypt's economy was under heavy strain from the burden of military spending and from the lack of foreign exchange to pay for spare parts and raw materials to keep industry going. Egypt's future development obviously depended on whether there was to be peace or more war with Israel, and particularly on the reopening and future prospects of the Suez Canal along the Eastern bank of which the Israeli army was still strongly entrenched. President Sadat tried to meet the situation in two ways. He introduced a more liberal 'open door' economic policy to encourage private business and attract foreign investment. And he launched a diplomatic initiative for a step-by-step settlement with Israel which would begin with a partial Israeli withdrawal in Sinai and the reopening of the Suez Canal to international shipping. In case this peaceful initiative failed, he began to prepare for the recovery of control of both banks of the Canal through a limited war.

Diplomacy having failed, the war was launched in alliance with Syria in October 1973. The initial Egyptian victory in crossing the Canal and seizing control of the East bank, was followed by a setback when Israel in turn crossed the Canal to the West Bank and threatened the town of Suez. Eventually, the war led to an American-negotiated disengagement agreement which left Egypt in control of both banks of the Canal. President Sadat's limited objective had been achieved but the cost of the war to Egypt was enormous. The war itself was estimated to have cost Egypt over £1,000 million. The cost of the armed forces between 1967 and 1973 was some £E5,000 million – or enough to have spent a million pounds on each of Egypt's 5,000 villages. On top of this had to be added perhaps another £E5,000 million for war losses of various kinds, including compensation for victims and refugees, loss of oil fields and minerals in Sinai, and industrial firms closed or destroyed. About £E500 million a year that might in peace conditions have gone to economic development had had to be diverted to the armed forces.

Egypt also owed Russia an estimated £1,500 million for arms supplied before and during the October war. The Soviet Government rejected Egyptian requests for a rescheduling of this and other debts. In 1975 Egypt was also believed to owe the Soviet bloc countries about 1,000 million dollars (£454 million) for non-military projects. Egypt's debts to Western countries, estimated at 3,000 million dollars (£1,362 million), including short-term borrowing, were rescheduled after the October war.

The severe strain of the war and preceding six years on the Egyptian economy showed in a thirty per cent inflationary rise in the cost of living, in shortages of consumer goods and of imported raw materials and spare parts for industry and public services. Strikes and demonstrations by workers and peasants in 1974 led to an official increase in the basic wage of workers from £9 to £12 a month and a rise in prices paid to farmers for their crops. Over £E1,000 million was earmarked for imports of basic foodstuffs and other necessities. In 1975 the average wage was £176 a year but agricultural workers who form nearly half the labour force got an average of only £58 a year. The average industrial wage was £269 but the minimum was £144 a year. Difficulties in financing the import bill were greater because of a fall in the price of cotton, the main export, and a rise in the price of imported wheat. Arab financial aid and medium-term borrowing helped to bridge the gap.

Soon after President Sadat took power he had announced a ten-year economic programme in two five-year plans to start in 1972. But the ten-year programme was never launched. Instead there was a continuation of the annual development budgets. The 1974 budget, the first after the October war, allocated £E564 million for development out of a total expenditure of £4,187 million, with continued stress on industrial expansion. The first stage of the big iron and steel complex at

Helwan was completed at the end of 1973 providing a production capacity of 900,000 tons a year. A further expansion was then planned to raise capacity to two million tons by 1982. There were also plans for a second iron and steel complex with three million tons capacity to be built near the Mediterranean coast.

Work began in 1973 with Soviet aid on the 100,000 ton aluminium plant at Nag Hammadi in Upper Egypt. Hopes of more industrial development were pinned on the exploitation of three natural gas fields. The first to begin operating at the beginning of 1975 was at Abu Madi in the north-east corner of the Nile Delta. Among its main users were to be two new nitrogenous fertiliser plants at Talkha near the city of Mansoura. The bigger of the two Talkha plants was planned to produce 570,000 tons of urea fertiliser a year which would meet Egypt's needs for nitrogenous fertilisers until the end of the 1980's, at a saving of £375 million in foreign exchange. The total cost of the plant was estimated at KD38 million (£57 million). The Kuwait Fund granted a loan of KD7 million (£10.5 million) to meet part of the foreign exchange element (68 per cent of the cost) together with IDA, the Arab Fund, the Abu Dhabi Fund and the Libyan External Bank.

The second gas field, at Abu Gharadeq in the Western Desert, was due to start operating when a 270km pipeline linking it with the Helwan iron and steel complex was finished.

A third field is offshore at Abu Qir where production is expected to reach nearly 100 million cubic feet a day. To help develop this field, which was discovered in 1969, the Kuwait Fund granted two loans of KD4.5 million (£6.75 million) and KD3.5 million (£5.25 million). The first loan at four per cent for 20 years provides nearly half of the total cost KD9.62 million (£14.43 million) of the proposed work and 85 per cent of the foreign exchange component, the remaining 15 per cent being met by the Arab Public Oil Corporation. The work planned under this agreement includes the drilling of nine wells, the building on an offshore platform, and a submarine pipeline linked to the processing plant. There is also a pipeline network to distribute gas to the consumption centres in Alexandria, Kafr Al Shawar and Damarkur, as well as arrangements to convert some plants to burn gas instead of fuel oil, thus saving about 500,000 tons of fuel oil a year. In 1975 the Kuwait Fund also made a loan of KD10 million (£15 million) to Egypt for the construction of a new thermal power station of 173 mgw capacity at Abu Qir. The loan is for twenty years at 4 per cent and the work, begun in mid 1975, is expected to be finished by the end of 1979.

The Fund has also been considering a loan for an oil pipeline from the Ras Shukair oil fields to Suez and Cairo.

Some critics believed that Egypt was devoting too much of her investment resources to major industrial projects of high prestige but uncertain or only long-term economic value, such as the Helwan iron and steel complex. Even the Aswan High Dam became the centre of controversy, although this was partly a political rather than technical dispute between those wishing obliquely to attack the results of the late President Nasser's regime and those defending its social and economic performance. While there seemed no reason to accept the judgement of some critics that the Dam had been an ecological disaster and an economic failure, there was common ground in the recognition that the full potential of the dam for both agriculture and electric power generation was not being used because of failure to develop the necessary ancillary services in the form of drainage and electric power lines. Nor had sufficient measures been taken to deal with the side effects, such as increased erosion of the Nile banks, increased salinity, the retention of silt behind the dam, and the spread of bilharzia, which had been foreseen and taken into account when the Dam was built.

The Egyptian authorities claimed nevertheless that the Dam had already more than paid for its cost in the form of increased production and that it had twice saved the country from disaster – once from floods in 1967 and again from drought in 1972. Measures to improve drainage on reclaimed land were put in hand with financial help of the World Bank. But a clash looked possible in the future between the demands of industry for power, and of agriculture for water, since the power generation from the Dam's hydro-electric plant depended on the amount of water allowed to pass through the Dam for irrigation purposes. A special committe reported to President Sadat in 1975 that priority should go to power projects.

In 1975 Egypt's budget expenditure was increased to £E6,194, of which £E2,277 was earmarked for industry and mining. In the same year the government announced the outlines of a new five-year plan for 1976-80. According to the Minister of Finance, Ahmad Abu Ismail, total investment was expected to reach £E7,000 to £E8,000 million. The first priority would be to complete unfinished projects and take up idle capacity in industry. Stress would be laid on resconstructing run-down public utilities and improving the performance of agriculture through new incentives and techniques. The next priority would be the oil industry with the aim of producing 50 million tons a year by 1980, and then tourism.

Fourth was the widening and deepening of the newly opened Suez Canal. Revenues of £E80 million were expected from the first six months of the Canal's operation in 1975, with a target of £E200 million for 1976.

The fifth priority was shipping. The port of Alexandria was to be expanded and a new additional port built.

In April 1974, after the first Sinai disengagement agreement, the Egyptian Government began work on clearing and repairing the Canal with the help of the British and American navies, and later the French and Soviet navies. It was an enormous task. It involved the removal of 656,000 land mines on both banks, 3,559 unexploded bombs near the Canal, 41,539 bombs or explosives in the waterway, ten wrecks of big ships and 80 smaller wrecks. In addition the Canal had to be dredged of silt and its banks, navigation facilities and control installations repaired and re-equipped.

The Kuwait Fund contributed a loan of KD10 million (£15 million) towards the cost which was then estimated at KD32 million (£48 million). The loan, for 18 years at four per cent interest, was to cover over half of the foreign exchange cost of KD18 million (£27 million).

According to Egyptian official sources, the eventual total cost of clearing and reopening the Canal was £118 million, mostly covered by Egypt, the United States and the World Bank, but clearance work by the Western and Soviet navies saved Egypt £68 million.

The Canal was eventually reopened to traffic on 5 June 1975, the eighth anniversary of the 1967 war which had led to its closure. Some doubts surrounded its future economic value in a world of super-tankers (in 1967 only one vessel of over 200,000 tons existed and by 1975 there were 479), of economic recession and slackening oil consumption in the West. Much depended on how far the expansion and development of the Canal could meet new conditions. The Suez Canal Authority was confident it could do so by the resumption and adaption of the programme of continuous improvement that had been begun before 1967 and had been interrupted by the war.

When the Suez Canal Company was nationalised in 1956 work was in progress on the eighth improvement programme for the Canal since the great waterway was first opened in 1869.

The Canal is 101 miles long and when it was opened it could take ships with a draught up to 24 feet 5 inches. Since then the amount of traffic and the size of ships have constantly increased except during the first and second World Wars. By the time of the eighth programme, the draught was being increased to 36 feet and the Canal had also been widened and double-tracked along part of its length.

After the Suez-Sinai war the eighth programme was expanded and merged with the first stage of the new long-term 'Nasser Programme' worked out by the Egyptian Suez Canal Authority. The Nasser Programme was geared to the expected rapid expansion of oil exports from the Middle East to Europe where demand was rising by eight to ten per cent a year – and the development of bigger tankers of up to 250,000 and 300,000 tons. Before 1967 eighty-five per cent of north-bound traffic through the Canal consisted of laden oil tankers, and most of the south-bound traffic was made up of tankers in ballast.

The programme's general aims were to double the Canal over its whole length and deepen it to take the biggest tankers: to improve communications, pilotage and salvage services and modernise equipment. In addition it was intended to reorganise and expand the Suez Canal Authority's workshops, mostly located at Port Fuad, and to fit out a complete fleet of dredgers and other craft to provide continuous maintenance of the Canal.

The first part of the Nasser programme was completed in 1963 at a cost of £E47,400,000 of which £20 million was provided by a loan from the World Bank.

It included deepening the whole length of the Canal to take ships of 37 feet draught, which means tankers up to 47,000 tons dead weight, and the deepening and widening of the approaches to Port Said. It involved the excavation over a period of seven years of nearly 1,000 million cubic metres of sand and rock. A new railway bridge had to be built to replace a too narrow old one. The Port Fuad shipyards were expanded and equipped to build ships up to 6,000 tons and a floating dock acquired to take ships up to 50,000 tons for repair.

The second stage of the Nasser programme was planned in two parts. The first part was aimed at increasing the draught depth in the Canal to 40 feet to take tankers up to 55,000 tons dead weight and at improving Port Said harbour. The ship-yards at Port Fuad were to be expanded to allow the building of two ships of up to 12,000 tons at a time and the Canal Authori-ty's repair workshops were to be extended. There was to be a further increase in the Canal Authority's fleet of dredgers, tugs, launches, floating cranes, ferries and other craft and an expan-sion of its electric power generation, road network and tele-communications.

This part of the programme was to cost £E36 million and to be completed by mid-1966.

The improvements carried out were expected to increase Canal revenues by £E3,500,000 a year and income net of operating costs by £E1,750,000. In addition there would have been a net benefit of £3 million a year to the oil transport industry (because partly laden tankers using the Canal would be able to increase their load without paying more dues – unless they are in ballast, tankers pay according to the size of the ship not the size of the cargo).

Work on this part of the programme had already begun by mid-1963 when the Suez Canal Authority approached the Kuwait Fund for a loan. The design and planning of the project had been done by the SCA's own staff and the SCA itself was also doing most of the construction work. It had taken over the dredging from foreign contractors, except for one Japanese firm employed to excavate the most difficult southern section of the Canal.

The Canal was then a very profitable undertaking, with revenue from tolls increasing at an average rate of 5.6 per cent per annum. Operating costs were only a quarter of operating revenues and the Canal supplied thirty per cent of Egypt's export earnings.

In 1964 the Kuwait Fund gave the Canal Authority a loan of £E11,760,000 or KD9,800,000 for sixteen years at four per cent.

The loan agreement, guaranteed by the Egyptian Government, provided the foreign exchange needs of this part of the Canal programme, and the rest of the cost came from the SCA's reserves.

The project was not completed by 1966 as planned, but when the war closed the Canal in June 1967 more than two-thirds of the work had been done, including the re-equipment of the Port Fuad shipyards. There was still KD1 million of the loan unspent, but the rest of the project, including the second part of stage two (which was to deepen the Canal to take ships up to 43 feet draught and 80,000 tons) has since been merged into new plans for the Canal now that it has reopened.

Although the Canal was closed in June 1967 and for the next six years became the front line between the Egyptian and Israeli armies, it was not until 1969 and 1970 in the intermittent 'war of attrition' that the heaviest damage was done to the Canal installations and the towns along its banks – Port Said, Port Fuad, Ismailia and Suez-Port Tewfik – by Israeli artillery shelling and air bombardment. Further extensive damage was done in the 1973 war. In the first Israeli bombardment the Canal transit stations and the villages behind them were completely destroyed. The Canal Zone towns were severely damaged, especially Suez and Ismailia. After many hundreds of civilians had been killed, most of the population to a total of 700,000 were evacuated to other parts of Egypt. Out of Port Said's population of 300,000 only 4,000 were allowed to stay. Out of Ismailia's 200,000, only 10,000 were left behind. In the Suez-Port Tewfik area out of a population of 210,000 all but 10,000 left – 5,000 stayed in Suez town, to run the services, and another 5,000 farmers went on working in the villages. Several thousands of Egyptian soldiers and civilian workers were killed in a massive Israeli bombing campaign while building anti-aircraft missile sites in the Canal Zone in 1970.

In June 1969 the Suez Canal Authority had to move its headquarters from Ismailia to the outskirts of Cairo and transfer its workshops and other facilities to improvised sites all over the country. Its first concern, however, was to keep together its skilled labour force totalling 14,000 men, a problem of morale rather than finance, since the workers' families were scattered all over Egypt. To anyone remembering its efficient peace-time administration and the pleasant, well-ordered air of the towns along its banks, the derelict Suez Canal before and immediately after the 1973 war was a sad sight.

The road from Cairo to Suez runs for ninety miles across hot brown desert. In the spring of 1971 the rare traffic was all military. Flanking the road at intervals were military positions, camps and gun emplacements. The first sight of Suez town at the southern end of the Canal was the low dark silhouette of its burnt-out oil refinery, destroyed by Israeli shelling, with the sea beyond. Then the town, devastated and empty. On the outskirts stood block after block of new workers' flats, now deserted, with their smashed windows boarded up and shell holes or shrapnel marks in the walls. Nearer the centre of the town, especially in the older, poorer and more heavily populated areas, the destruction was much heavier. Street after street off the main avenue was blocked by rubble and every other building an empty shell. There was no one about, no life, not even a stray cat or dog. Nearer the administrative centre of the town, there were a few people, mostly soldiers and policemen. There among some less damaged streets stood elegant old colonial-style houses with yellow-ochre washed walls and long delicate balconies of ironwork or faded green wood.

The harbour was empty except for a derelict Greek ship near the entrance and another aground by the shattered quays of Port Tewfik which lies on the other side of the harbour next to the Canal, linked with Suez by a causeway.

Before the 1967 war Suez was one of Egypt's main ports, with an average of seventy to eighty ships passing through the Canal daily in both directions. It was also an important commercial and industrial centre, with industries, such as petro-chemicals, derived from its oilfields, as well as being a winter tourist resort. Sixty per cent of the buildings in Suez and 95 per cent of those in Port Tewfik had been destroyed or damaged in the bombardments which had also killed 482 people and wounded 1,242. The gutted oil refinery had not been rebuilt but crude oil from the Suez wells was going through the pipelines to Cairo and Alexandria. The harbour was not seriously damaged. From the Egyptian army's front-line trenches in Port Tewfik the Israeli advanced positions were less than 200 yards away across the Canal. Two Israeli soldiers stood there on top of the raised bank scanning the Egyptian side through powerful binoculars. A cease-fire had been in operation for six months.

Port Tewfik was once a pleasant suburb of handsome red-roofed villas set in gardens and well-laid-out streets. Now it looked like a German town at the end of World War Two. Scarcely a building was untouched. Many streets were blocked with debris and others were mined as part of the Egyptian defences. Fallen lamp-posts and palm trees lay incongruously together across the wreckage and a buckled electric pylon bent to the ground like a grazing giraffe. Two fine white vapour trails curled through the blue overhead. 'Israeli Phantoms on reconnaissance', said an Egyptian officer. There were loud echoing bangs as they broke the sound barrier. Then once more silence.

One's first despairing impression on that visit was that the Canal would never reopen but would stay forever as a line of death across the desert. But by 1974, eight months after the October war, although most of the damage was still visible and the Canal was still closed, the atmosphere had quite changed. Hope and optimism had returned. The Egyptian army was in control of both banks of the Canal with a United Nations force in a buffer zone between it and the Israelis. Work had already begun on clearing the Canal in preparation for its reopening a year later. People had begun to return to the Canal towns and the clearing of rubble and rebuilding had started. A new Ministry of Housing and Reconstruction, under Osman Ahmed Osman, a leading businessman whose Arab Contractors' Company had helped to build the High Dam, was drawing up plans for the rebuilding and redevelopment of the Canal Zone parallel with the expansion of the Canal itself. The plans included the rebuilding of the damaged towns and villages, the creation of an industrial free zone, the reclamation of almost a million acres of land on both banks of the Canal, a fishing industry and a tourist complex at the Mediterranean end of the Canal Zone. In addition to an estimated nearly £1,000 million for the improvement of the Canal itself, the rebuilding of the Canal towns was expected to cost another £600 million. The Arab oil states had contributed £140 million to build 40,000 dwellings.

The long-term plan for the Zone up to the year 2000 envisaged the expenditure of £E3,300 million and the building of 600,000 housing units.

By the summer of 1975 the new Saudi-financed 'Faisal City', a garden suburb of 4,000 apartments, was rising on the outskirts of Suez. Another suburb of 10,000 dwellings, 'Sabah City', financed by Kuwait, was to be built nearby. In Suez city itself, emergency repairs were being carried out to those buildings capable of repair, and to the public services, pending the complete reconstruction of the city over the next six or eight years. The oil refinery was working again. Nearly 100,000 people were believed to have returned to the Canal zone by the beginning of 1975. In 1974 and 1975 the Government allocated a total of £E273 million for the Canal region, but it was clear that the financing of the development plans would depend heavily on foreign and especially Arab aid, at least in the early stages. However, the Egyptian authorities expected that the operation of the Canal itself would eventually provide nearly £300 million a year in revenue, in addition to another £48 million from servicing, shipyards and tourism.

But might not the reopened Canal become a white elephant, as some foreign observers suggested? Wouldn't the oil traffic, its chief source of revenue, by-pass it and find it cheaper to go round the Cape in giant tankers?

The Canal authority naturally believes otherwise and has plans for expansion to take eventually much bigger tankers of up to 260,000 tons fully laden. They point out that the future of the Canal depends on two main factors – the rate of European consumption of Gulf oil and the dimension of the tankers carrying this oil. Oil tanker transit dues had provided 73 per cent of the Canal revenue. Of the oil which went through the Canal in 1966 the last year before its closure, 95 per cent came from the Gulf and 92 per cent of this went to Europe. A recent study made by the Egyptian authorities with Western consultants showed that in 1973 Europe imported some 440 million tons of Middle East oil. Of this some 60 million tons went through pipelines to the Mediterranean, leaving 380 million tons which could have gone through the Canal if it had then been open. Apart from supplies from North Africa, the North Sea and other sources, it was calculated that Europe might need up to 500 million tons of Gulf oil to come through the Canal in 1976, increasing to 620 million tons by 1980. By that time the Canal is expected to be able to take an oil traffic of 1,000 million tons a year.

Since 1973 the rate of increase of European oil consumption has slackened, but may well increase again as the world economy climbs out of recession. But how far the tankers choose the Canal route for transporting Europe's oil will depend on the size of the tankers and the width and the depth of the Canal, as well as on the level of freight rates. (Egypt will obviously fix Canal dues at the highest competitive figure).

The calculations involved here are too complex to be examined in detail, but it is necessary to note a few special underlying features of the economics of the Canal. To begin with, the capacity of the Canal to take a ship depends not only on the vessel's size but on whether or not it is laden and the size of its cargo. Similarly the comparative cost of sending a tanker through the Canal or round the Cape does not depend simply on its size but also on how much oil it carries and on current freight rates. A tanker which was too big to go north through the Canal fully laden might nevertheless be able to use the Canal on its return voyage in ballast. Or, depending on the freight rate, it might be cheaper per ton of oil transported to send a big tanker north through the Canal only partly laden rather than round the Cape with a full load. So the Canal could earn money on three types of tanker traffic: medium-size tankers going both ways through the Canal, north fully laden and south in ballast; bigger tankers going north partly laden and returning in ballast; and even bigger vessels going laden round the Cape and returning in ballast through the Canal.

By 1965, with new developments in shipbuilding technology, the trend had begun towards bigger tankers of over 200,000 tons (with a change in the loading line convention 210,000 tons became 260,000). The Canal Authority then began to restudy the Canal's development, at first independently and then in cooperation with the oil industry. At a conference at Ismailia in February 1966, the chairman of the Authority met the oil company chiefs and representatives of the international maritime organisations to discuss future plans. The oil companies confirmed their belief that the biggest tankers were the most economic size for transport from the Gulf. At that time there were only a few tankers of 120,000 to 150,000 tons in existence, but the studies by both sides had come to the conclusion that the best size for tankers passing through the Canal would eventually be 250,000 tons.

The Canal Authority then revised the 'Nasser programme' so that the second part of stage two would be overtaken by a third stage of expansion greater and faster than planned. Preliminary work on the third stage had already begun in February 1967 but was halted by the war. Subsequently the plan was revised again, because the closure of the Canal had speeded up the building of very big tankers.

Now the plan has two phases. In the first phase the aim is to deepen and widen the Canal to take vessels with up to 53 feet draught, or oil tankers of 150,000 tons fully laden and up to 250,000 tons unladen or partly laden. In the second phase the draught would be deepened to 67 feet to enable the passage of tankers up to 260,000 tons fully laden, 290,000 tons partly laden and, perhaps, more than 300,000 tons in ballast. The first phase was expected to take about three and a half years to complete from the reopening of the Canal and to cost £386 million. The second phase might take another three or four years, at a cost of £523 million, but the time needed will depend on the capacity and availability of the world's dredging fleets, since the whole project will involve dredging a total of 650 million cubic metres of sand and rock, twice the total excavated in the cutting of the original Canal.

In addition, it is planned to make a by-pass canal which will start just over ten miles south of Port Said and cut through the Sinai desert to the Mediterranean near Port Fuad. This will enable big tankers to avoid congested traffic at Port Said.

The Canal Authority believes that the cost of improving the Canal will be covered by increased revenues within the time of the execution of the projects. But meanwhile the financing of the plans was being discussed with potential international aid sources including the World Bank, the Kuwait Fund, the Arab oil states, oil companies and Japanese and American interests.

Looking further ahead, the Canal Authority has discussed the next generation of tankers with world ship owners. The Authority says it has been assured by the shipping interests that, for financial and technical reasons, there is likely to be a plateau in the size of tankers: they will mostly have to stay for a long time at about 260,000 tons. There are several reasons for this. Above 250,000 tons there is no reduction in freight costs per ton. In bigger ships a huge capital commitment is involved and an enormous load of oil is at hazard. For very big tankers insurance rates have been sharply increased and so has insurance against pollution accidents. Few world ports are equipped to take the biggest tankers, to store their loads or handle such big consignments at a time economically. There are also limits on tanker size imposed by navigation in other canals or even in natural waterways such as the English Channel or the Malacca Straits.

The Egyptians have not hitherto had the same seafaring reputation as other Mediterranean or other Arab people. But their efficient peace-time operation of the Suez Canal is not the only reminder that from earliest times they have been a maritime as well as a river people. When Thor Heyerdahl traversed the Atlantic in a papyrus reed boat built to an ancient Egyptian model, he may or may not have proved the theory that the Egyptians crossed the ocean to influence the ancient civilisations of Central America, but he at least gave a romantic and convincing demonstration of Egypt's early ship-building skills.

The medieval Arab scholar and traveller, Abdulatif al Baghdadi, notes in his account of Egypt at the beginning of the thirteenth century that 'they have in Egypt ships of many different forms and divers kinds'.

Egypt's modern merchant marine dates from 1857 when the country's first shipping company was formed. By the nineteen-thirties there were three companies operating a merchant fleet on international lines, sailing under the Egyptian flag in the Mediterranean, the English Channel, the North Sea, the Baltic and Red Seas, the Indian Ocean, and over the Atlantic to North America and West Africa.

In the early sixties all the Egyptian shipping companies were nationalised, when President Nasser began to develop his 'Arab Socialism'. All ships sailing under the Egyptian flag have since then been owned and operated by the United Arab Maritime Company which is a subsidiary of the General Maritime Transport Organisation, a state body.

The UAM developed a modest but expanding and profitable business. In the last year before the 1967 war it was operating a fleet of 35 ships – 24 cargo vessels, five oil tankers and six passenger ships totalling 192,000 tons dead weight – and earned nearly £E8 million. It ran regular services on four main lines: to North-west Europe, including the Baltic; to Britain via the Eastern Mediterranean and southern Europe; to the Adriatic and to the Black Sea.

But many of the cargo ships – which earned the most money – were old and obsolete, though some had been modernised by conversion from steam to diesel power. At the same time there appeared to be scope for expanding the fleet, since the UAM was still carrying only three per cent of Egypt's sea-borne foreign trade, and under its bilateral trading agreements Egypt can claim to carry fifty per cent of the trade arising from the agreements in her own ships. Moreover, Egypt's shipbuilding capacity had been expanded at the Port Fuad and Alexandria shipyards as part of the Suez Canal expansion programme and the Five Year Plan. Between 1961 and 1964 the Port Fuad shipyard, owned by the Suez Canal Authority, built five ships of 3,2000 tons dead weight each for the Egyptian merchant fleet. Under the second Five-Year Plan the UAM was expected to acquire some 17 vessels of between 4,000 and 12,000 tons, a total of 115,000 tons, as well as six bigger tankers and carriers. Ships of 12,000 tons or less were to be ordered from the Port Fuad shipyard which had a capacity of 30,000 tons a year.

But at the beginning of 1967 Egypt's shipbuilding capacity was mostly standing idle because of the industrial slow-down caused by shortage of foreign exchange. There was not enough foreign currency to buy the imported materials and parts used in the shipyards.

The UAM then turned to the Kuwait Fund with an ambitious plan to increase its fleet and reactivate the shipyards. It proposed doubling its tonnage by building 20 cargo ships, four oil tankers, three ferry boats and 150 small river barges, at a cost in foreign exchange equivalent to £E25.8 million.

The Fund found the project too ambitious for the UAM's administrative, technical and financial resources, but it eventually agreed to help finance a more modest programme of building eleven cargo ships, four of 6,5000 tons dead weight and seven of 4,000 tons dead weight in the Port Fuad shipyard of the Suez Canal Authority. The total cost of the project was expected to be just over £E10 million, of which £5,620,000 in foreign exchange.

In January 1968 the Kuwait Fund granted a loan of KD3,500,000 (£3.87 million) for twelve years at four per cent. The loan was to cover three-quarters of the foreign exchange cost.

When the June war broke out, the improvement in the Port Fuad shipyard, provided for in the Suez Canal project which the Kuwait Fund had helped finance, had been completed. The yard was capable of building two ships of up to 12,000 tons at a time.

The war delayed but did not stop the ship-building programme. The Port Fuad shipyard, with the Israeli army on its doorstep, was no longer usable and work had to be concentrated in less vunerable Alexandria. In 1971 the first 12,000 ton ship to be built in Egypt was launched there.

At the end of 1971 plans were being made by the Egyptian Ministry of Maritime Transport for a further big expansion of the Egyptian merchant marine, including a bigger fishing fleet. Over the next ten years it was hoped to increase the capacity of cargo ships to 568,000 tons, and of tankers to 280,000 tons to secure a higher share in the expanding foreign trade. The cost was estimated at £E145 million. Like earlier projects, these plans may have to be scaled down to fit Egypt's difficult foreign exchange position, unless some foreign financing can be found.

As part of the five year plan for 1976-80 the Egyptian Government hoped to attract private investment into shipping and talks were also in progress in 1975 with the Kuwait Government on the establishment of a joint Egyptian-Kuwaiti maritime company.

The reopening of the Suez Canal and further steps towards peace in the Middle East should make many more things possible, both for Egypt and the Kuwait Fund.

8 Sudan

'Keep Left – One Way Only' – the sign in English and Arabic at the Khartoum traffic roundabout was not a political exhortation. In fact, after its defeat of the attempted Communist coup in the summer of 1971 the Sudan's military revolutionary regime had been moving politically towards the right and the middle of the road. Driving on the left is just one of the legacies of the fifty-six years the Sudan spent under British (theoretically Anglo-Egyptian) rule until it gained its independence in 1956.

There are still many other signs of the British connection. English is still widely known among educated Sudanese, though the standard of its use is declining. Khartoum university conducts most of it faculties in English, and British expatriates form the majority of its foreign teaching staff. The Gezira cotton-growing scheme along the Blue Nile, which earns most of the Sudan's foreign exchange, has long been run entirely and efficiently by Sudanese but on a structure largely created under the British. The army retains its British style despite its Russian arms. And there is nothing so indestructibly Anglo-Sudanese as the monumentally comfortable railway hotels and their awful cooking – although on their spacious terraces overlooking the Nile you were in recent years more likely to see a pale Russian drinking Coca-Cola than a beefy ex-Blue downing pink gins. Khartoum has a leisurely, unrevolutionary air and at the Grand Hotel in November 1971 it was hard to believe that tanks had been battling it out round the presidential palace just down the road only a few weeks before.

Until 1969 Britain was still the Sudan's biggest trading partner and British firms had a big share in the handling of the Sudan's commerce which still ran more or less in the traditional business channels of colonial times. Foreign firms of one kind or another controlled seventy-five per cent of the country's commercial activity, including banking, insurance, import and export business and cotton marketing. This situation contributed to the feeling among many Sudanese that although they had won political independence they had not yet achieved economic independence. This feeling was one of the causes of the army-led Nasserist-style revolution which put General Numeiry's 'Arab Socialist' regime in power in 1969.

The regime nationalised the main foreign commercial firms in 1970 and increased trade with the Communist countries. A trade agreement signed with Russia made Moscow the single biggest purchaser of Sudanese cotton with a promise to take a quarter of the crop for £14 million out of total purchases of £16 million. The Chinese gave the Sudan a 40 million dollar loan on easy terms mostly for road building. Other East European states gave small credits or loans. A team of Soviet experts was brought in to draw up a new five-year development plan (the Russian advisers were not told in advance of the government's nationalisation programme and they themselves provided in the plan for 45 per cent of the economy to stay in the private sector).

After the failed Communist coup in 1971, there was a sharp reduction in economic connections with the Soviet bloc, especially with the Soviet Union. The Numeiry regime began to look again to the West and increasingly to the Arab oil states for aid and trade. By 1973 Russian purchases of Sudanese cotton had fallen to zero and China had become the biggest buyer, followed by Japan, Italy and India. Sudanese exports to the Soviet Union fell from £S18.3 million (£24 million) in 1971 to £S3,000 (£4,000) in 1973.

At the same time the Government adopted a more liberal economic policy, even to the extent (in 1972 and 1973) of returning some local nationalised firms to private ownership. American aid, which had been suspended after Sudan broke off relations with the United States as a result of the June war in 1967, was restored in 1973 with loans and grants in that year totalling £S17.2 million (£23 million). In the same year the World Bank contributed £S25.7 million (£35 million) for irrigation, railway and electric power projects. United Nations and other foreign aid agencies contributed at least 17 million dollars (£7.8 million) to the relief and rehabilitation of refugees in the South Sudan after the war there ended in 1972. During 1974 a proportionately bigger influx of Arab aid raised the Sudan's external debt from £S111.8 (£148 million) to £S275.5 million (£363 million). Of this some 45 per cent was accounted for by loans from Arab sources including £S55.8 million (£74 million) from Kuwait. Over half the total consisted of loans not yet paid out.

The Sudan is the hinge between the Arab world and Africa. With an area of nearly a million square miles, it is the biggest country (in area) of the Arab world or Africa. It is a member of the Arab League and of the Organisation for African Unity. But only two-thirds of its sixteen million people are Arab: the other third in the South are neither Arabic-speaking nor Muslim, but African and pagan or Christian. For fourteen years the South was ravaged by a separatist rebellion which ended in 1972 with an agreement on Southern autonomy. The Sudan's political commitments to the Arab world are therefore limited by its needs to preserve its own internal unity by holding the balance between the interests of the Arab north and African south.

While the South is tropical, the northern part of the Sudan is geographically in two sections. The most northerly is desert except for a strip along the Nile. Then there are the central plains with good land and with water from irrigation and rain. The Sudan is thus one of the Arab countries which lacks capital but can use aid effectively because it has resources of land and water that can be developed and because it has retained at least the elements of a capable administration. It is an obvious place for Arab oil countries to invest some of their surplus revenues.

It was the first country to apply to the Kuwait Fund for a loan and the first to receive one. Over the last few years, Kuwait has given the Sudan substantial and increasing help, especially in Fund loans which by 1975 totalled KD36.25 million (£54.3 million).

In 1975 the new Arab Fund for Economic and Social Development, in which Kuwait has, via the Kuwait Fund, a 30 per cent share, was considering an ambitious inter-Arab plan to develop Sudanese agriculture at the cost of several billion dollars over the next ten years so as to reduce the present dependence of the Arab world on food imports. A team sent to the Sudan by the Arab Fund completed a feasibility study for the plan in the summer of 1975. The study found the Sudan had a great potential for food production – upwards of 200 million acres suitable for agriculture and livestock. It is reported to have proposed investments totalling 6,000 million dollars (£2,727 million) in 130 projects of both the infrastructure and commercial type. The plan would aim at doubling the Sudan's cereals output to five million tons a year; and raising meat production from 350,000 to 850,000 tons, and sugar from 110,000 to 810,000 tons. Part of the financing of the infrastructure would come from grants and soft loans. If approved by the Sudanese Government the plan was to be put to a meeting of the pledging group of the Arab Ministers of Finance to authorise a ten-year inter-Arab aid programme. But help would also be sought from the World Bank, from other United Nations and foreign aid agencies, as well as from joint ventures using Western technology and Arab capital.

One of the economic weaknesses of the Sudan springs from its geography: its huge size and its limited access to the sea – only through the one outlet of Port Sudan on the Red Sea. Apart from political instability, the chief obstacles to development have been poor communications, lack of capital and, until recent years, restrictions on the Sudan's use of the Nile waters.

Its great distances and sparse population made the Sudan dependent for transport on railways rather than roads.

Railways link together the country's widely dispersed regions with the ports and main towns. They are a vital element in the Sudan's economic development for two reasons. The movement of agricultural products and industrial goods from the centres of production to the markets and ports of export depend almost entirely on the railways. Rail transport is also used to carry most of the materials and equipment needed for important development schemes.

In 1962 the Sudan was engaged on a seven-year scheme to extend and modernise the railway system. Existing lines were to be renewed, new lines built to the developing agricultural areas and the signals and workshop system expanded. The plan also provided for the modernisation of Port Sudan with the building of two new berths and the installation of more cargo-handling equipment.

The cost of the whole scheme was estimated at £S27 million (£32.5 million) of which two-thirds was in foreign exchange. The Sudan Government approached the Kuwait Fund for help and in May 1962 the Fund made a loan of KD7 million (£8.1 million) at four per cent for sixteen years. It was the first loan to be made by the Fund to any government.

Subsequent Fund loans to the Sudan included three totalling KD19.71 million (nearly £30 million) for irrigated agricultural development; two amounting to KD6.2 million for two sugar factories; one of KD1.6 million (£2.4 million) for mechanised dry farming; KD1.5 million (£2.25 million) to the Sudan Industrial Development Bank; and another KD450,000 (£675,000) in grants for three techno-economic studies.

Although the Sudan has more potential for development than other Arab states, it it still one of the poorest, with a per capita income of only £42 a year. Its main source of domestic income and foreign exchange is agriculture which employs 86 per cent of the population and produces 42 per cent of GDP and nearly all the country's export earnings. Agriculture is mostly for subsistence but surpluses of cash crops for export, especially cotton, are grown in government-encouraged schemes. These schemes are of two main kinds: on irrigated lands between the two Niles, especially the famous Gezira scheme, and on the rainlands of the central plains where there is extensive, mechanised dry farming. The irrigated lands provide most of the cotton for export and the rainlands chiefly durra (sorghum) as a food for home consumption.

The Sudan has been bold in experimenting to find the best economic, social and technical forms of agriculture for its needs. It has been helped by the Government's own role in development. The Gezira scheme, for example, evolved a unique combination of state technical and marketing control, of cooperatives and tenant farming, an attempt to secure the advantages of both individual cultivation and collective scientific and production planning. In one of the extensions of the irrigated land, at Guneid, another experiment was made in a simpler form of tenancy under which the tenants paid a straightforward rent to the Government including payment for water. But so far it has not worked well.

In the rainlands, the first method used was private enterprise. The government gave help and encouragement and rented out the land to private owners. Then came cooperatives and later the development of state farms. This progression reflected not only experience but also Sudan's political move towards the left.

In the national development plans agriculture has usually

had first priority though recently more investment has gone to transport and communications. The ten-year plan for 1961-71 achieved an average growth rate of 4.9 per cent with an expenditure of £336 million. It was followed by a five-year plan for 1970-75 which in June 1974 was amended and extended to 1977.

The plan originally aimed to boost the growth rate to 8.1 per cent and to create an investable surplus from agriculture. It hoped to increase agricultural production by 77 per cent and to increase public investment in education and culture by 60 per cent, health by 82 per cent and public utilities by 58 per cent. It envisaged development expenditure of £372 million, of which £230 million would come from public funds, over half of it from foreign loans.

But in the years 1970 to 1973 actual development expenditure totalled only £S115 million (£153 million). It declined both in real terms and as a share of total government expenditure, partly because of lack of foreign exchange and partly because problems with transport and communications slowed down development projects. In the 1974-5 budget, with more Arab and other foreign aid available, £S194 million (£260 million) was allocated for development, although actual expenditure during the year was not expected to exceed £S65 million (£86.4 million).

The Sudan government has applied to the World Bank and other United Nations agencies as well as to the Kuwait Fund, the Arab Fund and other Arab governments for help for various schemes, especially for a large-scale increase in cultivation of the rainlands. It has looked to the World Bank and IDA chiefly for financing private farms and to the Kuwait Fund for money for state farm schemes.

The Gezira scheme has been described as the 'biggest farm under one management in the world'. It was the Sudan's first large agricultural development project and a pioneering experiment in government participation in agriculture. It was mostly created between 1920 and 1937 on an area of 982,000 feddans (4 million acres) on the west bank of the Blue Nile, between Khartoum and the Sennar Dam. Until 1950 it was a joint operation of the privately-owned Sudan Plantations Syndicate and the Government. Then, after the Syndicate's concession ended, the scheme was taken over by the government entirely, under the management of the Sudan Gezira Board. The Board is an autonomous body, not the servant or agent of the Government, though its members are government-appointed. The irrigation and agricultural technical management are the responsibility of the Ministries of Irrigation and Agriculture.

Between 1952 and 1964 another 780,000 feddans was added to the Gezira scheme in the Managil area, and then both the original Gezira scheme and the Managil area were extended until the area cultivated under both rose by 1967 to just under two million feddans.

When the Gezira scheme began it was based on the one cash crop of cotton, the rest of the crops being for the farmer's subsistence. But cotton cultivation remained at a low intensity because of the limits placed on the Sudan's use of water by the Nile Waters agreement made with Egypt in 1929. This situation was improved by the revised Nile Waters agreement in 1959 which greatly increased the Sudan's share of the water. The Sudan was able to build two new dams at Khasm el Ghirba on the Atbara river in 1964 and the Roseires Dam, built with World Bank help, on the Blue Nile two years later. This meant there was more water available to intensify cultivation in existing schemes and to expand irrigation into new areas.

In 1967 the Sudanese Government applied to the Kuwait Fund for help in extending irrigation to another 260,000 feddans of land, 100,000 feddans of it in the Gezira-Managil schemes and 107,000 feddans in the Khasm el Ghirba area. Another 53,000 feddans were also to be added to a small pump irrigation scheme at Guneid on the Blue Nile.

The estimated cost of the schemes was KD13,489,000 (£15,680,000) nearly half of it in foreign exchange. The Kuwait Fund provided a loan of KD5.07 million (£5.69 million). The schemes included the building of irrigation canal works and cotton ginning and decortication plants, as well as the supply of domestic water, electricity, telephones, schools and clinics for the new villages to be established.

The Khasm el Ghirba scheme was first developed in order to resettle some 50,000 people who were displaced from the Wadi Halfa area on the Egyptian border by the building of the Aswan High Dam and the creation of the huge Lake Nasser behind it. The scheme was based on the Khasm el Ghirba dam which is capable of providing irrigation for 600,000 feddans on the left bank of the Atbara. The first phase of the project, completed in 1964, covered 165,000 feddans and included the resettlement of the people from the Wadi Halfa in thirty villages built by the government. The railway was extended to the area and a sugar factory built. The Kuwait Fund gave a loan of KD1.7 million (£1.9 million) for the factory. In the second phase, another 95,000 feddans were brought under irrigation, and the third phase, for which the Kuwait Fund gave a loan, added another 107,000 feddans. The area included in the third phase was land sparsely covered with patches of grass and thorn trees and virtually uninhabited except for occasional nomads. The project involved building 56 miles of major canals and 280 miles of minor canals in the course of which over ten million cubic metres of earth had to be excavated. Twenty new villages were built and new cotton ginning and groundnut shelling plants established.

The Gezira-Managil and Guneid schemes are situated in the Blue Nile province, the capital of which, Wad Medani, lies about 110 miles from Khartoum. The road from Khartoum to Wad Medani is busy and dangerous. It has barely room for two streams of traffic; the potholes and an endless thundering flow of big lorries and buses add to the hazards. It runs through partly cultivated scrubland on the west bank of the Blue Nile. On the outskirts of Khartoum it goes past the new suburbs of 'first, second and third class' housing estates. (The first-class houses cost £10,000 upwards, the second £6,000 and the third-class, in traditional mudbrick style within a compound wall, cost £1,000). Further out there are simpler mud villages by the Nile. Few have any trees. The wide dry plains were dotted with thorn bushes and patched with intermittent cultivation; the golden stubble of durra fields was being grazed by flocks of goats and sheep or sometimes small, hump-backed cows, showing their spiky bones. Occasionally by the roadside there was a carcass of a cow, a goat, or a dog, eaten hollow.

Wad Medani with a population of about 100,000 is the second most important town in the Sudan, after Khartoum-Omdurman. It is a crowded, bustling market town and administrative centre. Near its neat little municipal garden stand the headquarters of the provincial commissioner. In the anteroom to his office a brown wooden board on the wall bears the names in gold letters of the previous British governors of the

Blue Nile, like a school roll of honour. Under a new system of local government then (in 1971) being introduced by the Numeiry regime, the Provincial Commissioner was a political appointee and was assisted by an executive director, a senior official from the local government hierarchy. There is an Executive Council which includes local appointees as well as representatives of the central government. The intention was eventually to make the provinces the main administrative units in the country, with a high degree of autonomy in economic and social development. In the same spirit of decentralisation, the Sudan Gezira Board, a self-financing body, should also have found its autonomy strengthened, but it still sometimes had to fight hard against a too tight control over its expenditures by the central ministries.

The headquarters of the Gezira Board and its research centre are at Barakat, a twenty-minute drive south from Wad Medani. The road follows the length of a canal through the heart of the Gezira scheme. An occasional palm tree curves elegantly over the shining line of water; fields of cotton and maize extend on one side and, on the other, neat stores and factories, cotton ginning plants and a light railway with diesel· locomotives. There is a feeling of order, prosperity and efficiency, a sharp contrast with the scrublands further north.

Because the Gezira Managil scheme lies on plains which tilt gently in the right direction, it can be mostly irrigated by gravity flow. Two main carrier canals take water from the Sennar Dam for 30 miles along the Blue Nile to a reservoir from which subsidiary canals branch out. The extension of the scheme which the Kuwait Fund helped to finance included a big expansion of these irrigation works, as well as the supply of equipment and services for farms and villages, and transport and housing for the management officials. The carrier and main canals were extended by 160 miles and the minor canals by 250 miles, as well as a big network of smaller canals. Two new pumping stations were required and other irrigation equipment, such as steel gate regulators, syphons and movable weirs, was supplied. The new villages were equipped with schools, clinics and veterinary stations.

On the Gezira and Managil schemes the land belongs to the government and is let on yearly tenancies of fifteen to twenty feddans apiece. The tenants have to follow the instructions about crop patterns, irrigation and other technical matters given by the management of the Sudan Gezira Board. The management is responsible for providing water and maintaining the irrigation system. In return it gets a share of the proceeds of cotton sales or, in the case of the Guneid scheme, a payment of rent. The management also carries out research, advises the tenants and supervises the general farming operations.

For all crops except cotton the tenant both bears all the costs and gets all the profits. But in the case of cotton, costs and revenues go through a joint account shared by the Gezira Board and the tenants. The proceeds from cotton sales are divided in the ratio of 48 per cent to the tenants, 40 per cent to the Government (part of which is reallocated to local councils in the area and to the local social development board), ten per cent to the Gezira Board and two per cent to a tenants' reserve fund (this is usually handed over to the tenants the same year, so making their share effectively up to one half).

This system of profit-sharing has been criticised by some experts as inadequate to provide full incentives to the farmers, partly because it is restricted to cotton and partly because it encourages the tenants to ignore the real cost of the water and other services the government provides.

The distribution of income as between different tenancy holdings and different schemes also tends to be unfairly haphazard. The World Bank, among others, has in the past recommended a reorganisation of the tenancy systems and it was probably in response to such suggestions that the Sudan Government introduced a different system in the Guneid scheme. There for the first time in a government project tenants were asked to pay land rents. The tenants there are responsible for all the costs and profits of all their crops, including cotton, but in return for the water and management services they pay a rent based on crop yields and prices. The aim of this system was to provide more incentive to individual farmers. But in practice it does not yet seem to have produced the hoped-for results.

The new extensions of the Gezira-Managil, Guneid and Khasm el Ghirba schemes, which were partly financed by Kuwait Fund loans, provided nearly 15,000 new farm holdings. The tenants were expected to earn an average net income of £S203 (£244) a year – the equivalent of a per capita income of

£S40 (£48) a year, which was double the estimated per capita income for the Sudan as a whole in 1967.

The project as a whole was expected to increase the Sudan's production of cotton, ground nuts and wheat by twelve per cent – four per cent more long staple cotton (of which the Sudan is the world's second biggest producer); 20 per cent more ground nuts and 67 per cent more wheat. Cotton provides over half of the increased net value of production, estimated initially at £S4.2 million (£5.06 million) a year.

In 1973 and 1975 the Kuwait Fund granted two loans of KD3.3 million (£4.95 million) and KD11.2 million for another big irrigation project patterned on the Gezira scheme. This was the Rahad project which aims at the reclamation of 820,000 feddans and their irrigation from the Roseires Dam on the Blue Nile. The first loan of £4.95 million for 30 years at three per cent was for the first stage of the scheme which involves the development of 300,000 feddans of semi-arid land on the eastern bank of the Rahad river. Only half of this area has been cultivated and that by primitive means. The irrigation and drainage works include a pumping station on the Blue Nile, a diversion dam and a canal to feed the irrigation network. In addition the scheme will provide farming equipment and transport, storage and processing facilities. There will be facilities for settling 13,700 farm families, including medical centres and advisory services. The scheme is expected to produce cotton and groundnuts for export and vegetables for local consumption, trebling the income of the settlers and creating jobs for about 9,000 seasonal workers. The total costs were initially estimated at KD32 million (£48 million) of which nearly KD21 million (£31.5 million) in foreign exchange were to be covered jointly by the Kuwait Fund, IDA and USAID. The first phase of the project was expected to be completed within five years and then to be run by a new administration similar to the Gezira Board.

Parallel with the extension of the irrigated areas, the Sudan Government has encouraged an expansion of large-scale mechanised farming on the non-irrigated rainfed lands of the Central Plains between the two Niles. This mechanisation began in 1948 with the creation of a government state farm of 9,000 feddans. Five years later the Government encouraged private enterprise to develop mechanised farming by making land available at a nominal rent and providing various services under the Mechanised Crop Production Schemes (MCPS). By 1967, 1.4 million feddans were under mechanised cultivation mainly in the Gedaref area (in the Kassala province) and in the Blue Nile province, mostly producing sorghum. In 1968, after a crop failure and shortages of sorghum had shown the need for a properly planned and controlled expansion, the Government set up the Mechanised Farming Corporation (MFC) to be responsible for all mechanised farming on rain-fed lands, including state farms.

The following year the World Bank gave the Sudan Government a five million dollar loan to help finance a private mechanised dry-farming project of 140,000 feddans near Gedaref. By 1970-71 the area of mechanised rain-fed farming had been extended to about two million feddans, of which 94,000 feddans were state farms.

The five-year development plan for 1970-75 envisaged more than doubling the area of mechanised rain-fed farming. The extension was divided between private enterprise, state farms and cooperatives. The plan was to expand the area by 2.7 million feddans of which 1.6 million feddans would be in the private sector, 700,000 feddans run by cooperatives and 400,000 in state farms.

The Sudan Government sought help from the World Bank and IDA for the creation of 1,500-feddan farms on 200,000 feddans in the private sector. In 1971 it asked the Kuwait Fund for aid in setting up a state farm of about 200,000 feddans in the Agadi-Garabin area of the Blue Nile Province. The location for the state farm, about 25 miles from the Roseires Dam, was chosen because of suitable soil, enough rainfall, adequate communications, availability of labour and ease of development. There is a road to a nearby railway which goes on to Port Sudan. The farm was to be 25 miles long and 12½ miles wide. When work began on creating it in November 1971, it was covered by virgin vegetation, occasional trees and savannah grasslands. The work, to be completed in 1975, included clearing this vegetation, digging for water and building local roads, as well as offices, houses and huts for the management staff and farm workers, and sheds and workshops for farm machinery and vehicles. The machinery was to include 140 tractors and disc harrows, 60 combine harvesters as well as various tankers and trucks. The project was to cost KD3.28 million, (£3.81 million) of which just over half would be in foreign exchange. The Kuwait Fund granted a loan of KD1.6 million (£1.86 million) for twenty-five years at three per cent. It was estimated that the project would increase the Sudan's output of sorghum by 66,000 tons a year and of sesame by 3,325 tons. This output would be exported and earn about £S1.76 million (£2.12 million).

The management of the project was initially entrusted to the Sudan Government's Mechanised Farming Corporation, but the Kuwait Fund pointed out, when it investigated the project, that the MFC was originally conceived as an institution for providing technical services, credit and marketing and not as a business enterprise engaged directly in farming.

The Sudan Government and the Fund agreed that the MFC should be reorganised and that eventually the project should be run by an institution primarily dealing with state farms and with enough administrative and financial independence to operate like a farm business concern. At the same time it was agreed that a thorough study should be made in consultation with the Fund of the organisational, administrative and financial aspects of state farms in general. The Fund loan included money for this study and for specialised staff to carry out the recommendations the study might make.

Apart from the mechanised state farm project, the Sudan Government also approached the Kuwait Fund in 1971 about help for four other projects: another railway expansion, a grain silo, a sugar project, and the development of livestock.

The Fund gave technical assistance grants totalling KD450,000 (£675,000) for techno-economic studies of the planning of the Sudan's transport system, of the grain silos and sugar projects, and of livestock development. In 1973 a loan of KD4.5 million (£6.75 million) for 16 years at four per cent was granted for a sugar factory, the third in the Sudan and the second to be financed by the Fund. Under the project 32,000 feddans in the north-west Sennar area, 300 kilometres south of Khartoum, was to be brought under sugar-cane cultivation and a factory built with a capacity of 100,000 tons a year by 1980, rising to 150,000 tons by 1985. The aim is to reduce sugar imports and the project will provide work for over 5,000 people. The total costs were estimated at KD19.35 million (£29.5

million). The Kuwait Fund's loan was to meet a third of the foreign exchange component, the rest being covered by a credit from Lloyds Bank with the backing of the British Export Credit Guarantee Department.

In 1975 the Kuwait Fund granted a loan of KD1.5 million for 17 years at four per cent to the Sudan Industrial Development Bank, as part of its growing policy of giving aid through local development institutions, such as industrial banks, which can channel money into smaller projects.

9 Jordan

Jordan is unique among the Arab countries in at least two respects: it has needed outside economic aid not merely to develop, but even to survive; and it has suffered more proportionately than any other from the vicissitudes of the recurrent wars with Israel, civil strife and inter-Arab conflict.

Indeed, the losses of territory and revenue it has suffered, especially from the 1967 war with Israel, and the enormous burden of refugees and displaced persons it has had to bear, together with the lack of natural resources in the country, make some experts doubt whether even with large-scale foreign aid it can ever provide a decent living for all its present inhabitants.

But it has made great and often successful efforts to help itself: there is something admirable and moving in the resilience and energy with which its people seem able to pick themselves up from the floor after every disaster and start building again.

Jordan is, in fact, the classic case of an Arab have-not country which needs and can use aid from those Arab states whose huge oil revenues and small populations give them surplus capital to invest. Jordan has had a special demand on the sympathies and aid of the richer Arab states because for long she bore the main brunt of the Arab struggle with Israel. She was the main host country to the Palestinians, refugees and others, who came to form two-thirds of her population; she was also the state which had to defend the longest Arab frontier with Israel. But Jordan's geographical position, surrounded by more powerful neighbours – Israel to the west, Syria to the north, Iraq to the east, Saudi Arabia to the south, and Egypt nearby, has meant that she and especially her Palestinian citizens have been the targets of many contending pressures and influences. In fact the political fate of the Palestinians was a major question-mark hanging over the future of the Jordan state as moves towards a peace settlement between the Arab states and Israel began to develop after the Middle East war of October 1973. The question was whether, if the Israeli occupation of the West Bank ended, the Palestinians there would prefer to remain part of Jordan or to have a separate state of their own. And since all these conflicts have been seen by the Great Powers as affecting their own balance of power and interest in the region, Jordan has also been an object of wider international rivalries.

This entanglement has cost Jordan dear in many ways, but it has also had one compensatory result: for long it was easier for her to obtain economic aid from interested outside powers, in this case chiefly other Arab countries and the United States and Britain.

The Jordan state was born with heavy handicaps. It was created in 1949 by the union of the former kingdom of Transjordan, then under King Abdullah, grandfather of the present King Hussein, with the West Bank, that part of Arab Palestine which had been occupied by the Transjordan army and held against the Israelis during the first Palestine war.

Of the one million Palestine Arabs who fled from their homes before the Israeli advance, half took refuge in Jordan. Of the half-a-million who stayed in place on the West Bank, at least a hundred thousand in the border villages had lost their lands and livelihood. In addition, the West Bank and Transjordan itself had lost their normal markets and their access and trading routes westwards to the Mediterranean ports of Haifa and Jaffa.

With at least a third of its population homeless (Jordan alone of the Arab countries automatically gave citizenship to the Palestinian refugees), and almost a half of the working population jobless, Jordan was a depressed area in the Arab world with an unemployment ratio unheard of in a Western country even in the deepest depths of the Great Depression. It was kept alive by foreign aid. The refugees, whose natural increase far outstripped the numbers who could be absorbed or resettled, were provided with a meagre subsistence ration and some basic health and education services by UNRWA (United Nations Relief and Works Administration), most of whose funds were contributed by the United States and Britain. At first, Britain, the mandatory power originally responsible for both Palestine and Transjordan, also paid for most of the upkeep of the Jordan army, the Arab Legion, and gave some economic and technical assistance to the Jordan Government. The army subsidy was in itself a form of economic aid – though not necessarily the most effective kind – because the army was in a sense Jordan's biggest national industry, employing directly up to 50,000 men and providing support indirectly for perhaps five or even ten times as many people.

Economic development was slow at first and concentrated on the capital, Amman, which expanded rapidly from a small market town of 30,000 to a handsome city (now about 400,000). Palestinians from the West Bank middle-class set up businesses and built houses on the surrounding hills in the beautiful local stone, like their former houses in Jerusalem and other Palestinian hill towns, while their less fortunate compatriots huddled in refugee camps of tents or huts nearby. A troubled border with Israel and internal disturbance, stirred by the impact of the pan-Arab nationalist movement inspired by President Nasser of Egypt, deterred investment, especially on the West Bank.

Jordan was able to avoid direct involvement in the war between Egypt and Israel in 1956, except for suffering two or three big Israeli border raids. But Arab nationalist sentiment brought a break with the British treaty of alliance and the consequent replacement of the British military subsidy by a joint subsidy from Egypt, Saudi Arabia and Syria. This Arab subsidy was withdrawn and replaced by American aid in 1957 when King Hussein decided to endorse the new American post-Suez policy, known as the Eisenhower doctrine, of forming an anti-Communist front in the Middle East.

In the sixties there was for some years comparative quiet on the border with Israel and rivalries between Egypt, Syria, Iraq and Saudi Arabia to a certain extent relieved the pressure on the Jordan regime from its Arab neighbours. It was during these years that the Jordan economy began to develop more rapidly and to show some prospects of being able eventually to dispense with foreign aid – except for the United Nations relief to the remaining Palestinian refugees. There remained a large hard core of refugees who could not be absorbed in jobs, or who still lived in camps and were a kind of terrible enclave within the Jordan economy and society.

A five-year development plan was begun in 1962 and then revised to put greater stress on achieving self-sufficiency, becoming the seven-year plan for 1964-70. In the uncertainty after the 1967 war, planning was on a year-to-year basis until November 1972 when a new three-year plan was published and explained to a specially-called international conference. The new plan, calling for an expenditure of JD179 million (£200 million), was drawn up by a National Planning Commission under the chairmanship of the Crown Prince Hassan. The National Planning Commission then occupied modest offices in a stone villa in one of the hill suburbs of Amman. The Commission's secretary was Dr Hanna Odeh, a quiet, precise civil servant.

By 1966 development expenditure was JD(Jordan dinars) 15.9 million (£18.5 million) a year compared with JD2.8 million (£3.26 million) in 1954. Over the same period Gross National Product had increased to JD185.8 million (£216.4 million) from JD52.4 million (£61.1 million). Per capita income, despite a population increase of over fifty per cent, had risen from JD37 (£49) in 1954 to JD93 (£113) per annum in 1966. Exports of goods and services went up largely as a result of big increases in the three main export earners – fruit and vegetables, phosphates and tourism.

Jordan remained heavily dependent on foreign aid, especially for development purposes, though a reduction in direct budgetary support showed some movement towards self-sufficiency. In 1954 aid amounted to JD12.9 million (£15.5 million). In 1966, foreign aid totalled JD31.4 million (£36.6 million) of which JD13.4 million (£15.6 million) came from the United States, JD11.1 million (£12.9 million) from Arab governments, JD1.3 million (£1.5 million) from Britain, and JD5.6 million (£6.5 million) from UNRWA and other UN agencies. But it had begun to represent a smaller proportion of GNP. Aid, together with invisible earnings from tourism and some JD12 million (£14 million) worth of remittances from the thousands of Jordanians working in other Arab countries, helped to offset the trade deficit of some JD56 million (£65 million) in 1966.

The outlook at the beginning of 1967 was promising. Jordan seemed to be moving towards the point of economic 'take-off'. In the 1967 budget JD28.3 million (£33 million) was allocated for development out of a total of JD69 million (£80.5 million).

Then came the catastrophe of the June war and the Israeli occupation of the West Bank. Within a few hours, Jordan lost half of her economic resources. A third of her population was left under Israeli occupation. The East Bank received the additional burden of 400,000 people who fled from the West Bank – 100,000 of them already refugees from the 1948 war and 300,000 'new' refugees who had to be fed, housed and educated. The West Bank had provided 45 per cent of Jordan's GNP, and half of its government domestic revenues and foreign exchange earnings. It formed a quarter of Jordan's meagre cultivable area and produced two-thirds of its fruit and vegetables. With the Old City of Jerusalem, Bethlehem and other Holy Places, it was Jordan's main tourist attraction.

As if this was not enough, Jordan suffered two more serious setbacks. The first was the devastation and depopulation of the Eastern side of the fertile Jordan Valley in 1968, 1969 and 1970 as a result of border guerrilla operations and Israeli reprisals. The second was the civil war of September 1970 and July 1971 between the Jordan army and the Palestinian guerrillas. Jordan was able to meet the shock of these events with the help of some JD20 million (£23.3 million) emergency aid from Arab and other friendly governments in 1967 and subsequently a subsidy of £40 million a year from the wealthier Arab oil countries, Saudi Arabia, Libya and Kuwait. The economy was showing signs of revival by 1969 and this resurgence continued until the civil war in 1970 which was estimated to have cost the country some JD16 million (£18.7 million) and a drop in GNP for the year of 12 per cent. After the final round of the civil war in 1971, Kuwait and Libya suspended their aid, amounting to £23 million, though the gap was partly filled by a resumption of budgetary support from the United States. (Kuwait resumed her aid after the 1973 war.) The closure of the Syrian border and air space to Jordanian traffic (Iraq also closed her borders with Jordan but reopened them three months later) did serious damage to Jordan's foreign trade. But by the spring of 1972, Jordan, in its seemingly irrespressible way, had bounced back again and begun yet another recovery.

However, more ups and downs were at hand. The first year of the 1973-5 plan coincided with one of the worst droughts in the country's history and with the October war against Israel. The drought severely curtailed agricultural production but the war brought some gains as well as difficulties. Jordan territory was not directly involved in the fighting but Jordanian armoured units went to fight on the Syrian front. There was an inevitable disruption of trade and tourism but also subsequently a bigger inflow of Arab aid as oil price increases swelled the surplus funds of the Arab oil states. Relations were also eased with Syria and Iraq and other Arab states, but the recognition by the Arab summit in Rabat in 1974 of the Palestine Liberation Organisation rather than the Jordan Government as the official representative of the Palestinians, increased the uncertainty about Jordan's future political shape. In 1972 King Hussein had proposed that, after Israel's withdrawal from the West Bank, the Palestinians there should be free to choose whether they wished to remain separate or to join with the East Bank as an autonomous region within a federal kingdom. After the Rabat decision, the Jordan Government began more seriously to consider the future separate economic and political development of the East Bank, in case the Palestinians chose a separate existence. This had in any case been happening by force of circumstances and was reflected in the 1973-5 development plan.

The expenditure envisaged under the plan included JD27.6 million (£40 million) for agriculture and irrigation, JD26 million (£37 million) for mining and industry, JD35.8 million (£51 million) for transport and JD34.9 million (£50 million) for housing and government buildings.

The aim was an average annual growth rate of 8 per cent, of which 6.4 per cent would be for agriculture and 14 per cent for industry, and the creation of 70,000 more jobs. An expenditure of just under JD100 million (£143 million) was to be in the public sector. The plan fell short of these targets but registered some significant progress. Growth was at the rate of five per cent and only sixty per cent of the planned public sector projects were implemented. But a combination of good harvests after the drought year, the quadrupling of phosphate prices (Jordan's most valuable export) and increased Arab and international aid enabled expansion to be continued and to offer good prospects for the five-year plan which was being prepared for launching in 1976 with an expected investment of some £350 million. The aims of the new plan included the raising of phosphate production to ten million tons by 1980 and the reduction of dependence on foreign aid. The new plan would carry over some projects from the three-year plan but it also envisaged new projects including more dams and irrigation works on the Yarmouk and Jordan rivers, a new fertiliser plant, a million-ton capacity cement plant and the development of potash and copper mining.

Jordan's state budget for 1975 provided for an estimated expenditure of JD218 million (£310 million) of which 40 per cent was allocated for development and 22 per cent for defence. More than half the budget revenues of JD206 million (£294 million) were to come from various forms of foreign aid. This included JD60.4 million (£86.3 million) in direct budgetary support chiefly from Saudi Arabia, Kuwait and the United States, and JD50.15 million (£71.6 million) in development loans and grants. Total aid from the Arab states during 1975 was estimated at JD46 million (£65.7 million).

However, Jordan's chances of progress still hinged on the prospects of peace and stability – if not a permanent peace settlement with Israel, then at least a form of peaceful coexistence with Israel and its Arab neighbours which would provide greater outlets for its trade and better security for investment. In 1975 some steps seem to have been taken in this direction: the reopening of the Suez Canal and the freeing of Syrian trade routes encouraged hopes of expanding exports to Europe as well as to the other Arab states.

From the earliest days of the Kuwait Fund, Jordan was an obvious and deserving client for the Fund's operations. Jordan was the second country after the Sudan – both inheritors of a British-trained civil service with a business-like approach – to apply for and receive loans from the Fund. Jordan's need and her special position as the main haven for the Palestinians no doubt increased sympathetic interest in Kuwait where exiled Palestinians were also becoming a large, productive and intellectually influential part of the population. But special sympathy did not deflect the Fund from applying to Jordan the cautious criteria for loans it was seeking to establish for all applicants. In March 1962, agreements were signed for a series of Fund loans totalling KD7,500,000 (£8.29 million) for projects in Jordan in the three most promising fields of development, especially for foreign exchange earning, namely irrigated agriculture, phosphate mining and tourism, as well as for an expansion of electric power.

The tourism projects were for two modern hotels in

Jerusalem and Amman, which received loans totalling KD260,000. Another small loan of KD240,000 was for the expansion of the Jerusalem electric power station. The fate of these projects is a small indication of the difficulties Jordan has had to face in her development. They were all completed by 1966, the two hotels, as I know from personal experience, being handsome and well-run establishments.

By that year Jordan's income from tourism had risen from JD2.2 million (£2.5 million) in 1954 to JD11.26 million (£13.1 million), providing 25 per cent of her foreign exchange earnings. But the following year the Jerusalem hotel and power station fell under Israeli control with the conquest of Jerusalem in the June war. The Jordan hotel in Amman alternately languished for lack of tourists and was full to overflowing with journalists and other foreigners during Jordan's periods of internal crisis, achieving world-wide fame – and sustaining some military damage – as the headquarters of the beleaguered international press during the battle of Amman in September 1970. In the spring of 1972 it was flourishing again, though without a political crisis, and had even resumed the construction of a new wing which had been planned but held up for several years past.

But the biggest Kuwait Fund aid was in two loans totalling KD6.5 million (£7.18 million) to finance the Yarmouk project and the later Zerqa River project for the extension of irrigation in the Jordan Valley, and two others totalling KD3.22 million (£3.78 million) for the development of phosphate mining.

Since then the Kuwait Fund has granted Jordan two further loans. The first was of KD3.02 million (£4.53 million) for 14 years at four per cent to help finance a new power station at Zerqa. The second loan was of KD1 million (£1.5 million) to the Jordan National Bank for Industrial Development.

The Jordan Valley is the most fertile part of a country of which a very large area is desert or steppe with little or no rainfall and only 13 per cent of which is cultivable land. The Valley is in three sections: the Zor which is the flood bed of the Jordan River; the Qatar which is the non-irrigable lip of the valley; and the Ghor which is the name given to the higher irrigable ground on each side of the Valley.

The original 'Yarmouk Project' was to build two main storage dams on the Yarmouk and Zerqa rivers which flow into the

Jordan, with smaller dams on the other tributaries further south. There would also be a network of main and subsidiary irrigation canals and flood protection, drainage and land improvement work. The total cost of the scheme, together with hydro-electric installations, was expected to be JD60 million (£70 million). It would put about 550,000 dunums (about 50,000 hectares) under irrigation and eventually add over JD24 million (£28 million) a year to the value of agricultural production.

Part of the scheme had already begun in 1958 when with the help of American aid a start was made on building the East Ghor main canal. The Yarmouk waters were diverted by gravity through a one-kilometre tunnel into a 69 kilometre-long canal running down the eastern side of the Jordan Valley. From this another 600 kilometres of subsidiary irrigation and drainage canals supplied 3,500 farm units and 120,000 dunums of land. All these installations, including ancillary maintenance roads and a telephone system, had been completed by July 1966.

One of the smaller side dams (the Sharhabil Bin Hasna at Ziglab) had also been completed in March 1967. Work began on two others, at Shueib and Kafrein, in September 1966 and was completed in 1968 and 1969, despite the fighting then going on in the Jordan Valley.

Meanwhile, the Yarmouk project as a whole had been complicated by 'the immediate Arab project'. This was the Arab states' plan for countering the Israeli diversion of the Jordan head waters by diversion schemes of their own. The Israeli diversion begun in 1964 had posed two serious problems for Jordan: it not only reduced the flow of the Jordan, but also, in the view of Arab experts, made it saline and unsuitable for irrigation purposes.

Jordan's share in the 'immediate Arab project' was to make greater use of the Yarmouk water in place of the saline Jordan river flow by three developments. (1) To double the capacity of the East Ghor Canal. (2) To build canals to carry Yarmouk water to the Zor flood lands and a syphon to carry it over the Jordan river to the West Bank, and (3) to build the main Yarmouk storage dam, the Khalid Ibn Al Walid dam at Mukheibe. The total cost of these projects was to be JD16.3 million (£19 million).

The doubling of the East Ghor Canal and the construction of most of the Zor Canals were completed by May 1967; work had begun the previous year on the Khalid dam. But the June war and the Israeli occupation of the Golan Heights led to the suspension of work on the Khalid dam and the Zor canals.

Of an initial Kuwait Fund loan of KD4 million (£4.64 million) for the Yarmouk project, nearly half had been spent by 1972 on feasibility studies, on the Khalid dam and other dams, and on an extension of the East Ghor Canal by eight kilometres. In early 1972 the Jordan Government was negotiating with the Kuwait Fund, the World Bank and several national governments for help in financing a revised form of the Yarmouk scheme, concentrating on the Zerqa river. This included the building of the Zerqa Dam and a further extension of the East Ghor canal, together with feeder canals and land levelling. The extension would put another 34,000 dunums under irrigation.

The Jordan Government eventually reached agreement in 1972 for the Kuwait Fund to supply KD4.6 million (£5.1 million) out of the total cost of £11.1 million for the new Zerqa River project. This would be made up of KD2.1 million balance from the original Fund loan for the Yarmouk project and an additional Fund loan of KD2.5 million.

During the border fighting between 1967 and 1970 the East Ghor canal was several times damaged by Israeli shelling and bombing. Thousands of Jordanian farmers were forced to leave their fields in the valley and take refuge in the hills. By 1972, after the expulsion of the Palestinian guerillas from Jordan, the canal was repaired and the rehabilitation of the farmlands had begun. The Jordan Government was working with the USAID agency on an integrated plan for the restoration and development of the Valley.

The World Bank granted a loan of 7.5 million dollars (£3.4 million) for Jordan Valley development and USAID lent 18 million dollars (£8.2 million) for connected agricultural projects. The Jordan Valley development plans include new roads and irrigation schemes, power stations and the creation of 38 new villages for 137,000 people.

Apart from farming, minerals – chiefly phosphates, rock for cement-making and the potash and other salts of the Dead Sea – are Jordan's only other important natural resource. So far, no exploitable oil has been found, though the search is continuing. But there are hopes that copper ore deposits found in southern Jordan and estimated at 55 million tons may prove worth exploiting.

Jordan's phosphate industry is run by the Jordan Phosphates Company which is two-thirds government owned and has one-third private capital (including 4,000 small shareholders). The industry has both potentialities and problems.

Jordan has large phosphate deposits in many places and proven reserves of 130 million tons, with another 140 million tons estimated but unproven. But the economic working of the deposits depends on how deep they lie, what ground covers them and how far they are from the nearest port for shipping. Then there is also the question of their grade. The keenest world demand now is for super-phosphates; for the average grades which Jordan mostly produces the market is very competitive.

In the nineteen-fifties, phosphate mining was located near Amman in central Jordan and output was less than 100,000 tons a year. The location was a handicap on exports because it meant sending the phosphates by road either 380 kilometres south to Aqaba or 350 kilometres north through Syria and Lebanon to Beirut.

So a location was sought nearer to Aqaba, which was then being developed as Jordan's only port of its own. Suitable deposits were found at Al Hasa, 180 Kilometres north of the port.

It was there that a Kuwait Fund loan of KD3.0 million was used to set up the mining installations, together with a small town or village for the employees. There are 1,500 men directly employed by the company as well as others working on contracts given to small local enterprises which use their own bulldozers and are paid by the cubic metre excavated. Contractors also run the fleet of trucks carrying the phosphates to the ports. The mine installations include a benificiation plant for purifying and improving the grading of the phosphate, as well as furnaces and an electricity generator.

With the help of loans from the West German Government the port of Aqaba was expanded to take ships in deep berths up to 50,000 tons. There is a special berth for phosphate ships with a modern handling system capable of dealing with 10,000 tons a day.

By 1967, the company was producing and exporting over a million tons a year and was making a profit. Its exports, valued at over £3 million, represented 35 per cent of the country's total commodity exports. Markets had been found in Turkey, Eastern Europe, Yugoslavia and the east coast of Italy and other sales were being developed in the East in Asia and Africa.

But this promising outlook was seriously affected at least temporarily by the aftermath of the June war. The closure of the Suez Canal meant that phosphates intended for Mediterranean or Black Sea ports could no longer be shipped from Aqaba but only through Beirut, involving a long and costly road journey to the port. Then, after the civil war in Jordan, even this route was interrupted completely for seven months in 1971-2 when Syria closed her borders as a reprisal for the expulsion of the Palestinian guerrillas. Some of these European markets were retained by continuing the contracts at a loss, in the hope of an eventual reopening of the Suez Canal. For technical reasons, a contract once lost is difficult to regain. The Syrian blockade was lifted for phosphate consignments early in 1972 when it was pointed out to the Syrians that the chief gainers from the blockade would be the Israelis who were trying hard to replace Jordan in the Turkish market. Since then economic cooperation has grown closer between Jordan and Syria.

At the same time, Jordan sought to expand her exports to East Asian and African markets, for which Aqaba is well situated as a port of shipment. In these areas, especially in India and Japan, an increasing demand for fertilisers is expected as a rising population requires greater food production. India signed a contract for 350,000 tons a year and Japan also expanded her imports.

The company optimistically looked round for money to expand production, especially of higher grade phosphate, and to improve its transport and shipment. In 1972 it was hoping to build up production and export to two million tons a year over the next two years – doubling current output. In fact, exports in 1974 reached 1.6 million tons and were expected to attain 2.75 million tons in 1975. But more important financially was the big increase in the value of these exports – from JD4.02 million (£5.7 million) in 1973 to JD19.53 million (£28 million) in 1974, as a result of the quadrupling of world phosphate prices. One of the targets of the next Jordanian five-year plan is to raise phosphate production to ten million tons a year by 1980. At present Jordan is still fairly low down in the world phosphate league. Her output compares with a production of 30 million tons in the United States, 14 to 15 million tons in Morocco, three to four million tons in Tunisia, and about 700,000 tons of low grade phosphate in Israel.

To improve transport, a special railway is being built with West German help at a cost of £14 million to link the Al Hasa mines with Aqaba. The railway, connecting also with the main railway system in Jordan, will be able to carry three to four million tons a year. Aqaba port can already cope with that amount. The reopening of the Suez Canal in 1975 improved the prospects of expanding phosphate exports to Europe through Aqaba.

The last instalment of the KD2.99 million Kuwait Fund loan was due to be repaid at the end of March 1972. But the Fund agreed to re-lend this last instalment of KD230,000 to expand the beneficiation plant at Al Hasa.

Another economic casualty of war, which could be revived by the return of peace, is the exploitation of potash on the Jordan shores of the Dead Sea. Just before the 1967 war, the Jordan Government was about to reach agreement with the Kuwait Fund, the World Bank and USAID on the establishment of a potash company and a plant with a capacity of 1.25 million tons a year. The company was to have 25 per cent equity and 75 per cent loan capital, and the Kuwait Fund was to have put up 30 million dollars (£12.5 m.) But a proviso of the Fund and of the World Bank was that the company should have a foreign industrial partner. Because of the war and the consequent military and political uncertainty in the area, it proved impossible to attract such a partner. So the project remained in cold storage.

The Kuwait Fund and the World Bank have also worked closely together, as well as with other potential aid donors, in providing aid for Jordan's new national electrification plan. This would centralise power generation for central and northern Jordan at a central thermal station at Zerqa. The Zerqa station, with two steam units of 33 megawatts each, would feed a high tension grid system linking Jordan's main towns. The total cost of the power station is just under £11 million. The

Kuwait Fund loan of £4.8 million, already mentioned, has provided half of the foreign exchange element, the other half being supplied by IDA, the World Bank affiliate.

The amount of the Kuwait Fund's loans to Jordan over the first thirteen years of the Fund's operations – KD14.4 million (£21.6 million) – may perhaps appear relatively small compared with Jordan's great needs, and compared with aid from other sources or with amounts lent by the Fund to other Arab countries in less desperate straits. But it has also to be remembered that between 1967 and 1971 and again from 1974 onwards the Kuwait Government itself was contributing £15 to £18 million a year to the Jordan exchequer as an outright gift, apart from more recent commitments to help finance Jordan's military needs. When Kuwait Government aid was suspended in the summer of 1971 as a protest in support of the Palestinian guerrillas, the Kuwait Fund continued its operations in Jordan unaffected – striking evidence of the Fund's success in keeping its operations free from political influences.

But, apart from the misfortunes of war, nowhere has the Fund better demonstrated than in Jordan its ability to make a disproportionate contribution to development by the well-chosen application of its loans to key projects and by its ability thereby to act as a catalyst for help and so also to attract help from other international aid agencies such as the World Bank.

And certainly nowhere more than in Jordan, still the main haven of the displaced Palestinians, could Kuwait's aid be applied to a better or more urgent human purpose or one more necessary for the future political and economic development of Arab Asia, indeed of the Arab world as a whole.

10 Lebanon

Until the death, destruction and commercial ruin brought by the tragic Lebanese civil war which began in 1975, Beirut was one of the most beautiful as well as one of the busiest ports in the Eastern Mediterranean. Whether approached from the sea or from the air it provided for the incoming traveller a splendid entrance to the Arab East. No doubt if there is a new political settlement in Lebanon, it will do so again.

In times of peace, its beauty lies mostly in its situation. On the one side is the Mediterranean in all its varying moods and colours, silky calm on a summer's morning or raging blue and white in a winter gale, purple and turquoise as it receives the setting sun. Behind are foothills of delicately-terraced orchards and olive groves, or slopes of pine and stone-built villages. They rise rapidly to the Lebanon mountains, snow-streaked on their bare upper ridges six thousand feet above the sea.

In between is the city itself. Beyond and sometimes within the old centre of tight-packed shopping streets and traditional Arabo-Turkish style houses with broad terraces, airy salons and graceful arches, rose tall modern blocks of offices, flats and hotels, some now, alas, fire-gutted shells or fortresses. The haphazard mixture had its own charm and was consistent with the city's character. For Beirut, the capital of the Lebanon, developed as a free-trade emporium with a chameleon-like capacity to adapt to the march of history and the clash of cultures, while always making of the amalgam something distinctive of its own. In the 1975 civil war this capacity and with it the ability of the Lebanon to survive as a single independent state, has been put to its most severe test.

In Lebanon the pattern of economic development has been strongly influenced by two inter-related political and economic factors which distinguished it from the rest of the Arab world.

The first factor was the almost equal mixture of Christian and Muslim Arabs in its population and the dominant role of the Christians in the economy and the structure of the state.

The second factor was its geographical position which made it, especially during the eight-year closure of the Suez Canal, the main gateway to the Arab East for people and goods coming from the outside world, particularly from the West. It was a centre of cultural as well as commercial interchange. These factors were normally conducive to a system of compromise in politics, both internal and external, and to free trade and free enterprise in the economy.

Most of the Arab states have minorities of some kind - – whether Christian or other religious groups within a predominantly Muslim population, such as the Copts in Egypt; or Muslim minorities, such as the Shia in Iraq among an orthodox Sunni majority; or racial or linguistic groups, such as the Kurds in Iraq and Syria, the Berbers in North Africa or the Africans in the South Sudan.

But the Lebanon's very existence as an independent state, separate from neighbouring and predominantly Muslim Syria of which most of it once formed part, was bound up with its communal pattern. For its original core was the community of Maronite Christians (originally Monothelites and linked with Rome since the eighteenth century). The Maronites have a long tradition of hard-won autonomy in their stronghold of Mount Lebanon, and were, at least until the civil war, the most powerful of the eleven communities – eight different Christian sects, two Muslim (Sunni and Shia) and the Druze – which made up the modern Lebanese state.

Lebanon's political independence and prosperity thus depended not only on an understanding between the communities about the share of power within the state, but also on maintaining a balance externally between relations with the West, to which most of the Christians traditionally look, and ties with the Arab world to which the Muslims are naturally drawn and on which both Christians and Muslims depend for employment, trade and commerce.

In times of stress when important parts of the Arab world and the West are in conflict, or the Lebanon is being drawn too closely into the military confrontation between the other Arab states and Israel, this understanding is threatened with breakdown. A breakdown occurred in the civil war in 1958; it came near to happening again in the clashes between the Lebanese army and the Palestinian guerrillas in 1969, and happened again more disastrously in the serious fighting in 1975 and 1976, involving Maronite Christian militants, the Phalangists, on the one hand and Muslims, left-wing Lebanese and Palestinian guerrillas on the other. The Lebanese system appeared unlikely to survive this last conflict without at least, some changes in the power sharing agreement. Indeed the war was imposing a form of de facto territorial partition. But the continued search for a new compromise, despite the loss of many thousand lives, was a confirmation of the extent to which both Muslims and Christians, especially the wealthier, had come to recognise a common interest in preserving Lebanon's independence and special position. They had previously shown great caution about any change that might upset the delicate local balance. But the balance now has to take account of two disturbing elements. The first is the growing consciousness of social and economic inequalities in the Lebanon (the disadvantages of which have often been felt most by the poorer Muslims) and the pressure for reforms to improve the efficiency and honesty of government. The second element is the presence of some 250,000 Palestinian refugees in the country and the increased use of Lebanon by the Palestinian guerrillas as a political headquarters, training ground and jumping-off point for operations against Israel.

The 1975 fighting led to demands for fundamental changes in the 'national covenant' to reduce its communal basis, such as allowing Muslims to compete for the presidency. (Hitherto, under the power-sharing covenant, the presidency had been a monopoly of the Maronite Christians, presumed to be the biggest single community in the state, while the Sunni Muslims have always provided the prime minister).

But such was the previous desire to preserve both the traditional political balance and the economic system which accompanied it, that in the political vocabulary of the Lebanon there were for a long time two dirty words: 'census' and 'planning'. The last population census was held in 1932 and the nearest approach to a census since then was a survey for wartime rationing purposes in 1942. A new census was continually postponed in case it should reveal that the Christians were no longer a majority in the state, or that the Maronites were no longer the biggest single community. It might also have revealed that the Shia Muslim community had grown substantially in numbers relative to the Sunni Muslims and could claim a bigger share of power than it now has. Such revelations would have upset the assumptions upon which a delicate and complicated political and constitutional structure was founded. So there was a tacit understanding, especially among those profiting economically from the status quo, to let well alone, unless pressures for change from outside the state or from the under-privileged from within it became irresistible.

The idea of economic planning had recently become slightly more respectable; the Lebanon set up a Ministry of Planning and had a series of development plans. But it was still supremely the country of *laissez-faire* where government inactivity was sometimes carried to lengths which would have astonished even John Stuart Mill or the fathers of the Swiss confederation – many Lebanese liked to think of their country as an Eastern Switzerland. (Beirut had no public rubbish-collecting service, for example.) There were two reasons for this free-for-all approach – apart from the fact that those at the top did well out of it. One was political, the other economic. The Lebanon depended for its prosperity largely on its activities as a centre of commerce, banking, entrepôt and transit trade, and other services, such as contracting and tourism. It was also a financial and a political haven for people and money in flight from more authoritarian or insecure Arab countries. For these purposes a free enterprise economy and a free money market were an advantage, perhaps a necessity. Moreover, a wide degree of political tolerance and a central government of limited powers were probably essential if the virtual confederation of different communites which was the basis of the Lebanese governmental system were to survive and at the same time to continue to give a refuge to the political casualties of the rest of the Arab world.

The supporters of the system would claim that it was due to its operation that the Lebanon was relatively prosperous and had a dynamic economy. For the Lebanon had other distinguishing features in the Arab world, apart from its character as a Christian sanctuary. It was one of the smallest Arab states and also the most densely populated.

A recent population survey – an estimate in the absence of a census – showed the population in 1972 to be 2,300,000 – some 400,000 less than had been thought. The total included 300,000 immigrants, mostly Palestinians and Syrians, while an unknown number of Lebanese emigrants – but probably at least as many – work and live abroad. Their remittances, totalling over £10 million a year, are an important element on the credit side of the Lebanese balance of payments. But with a natural population increase of 2.5 to 3 per cent per annum, there is heavy pressure on the land and emigration is likely to provide a declining outlet in future.

The Lebanon nevertheless had the highest pre capita income (about £318 in 1975) of any Arab country outside the main oil-producing states. It also has the highest literacy rate at seventy per cent; a large part of its educational system, like other social services, is privately financed, often through religious communal organisations.

Lebanon's increased attention to economic planning and greater stress on investment in the public sector dated from the early sixties. This may be because the 1958 civil war was an explosive warning. It showed that serious economic and social grievances underlay communal tensions and could aggravate them dangerously. Although the general level of wealth in the Lebanon was higher than in many other Arab countries, there were some sharp and glaring inequalities in its distribution. By any standards many in the more remote villages of the south and far north were – and are – miserably poor while in Beirut there could be seen a luxury and personal wealth unrivalled anywhere in the world.

To close this gap, to remedy these grievances and to avert the political disintegration which might flow from them required more than the traditional policy of *laissez-faire*: it needed positive public action.

The first evidence of an attempt at comprehensive planning in the Lebanon, as opposed to the study of particular projects, was the official investment plan of August 1961 which called for the expenditure of £5,600,000 during the five years 1962-6. It was followed by the five-year plan for 1965-9 which envisaged an expenditure of £187 million, of which two-thirds would come from government investment.

The latest six-year development plan was to run from 1972-7 with an estimated total expenditure of £218 million. Direct government spending was expected to provide £151 million, and £61 million was to come from the self-financing of autonomous services, such as the electricity and telephone authorities and municipalities.

The Lebanese Ministry of Planning, where I called to discuss details of the plan during a visit to Beirut in spring 1972, was a modest establishment, as one might expect. It then occupied half-a-dozen rooms on the fourth floor of a small office block, one of the many new buildings that had spread out beyond the city of Beirut on the way to the then busy international airport. The Minister's office was empty and there was a forlorn feeling about the place – not only because it was Saturday morning: it was also the eve of parliamentary elections and the Minister had just resigned.

The Director-General of the Ministry, then Dr Mustafa Nsouli, a kindly and precise middle-aged economist, (and an enthusiastic reader of Wordsworth) was at his well-ordered desk.

In impeccable English he explained that the six-year plan was very flexible. It was what the French call 'indicative' in character, that is to say it set out targets and a broad framework rather than laying down precise action to be taken. The plan, said Dr Nsouli, had eight principal aims:

1   A high annual rate of economic growth with the target of seven per cent per annum. Taking account of population increase, this would raise the Lebanon's per capita income by 4.2 per cent per annum.

2   To create more jobs, especially since emigration may provide less of an outlet for surplus population in future.

3   To establish a better balance between different sectors of the economy and to speed up the expansion of agriculture and industry, again with an eye on the future when the Lebanon may not be able to rely so heavily on its special commercial and financial skills.

4   To reduce the gap in wealth between income groups and different regions of the country. This was not only desirable on grounds of social justice but also necessary to maintain communal harmony, since on the whole Muslims rather than Christians predominate in the poorer classes and areas of the country.

5   To reduce the balance of payments deficit on current account – although Lebanon's overall financial and foreign exchange position was very healthy, with reserves in foreign currency and gold equivalent to the value of a year's imports.

6 A more rational distribution of the infrastructure in different parts of the country – some areas have few or poor roads and lack social services.

7 To increase exports mainly of manufactured goods.

8 To give a greater emphasis in education to the applied sciences and technology.

Some sixty per cent of the government expenditure envisaged in the plan when it was launched was intended for communications and social services. Roads at £31,250,000 and education at the same figure were to take the biggest share. Irrigation and agriculture were together allocated £34 million, but industrial projects only £5,750,000.

As with previous Lebanese plans, the intention was that the cost should not be met entirely out of the state budget, but at least £45 million should be raised from internal or external loans. How much of the Plan would actually be put into effect was then, of course, still problematic. The main obstacles appeared political rather than financial; it was not money which was lacking but firm conviction among the political leaders of the need for planning and agreement about how and where public money should be spent.

In practice the plan appears to have remained little more than a framework of ideas and aspiration; its original calculations about the economic outlook of the Lebanon were overtaken by the impact of the 1973 Middle East war, the big increase in Arab oil wealth and the civil strife in 1975.

The October war and the 1975 fighting temporarily disrupted trade and tourism – the first few months of the 1975 events alone were estimated to have cost £L2,000 million (£370 million) in damage and losses and the final bill will be much higher. But the new Arab oil money helped to make 1974 a boom year for the Lebanon. By 1975 several of the plan's targets were being exceeded while little progress was being made towards the fulfilment of others because of political delays. The annual growth rate was ten per cent a year in the first three years of the plan period (although inflation was also running in 1974-5 at 11 to 25 per cent). Industrial exports rose spectacularly from £L207 million in 1970 to £L845.7 million in 1974. Tourist earnings rose by 54 per cent and foreign exchange reserves doubled compared with the previous year. Electric power production rose to 1,975 megawatts in 1974 compared with 1,790 in 1973: Lebanon had excess power capacity and exported some electricity to Syria.

The budget approved in July 1975 provided for expenditure of £L1,636 million (£303 million) of which nearly a quarter was for defence, 20 per cent for education and 17 per cent for public works and transport. But major projects, such as the expansion of Beirut port and several big irrigation and land reclamation schemes were held up by government inertia or the pressure of private interests.

Lebanese governments have not liked to draw on the country's considerable foreign exchange reserves to finance investment projects requiring foreign currency, for fear that this should weaken confidence in the currency, especially since some of the big private holdings of foreign exchange were on call to foreign owners. Nor was there a well-organised capital market in the Lebanon, despite its well-developed international money market. Most of the banks did not engage in long-term financing. Hence the tendency of the Lebanese Government to look abroad for foreign financing of its development projects, whether through commercial loans or aid from governments or from international financial institutions such as the World Bank and the Kuwait Fund.

Lebanon's small size, its relatively high level of development, together with its lack of a highly organised framework for public investment and its comparatively easy access to private investment (much of it Kuwaiti private funds invested in Beirut in property development and to a certain extent in banking and commerce), may account for the fact that Lebanon, compared with other Arab countries, has had one of the smallest totals of loans from the Kuwait Fund.

The total of KD2.47 million (£2.9 million) from the Fund is made up of KD1.67 million lent in 1964 for a hydro-electric power station and KD800,000 in 1968 for the construction of a grain silo in the port of Beirut. Both projects have now been completed though the silo may have been damaged in the fighting. They were an important contribution to development in two key sectors of the Lebanese economy: the harnessing for power and eventually for irrigated agriculture of Lebanon's main water source, the Litani River; and the expansion of Beirut port, then the main Mediterranean outlet and port of entry not only for Lebanon itself but for traffic to and from the

Arab countries of the Fertile Crescent, the Arabian Peninsula and the Gulf.

The history of the Litani river project illustrates both the potentialities and problems of economic development in the Lebanon. It also shows the stimulus that even a relatively small amount of outside aid can give. The Litani is the biggest river flowing entirely within Lebanese territory. Its course is marked by the historical associations and natural beauty that together make Lebanon in normal times such an attractive country. It rises near Baalbek, the famous site of grandiose Graeco-Roman ruins, three thousand feet above sea-level. It runs south through the agricultural plain of the Beqaa, the vast green and brown chequerboard that spreads out so grandly before the eyes of travellers crossing the mountains from Beirut to Damascus. Some twenty miles from the Israeli border the Litani loops westward through the south Lebanon mountains with their dark gorges and Crusader castles, to enter the Mediterranean near the ancient Phoenician city of Tyre. The Litani has an annual flow of between 400 and 500 million cubic metres compared with 560 million cubic metres for the upper waters of the Jordan river. But until less than twenty years ago little attempt had been made to harness its waters for either irrigation or hydro-electric power.

The first serious study of the use of the Litani waters was made in 1951 by American experts under the US Technical Assistance Programme. A report on its use for power generation and irrigation was published in 1954 and in the same year the Lebanese Government established the National Office for the Litani as an autonomous agency to supervise the execution of the proposed plan.

The plan was for the building of a main storage and diversion dam at Karaoun at the southern end of the Beqaa. From there the Litani would be diverted westwards through a series of tunnels cut through the mountains. Three hydro-electric plants would be built along the diverted course of the river and some of the water would be used for irrigation. The first part of the scheme provided for the irrigation of 27,000 hectares (67,500 acres). The irrigation works were to cost £6,640,000. They were to begin in 1966 and be in full operation ten years later.

However, at first the new Litani authority gave priority in

the plan to the generation of electric power rather than to irrigation for farming. There were probably political as well as economic reasons for this decision. More electricity was certainly needed urgently to satisfy the increasing demands of the urban areas. The city of Beirut, in particular was expanding rapidly, and was the centre of the various services – banking, trade, commerce, tourism – which then provided over half the national income as compared with less than ten per cent from agriculture.

But if by 1975, nine years after the irrigation works were supposed to begin, little or nothing had still been spent on irrigation in the Litani project, it was also partly because of the little political weight carried by the farmers of the Southern Lebanon, the most neglected area of the country. The people there are poor and mostly belong to the Shia Muslim community, which was politically the least influential of the major religious communities in the Lebanon although it is now making its voice heard more loudly through a more dynamic leadership and its role in the civil war. Moreover, it is probable that investment in the south – at least after 1967 – was inhibited because of proximity of the area to Israel and the perennial fears in the Lebanon that one day the Israelis would try to expand northwards to the Litani.

Before the Litani project began to supply more power, about one-third of the Lebanese population were without electricity, although per capita power generation in the Lebanon was among the highest in the Middle East (in 1964 it was 375 kilowatt hours compared with 160 kilowatt hours in Egypt – before the Aswan High Dam power station became operative – and 80 kilowatt hours in Syria).

The aim of the project, incorporated in the national five-year economic development plan for 1965-9, was to provide electricity for the whole population, including all the country's 1,600 villages, by 1968. It was estimated that the demand for electric power would increase by 12 to 15 per cent a year, doubling in five years. Electricity and irrigation between them were expected to account for 15.2 per cent of the expenditure of £126 million envisaged in the five-year plan.

The Litani plan was designed in two phases. Phase A was to include the building of the Karaoun Dam with a capacity of 220 million cubic metres, and two of the three power plants. One plant, with a capacity of 34,000 kilowatts, would be built at Markabi about four miles south of the dam. The other with an initial capacity of 68,000 kilowatts and provision for an ultimate 102,000 kilowatts, would be placed at Awali, at the end of a diversion tunnel running through the mountains for nine miles north westwards from Markabi. Phase B was for the construction of the third power plant at Joun, four and a half miles west of the Awali station, together with a diversion tunnel and ancillary works.

For the first phase a French company, the 'French Group of the Litani', was appointed consultants in 1955. But when the work began in 1957 it was delayed by technical difficulties and management problems and then by the Lebanese civil war in 1958. One technical problem was the design of the dam: there were doubts about the weakness of the foundation material discovered along its proposed axis. Work was also held up on the diversion tunnel because of sandflows under pressure.

In 1961 new consultants, *Electricité de France*, were appointed. Work was started again and by the end of 1962 the technical problems had been overcome. The design of the dam was changed, the course of the tunnel was altered and the obstacle of the sandy soil was dealt with by injection.

Phase A of the plan was completed – except for the irrigation part – by January 1966, nearly a year ahead of time. Part of the cost of £26.8 million was financed by a World Bank loan of 27 million dollars (£9,650,000).

A start had already been made on Phase B, the third power station at Joun, in 1965 before the first phase had been completed. It was for this second phase that the Lebanese government approached the Kuwait Fund for a loan. The project included a power plant with two units each generating 24,000 kilowatts, diversion works and a tunnel bored through the mountain side. Water from the tailwater basin would be used for irrigation. By 1970, its first year of full operation, the Joun power plant would produce 188 million kilowatt hours which would increase the electricity output of the Litani Authority by 55 per cent. This was to be the output before water was used for irrigation. But as more irrigation schemes began to operate the power output would fall until by 1976, when the irrigation schemes were planned to be in full operation, power output in a dry year could go down to 112 million kilowatt hours.

The total cost of the Joun project was £5,150,000, of which just over half was in foreign exchange. After a mission had been sent to Lebanon in December 1965 and reported favourably on the project, the Kuwait Fund agreed to grant a loan of KD1.67 million (£1.95 million) for thirteen years with interest at four per cent.

The Joun project was successfully completed and the electricity side of the Litani Authority's operations was working as planned. But in 1975 irrigation plans were still mostly only on paper. Their implementation had been delayed partly through lack of government funds, partly for bureaucratic or political reasons, and partly because of the considerable social problems such as determining land and water rights, involved in introducing any new large-scale development scheme. In South Lebanon, outside the main towns of Tyre and Sidon, there are 412 villages with some 330,000 inhabitants. But in an area of 2,000 square kilometres only 75,000 hectares (225,000 acres) are now cultivated and only ten per cent of these are regularly irrigated.

In 1966 the Lebanese Government ordered the Litani Authority to prepare studies for the irrigation of a large area of the South and it also has had the help of the United Nations Development Programme in planning water development schemes. A 'Green Plan' was worked out to prevent erosion in the South. In 1970, one obstacle was cleared when the Government issued a decree laying down the proportions in which the Litani waters were to be shared between the different regions through which the river flows and between different kinds of use – for irrigation, domestic or industrial purposes.

The latest Six-Year Development Plan for 1972-7 included an estimated public expenditure on irrigation of £27 million. Part of this was to be spent on irrigating 33,000 hectares (82,500 acres) in the South, beginning in 1972 with a joint project of the Litani Authority and the UN Special Fund at the mouth of the Litani.

A new cause for delay arose from the politico-military tension in South Lebanon from 1969 onwards. The Palestinian guerrilla organisations began to use part of the border area as a spring-board for infiltration into Israel and the Israelis conducted heavy reprisal raids on Lebanese towns and villages and Palestinian refugee camps. The internal political repercussions in the Lebanon and the general uncertainty affected the country's economy as a whole and also contributed particularly to the apparent reluctance to invest in large-scale public works in the vulnerable south.

At the beginning of 1972, the work of the Litani Authority, at least as far as further irrigation development was concerned, appeared to be temporarily at a standstill and the head of the Authority was dismissed.

But a year later it was announced that plans for the development of the Litani were to go ahead. In March 1974 the Government allocated £L191 million (£36.8 million) for the first stage of the project and hoped for finance from the World Bank and Japan for the remaining stages. Technical studies for the project were completed in May 1974 but by the end of 1975 no contracts had yet been awarded, no work had begun and parts of the south were engulfed in the civil war.

In 1974-5 the Kuwait Fund was considering helping to finance an irrigation project in an area of 23,000 hectares in the Southern Bekaa. The total cost of the project is estimated at £L300 million (£57 million). The World Bank had agreed to contribute £22 million provided the Lebanese Government found other sources of finance to cover the balance.

The indications are, that the Lebanon, if it survives, may need to pay more attention to its relatively neglected agriculture in future as the development of other Arab countries or changes in Middle East communication, such as the reopening of the Suez Canal, reduce Lebanese pre-eminence in Middle East commerce and entrepôt and transit trade.

But meanwhile these and other services were still the main source of Lebanon's wealth and Beirut and its port were the centre of them.

Beirut's economic as well as political fortunes have fluctuated with those of the Arab hinterland beyond the Lebanon which it serves. Its role as a transit port for the Arab states was greatly increased when the 1948 Palestine war left the Mediterranean ports of Haifa and Jaffa in Israeli hands. Then within three years it suffered a partial decline when Syria ended her customs union with Lebanon. Syria and Jordan also sought to reduce their dependence on Beirut port by developing their own ports – Latakia and Tartous on the Syrian Mediterranean seaboard and Aqaba in southern Jordan giving access to the Red Sea and thence via the Suez Canal to the Mediterranean.

Though Lebanon's transit trade was dwindling by 1966 it expanded again after the 1967 Arab-Israeli war. Despite an expansion programme most of which was completed by 1966, the port of Beirut had to struggle to keep pace with the increasing traffic and until the civil war was still often congested. In March 1975 an average of 60 ships at any one time were reported to be waiting outside Beirut to enter the port and load or unload.

Part of the problem was that there were too many authorities in charge. The port was run by a private company with largely French capital, but it was also under the supervision of two different Lebanese ministries.

The Beirut port in 1974 handled over four million tons of cargo, an increase of 600,000 tons over the previous year. It can take thirty ships at a time in sheltered docks and twenty ships on the quays. One of the three docks has quays which can take tankers or bulk carriers of up to 65,000 to 70,000 tons. During 1975 berths were being provided for five more ships and the latest expansion plan envisaged another five berths in 1976. But this expansion was likely to prove inadequate to deal with the demands on the port which, given the return of internal peace to the Lebanon, seemed likely to grow, despite the reopening of the Suez Canal, as the Arab oil states increased their imports of goods to fulfil expanded development programmes.

One result of Lebanon's relatively small agricultural output and her rapidly growing population was a sharp increase in her imports of food grains, chiefly wheat. To handle these imports, the Beirut port expansion programme included a plan for the Lebanon's first modern port grain silo with an effective storage capacity of 90,000 tons. Between 1964 and 1968 when the silo project was drawn up, Lebanon was consuming an average of 311,000 tons of wheat a year, of which only 60,000 tons was grown locally. The rest was imported, chiefly in bulk shipments of wheat grain from Australia and the United States, consigned to the Lebanese Government's Cereals and Sugar Beet Authority. Only 35,000 tons a year came from neighbouring Syria, though Syria and Iraq between them supplied 75 per cent of Lebanon's barley imports.

Total grain imports were expected to increase from 325,000

tons a year in 1968 to an estimated 675,000 tons in 1985.

Before the silo was built, the unloading facilities for imported grain were slow and inadequate, Half of the wheat was unloaded by filling bags with grain in the hold of the ships by hand and then lifting them off by crane, while the other half was unloaded in bulk into waiting lorries by mobile grain suction units. Almost all the barley, corn and oil-seeds were also unloaded in bags. By increasing the off-loading in bulk instead of in bags, the silo cut the off-loading time and so helped to reduce freight rates.

The silo was completed by the end of 1970 at a cost of £2,220,000. The Kuwait Fund provided a loan of KD800,000 (£920,000) at four per cent interest repayable in eleven years. The loan covered almost all the foreign exchange cost of the project, the remainder of the cost being paid by the Lebanese Government.

By the spring of 1976 Beirut and its port were a battlefield. And beyond their immediate survival loomed another question. What would peace in the area between the Arab states and Israel do to Lebanon's commercial position and the trade through Beirut – always assuming that the Lebanon itself emerges intact from it own travail? The reopened Suez Canal might take away some of the trade that has passed through Beirut since 1967 and, if a full peace was achieved, Haifa and the new Israeli port of Ashdod might eventually begin to compete with Beirut for the trade of the Arab hinterland. But even on the coldest commercial calculations, peace would eventually favour the Lebanon more than the absence of it and the constant danger of war and military incursions. For peace could lead, especially with the new Arab oil surpluses, to a big upsurge in economic activity throughout the Arab East through the release of resources now wasted on military effort, and through a revived confidence in local investment. Lebanon's share in such a resurgence, together with the release from strife surrounding the presence of the Palestinian guerrillas, would probably more than compensate for any loss of the special commercial advantages that the deadlocked political situation in the Middle East had given her.

11 Syria

Almost every road into Syria has magic about it. From the north the road leads down from the blue Amanus mountains through the Gate of the Winds to Aleppo, with its glowing suq and red earth plains. From the east it comes suddenly from the desert into the streams and orchards of Damascus. From the west it leaves the Mediterranean coast past Crusader castles, mountains and pines. But none is more dramatic than the road from the South, the road to Damascus on which Paul saw his vision and was converted. Crossing the frontier from Jordan, it plunges through a strange spectacular landscape. The sweep of a high plateau is broken here and there by hills of black and brown stone and villages of the same. In spring massed fleets of clouds sail overhead and the light comes and goes as in a Suffolk sky. Blossoming fruit trees, almond or cherry, lean and tremble, pink and white, among the black stone. Women glide or cluster in long black robes and brilliant headscarves and sashes, green like the early wheat or purple and crimson as anemones. In summer, when the clouds are gone from the high blue sky, the dark earth is streaked with the gold of ripening wheat and barley as it was in springtime by the sunlight between the moving clouds.

This gold and black land, the Hauran, is one of the granaries – though not the biggest – of a country which has fed many empires in history. It was perhaps the first where wheat was ever grown but has yet to fulfil its rich potential in the modern Arab world.

Syria is a farming country with two great merchant cities in Damascus and Aleppo which are rivals in antiquity as in beauty. Although she has growing industries and magnificent artisans and craftsmen and an expanding educated class (in 1968, about 750,000 pupils were in primary schools, over 200,000 in secondary schools and 32,000 at Damascus and Aleppo universities) two-thirds of her seven million people still live off the land. In a good harvest year farm products provide 60 to 80 per cent of exports and over a third of national income.

With Iraq, Syria forms the heartland of the Fertile Crescent and lays sentimental claim to the historic guardianship of the cultural and political heritage of the classical Arab empires. Damascus in particular prides itself on being the 'beating heart of Arabism', and the Baath Socialist Party which, together with its army sympathisers, has ruled Syria since 1963 is doctrinally devoted to the pan-Arab ideal of a revived and unified Arab nation extending from the Atlantic to the Gulf.

The Fertile Crescent area, if it could be more fully developed – and both Syria and Iraq have substantial unused resources of land and water – would be the best-endowed and most natural basis for a regional union in the Arab world.

Yet curiously in recent times, until the 1973 Middle East war, apart from her two sudden jumps into Arab political union – first in the merger with Egypt in the United Arab Republic from 1958-61 and then in the loose confederation with Egypt and Libya launched in 1971, Syria had often seemed the most aloof and isolated of the major Arab states. Even with Iraq, itself run by another Baathist regime but of a different faction of the party, her relations have been severely strained.

Syria's aloofness was in part a result of her own political instability and fears that it would be exploited by pressures from her neighbours. This insecurity and the burden of war with Israel, which in 1967 displaced over 100,000 Syrian peasants from the now Israeli-occupied Golan heights and in 1973 led to some £700 million worth of war damage, have been two major obstacles to a fuller economic development in Syria. Others have been social, technical and financial.

Nevertheless the Syrian Government had made a considerable effort to overcome these development problems. Since 1963, when the Baath took over, it has done so within a partially socialist framework which includes limitations on land ownership together with nationalisation and self-management in industry and commerce. A big expansion of agriculture through privately-financed mechanisation and irrigation took place in northern Syria during the first decade of national independence after the second World War. Land reform and nationalisation began under the United Arab Republic. In 1958 land ownership was limited to 80 hectares of irrigated land and 300 hectares of unirrigated land. It was estimated that this made 275 million hectares of land available to be shared among 750,000 people or 150,000 families. The Baathist regime later reduced the limits to 15 hectares of irrigated land and 55 hectares of non-irrigated, but in deciding the maximum allowances were to be made for the location of land and its quality. The official aim is to organise farmers into mechanised cooperatives. By 1974 there were reported to be 1,700 cooperatives in existence covering some 15 per cent of the land. But over eighty per cent of the land was still privately owned and just over three per cent cultivated as state farms.

Syria's second five-year economic development plan for 1966-71 called for the investment of nearly £S5,000 million (about £500 million) of which the largest share was for agriculture and irrigation. Of the total, 13 per cent was for the first stage of the Euphrates Dam project, six per cent on other irrigation and land reclamation, and nine per cent on other agricultural development. Other major items on the plan were the development of the Karachuk oil field in north-east Syria, the building of a pipeline to the Mediterranean, a new oil refinery (destroyed during the 1973 war and now being rebuilt) and fertiliser plant at Homs, a new port at Latakia and an improvement of electricity supplies and communications.

The emphasis on agriculture was maintained and increased in the third five-year plan for 1971-5. The plan aimed at an annual growth rate of 8.2 per cent of GDP, of which 5.1 per cent would come from agriculture, 15.8 per cent from industry and 11.5 per cent from construction and buildings. In 1972 the overall growth rate was 5 per cent, of which 2.9 per cent was for agriculture.

The original target for public investment under the plan was just under SP6,500 million (£750 million) of which a quarter was for the Euphrates Dam project and another ten per cent for agriculture and irrigation. The Euphrates Dam project, which is being built with Soviet help, is a key element in the agricultural sector. When fully operational it will, it is hoped, double the area of land under irrigation and provide a large new source of hydro-electric power (800 megawatts in the first phase of the project, rising to 1,100 megawatts in the second phase and eventually to 2,000 megawatts). The diversion of the course of the Euphrates in July 1973 marked the completion of the first stage of the main dam. The use of the Euphrates water subsequently led to a serious dispute between Syria and Iraq (through which the river also flows), but it was eventually settled, at least temporarily, by Saudi Arabian mediation.

The Middle East war of October 1973 had a heavy double impact on Syria's economic development. The cost of the war itself and the widespread damage inflicted on key points such as power stations, ports, oil installations and communications by Israeli bombardment were a severe setback at a time when Syria was just beginning to benefit economically from three years of political stability under a more liberal and outward-looking regime. But the war also brought a substantial inflow of aid from the Arab oil states and credits from East European Governments. The oil crisis also led to an eventual increase in Syria's own earnings from oil production and transit dues. At the 1974 Arab summit conference in Rabat Syria and Egypt were promised 1,000 million dollars (£450 million) a year for defence from the main Arab oil states. Promises of Arab grants or gifts during the year following the October war to help to repair war damage, and for other purposes were estimated at another 1,000 million dollars.

The replacement of some of the oil refining installations at Homs which were destroyed during the 1973 war was partly financed with the help of a Kuwait Fund loan. Work began in March 1974 on a new refinery unit with a one million tons capacity at a cost of nearly £10 million to which the Kuwait Fund contributed a loan of £3 million for twenty years at one per cent interest.

In 1974 the Kuwait Fund also granted a 15½ year loan of KD9.9 million (£14.9 million) jointly with the World Bank to finance the first stage of a new 125 megawatt thermal power station at Mehreda near Hama to help make up for the heavy war damage to Syria's power network. Estimates put the cost at KD27.3 million (£41 million) of which two-thirds would be in foreign exchange.

Not all Arab commitments were fulfilled promptly but enough of the war damage was repaired within a year to enable some of the new funds to be used to finance an expanded development programme. In 1974 the Syrian development budget was doubled to SP3,500 million (£400 million) and increased again to SP5,800 million (£680 million) in 1975. In the 1975 development budget the allocation for agriculture, including the Dam project, was increased by three quarters to

SP1,300 million (£150 million). The third five-year plan was thus overtaken by the new availability of large surpluses of Arab oil money. In the 1975 Syrian budget, revenue from foreign grants and loans was estimated at SP2,700 million (£307 million). The fourth plan for 1976-80 was expected to set the ambitious growth target of increasing GDP by 75 per cent over five years. Once again the emphasis will be on agriculture (and this time also on oil) with the aim of achieving self-sufficiency in food production.

Although nearly half of Syria's land area of 18.5 million hectares is cultivable, only 3.3 million hectares or about 40 per cent of the cultivable area is in fact cultivated at one time. Half the remainder lies fallow or is not cultivated at all. Forests and pastures take another 5.8 million hectares.

Now, as in the past, Syria's wealth lies chiefly in wheat, barley and livestock, to which, since World War Two, has been added cotton and more recently a growing contribution from oil. As a result largely of private investment in the immediate post-war years, production of cotton (medium staple variety) for export expanded rapidly from 35,000 tons in 1950 to 180,000 tons in 1966, and to an average of over 400,000 tons in the years 1971-4. By 1972 cotton was providing 42 per cent of Syrian export earnings. In 1974 the value of cotton exports rose by 75 per cent to SP800 million (about £90 million). They were, however, overtaken by oil as the largest item in Syrian exports with oil export revenues of about £110 million.

But wheat has remained the main crop, grown on 37 per cent of the crop area. Since only about five per cent of the wheat land is irrigated, production has varied according to rainfall. The average of the ten years 1958-67 was 867,000 tons per annum; but in 1962, for example, it was 1,417,000 tons and in 1966 only 512,000 tons. Again in 1973 there was a record harvest of 1,808,000 tons but it was down to 593,000 the following year. Barley production also varies sharply. In 1972 it was 710,000 tons and in 1973 it was only 102,000 tons. Syria's livestock in 1972 included 5,160,000 sheep, 697,000 goats, 5,160,000 poultry and 488,000 cattle (of which perhaps ten per cent were good quality dairy cattle, the rest being used for farm work).

The biggest wheat-producing areas are in the north and especially the north-east of Syria on the great plains of the Jezira east of Aleppo and between the Euphrates river and the

Iraqi border.

An important part of the government's programme for agricultural development has been devoted to improving the production and marketing of grain, especially wheat, and raising the quality of livestock through better feed. The Ministry of Agriculture's plan for wheat was to expand production to a minimum of 1,300,000 tons per annum by the early nineteen seventies and to a minimum of 1,500,000 tons by 1980. It hoped to do so by three main methods: by reorganising crops on a regional basis so as to concentrate wheat-growing in semi-dry and semi-humid areas with more rainfall; by extending irrigation; and by improving seeds. By concentrating wheat-growing in the wetter north and north-east, which already produce 60 per cent of the country's wheat, it was hoped to increase production to an average of 1,200,000 tons a year (a minimum of one million tons and a maximum of 1,500,000). Irrigation and drainage projects were expected to increase the wheat area by 200,000 hectares of irrigated land by 1980. Half of this was to come from the first phase of the Euphrates Dam project. The other 100,000 hectares were to come from smaller irrigation projects. Altogether these irrigated lands were planned to add 300,000 tons to total wheat production.

The Ministry of Agriculture began a seed improvement programme in 1959 by studying and experimenting with different varieties of wheat. It showed that yields could be increased if seed were stored in better conditions and treated against disease before planting. But it was unable to put these lessons into practice on a national scale because of lack of facilities for cleaning and treating seed and lack of cooperation from the farmers who continued to keep their own seeds in primitive stores at home. Poor storage and the random use of seed, which mixes up different varieties, meant lower yields. The Ministry hoped to improve this situation by building seed processing plants in the main wheat areas capable of treating 30,000 tons of seed a year and by getting the farmers' cooperation in the handling, choice and storage of seeds. The new plants' output would equal only a fifth of the annual seed requirements, but the rest could be partially treated each year by cleaning and fumigation services at the new grain silos it was planned to build to improve the storage, transport and marketing of the wheat crop. It would also mean that over a period of five years all the seed wheat in Syria would be re-sorted, selected and fully treated.

The Syrians had long been aware of their need for a more efficient handling and storage of wheat. The need grew with the post-war expansion of mechanised production in the north-east and the problems of its transport, sometimes over several hundreds of miles with limited road and rail facilities, either to the coast for export or to the main consumption centres of Aleppo and Damascus. Obviously the problem was going to become even greater with the planned expansion of production in the nineteen seventies.

In recent years Syria's annual wheat consumption has been about 900,000 tons, including seed requirements of 130,000 tons. By 1982, when wheat output is expected to attain its planned peak of 1,500,000 tons minimum, the population will have reached an estimated 8 million and consumption will be 1,280,000 tons. In theory, all wheat should be handled after harvesting by the Grains Office, a semi-autonomous government agency which is responsible for marketing at home and for export as well as for managing the main flour mills and bakeries in the country. But, in fact, much of the wheat never comes into the hands of the Grains Office because the farmers keep about half a million tons a year for their own food and seed requirements. The main disadvantage of this is that the farmers' poor storage facilities lead to a high loss from rats, insects, damp or rain, which also affects the seeds.

The balance of the crop, averaging 400,000 to 500,000 tons a year, is bought by the Grains Office at officially fixed prices and transferred to storage centres in the main towns for supply to the flour mills, or for eventual export.

Syria's foreign trade in cereals (chiefly wheat and barley) fluctuates considerably – in 1971 she had net imports to the value of SP231,600,000 (about £23 million) with exports worth only SP100,000 (£10,000). In the following year imports and exports were almost evenly balanced at SP96,800,000 (£9,600,000) and SP94,900,000 (£9,500,000) respectively. In 1973 exports again fell to SP47 million (£4,700,000) against imports worth SP92,700,000 (£9,270,000). The fluctuations are caused not only by the size of the crop but also by the relative world prices of Syrian 'hard' and the cheaper European 'soft' wheat. It sometimes pays better to export more Syrian 'hard' wheat and import more wheat from Europe. But Syria's ability to exploit this price advantage to the full has been handicapped by lack of proper storage facilities. The same handicap has affected the domestic marketing system. Sometimes wheat which had been moved from the growing areas to city storage points had to be moved back again, involving double transport costs.

Substantial losses of wheat occurred in the process of putting wheat into bags on the farms, transporting the bags in trucks and storing them in inadequate sheds or in the open in tarpaulin-covered stacks. There was no bulk movement by truck and only one silo built in 1957 with a capacity of 37,000 tons, which was in the port of Latakia to load exports. But in the sixties grain exports were averaging nearly ten times the Latakia silo's capacity.

The building of the Latakia silo was the outcome of the first survey of the grain storage and handling problem made in 1954. In 1958 a report was made by a wheat storage expert from the Food and Agriculture Organisation and the Syrian Government then engaged two Danish and Swedish engineering firms to prepare a provisional report on a complete silo storage system.

In 1961 the United States Agency for International Development agreed provisionally to finance the silo project, provided a fresh study was made by an American firm. By 1964 a consortium of three American firms completed a full report and engineering study which recommended the building of eleven grain storage silos, together with three seed-processing plants and one animal feed mill.

The eleven silos, varying in capacity between 10,000 tons and 52,000 tons and with a total storage of 294,000 tons, were to be located in the main wheat-producing and wheat-consumption areas of the country. Each silo consists essentially of a series of concrete storage bins 120 feet high and 22 to 35 feet in diameter, together with necessary equipment and power facilities for handling grain in bulk and for partial treatment of seeds. The bigger silos can take incoming grain at the rate of 480 tons an hour from trucks and 240 tons an hour from railway wagons.

The animal feed mill, to be built in Aleppo, the main centre of the Syrian livestock industry, was to be linked with the silo in that city. With a capacity of 30,000 tons a year, it was intended as a pilot project for a bigger programme of improving livestock through better feed.

The Ministry of Agriculture had become convinced from its research that both the quantity and quality of Syria's farm animal production could be improved by better feed, especially what is known as 'formula' feed. They believed that by this method they could double the output of eggs and cows' milk and triple the production of sheep's milk. (Syria is a net importer of dairy products although she is a net exporter of live animals and meat). But if even only the best dairy cows were to be fed adequately it would require about 100,000 tons of concentrated feed a year, while another 1,300,000 tons would be needed for sheep and 160,000 tons for poultry.

Syria has the raw materials to make the required feed, but the only feed factory in the country was a very small and ineffective plant which supplied the local market in Damascus, using imported basic food concentrates and simply mixing them. So the Aleppo plant can supply only a small proportion of what will be needed if the aims of the livestock programme are to be fulfilled, a result which also depends on the farmers' using the new feed as it becomes available at cost price.

The negotiations for the financing of the combined project from USAID fell through, but the Syrian Government decided to go ahead with the scheme on the basis of the US firms' studies. It allocated £S34.4 million (£3.5 million) to the project in the second five-year plan. The total cost of the project (excluding what had already been spent on initial studies and land purchase) was estimated to be £S86.2 million (£8.5 million) of which just over a third was in foreign exchange.

By 1969 when the Syrian Government approached the Kuwait Fund for a loan for the project, no contract had yet been awarded for the project though the competing tenders had been reduced to a choice between a Russian and a Yugoslav offer (the latter in cooperation with two West German firms). The construction was expected to take just under three years to complete. The Kuwait Fund sent a mission to Syria which in June 1969 reported favourably on the scheme. It calculated that the benefits to the Syrian economy as a whole would be at least £2.3 to £2.8 million a year, as well as £3 million to £3.5 million a year gain in foreign exchange.

The Fund granted the Syrian Government a loan of KD3 million (£3.5 million) repayable over ten years at 3½ per cent, sufficient to cover the foreign exchange costs of the project.

Subsequently the project was expanded to increase the storage capacity of the silos to 334,000 tons and the costs went up to KD14 million (£16.3 million). As a result, in September 1971 the Kuwait Fund increased its loan to KD7 million (£8.33 million) over 12 years at the same 3½ per cent interest. The fact that after many years of discussion the project was at last begun owed much to the sustained interest and drive of the Kuwait Fund officials involved.

By 1974, when the existing silo programme was nearing completion, the Syrian Government planned a new expansion of grain storage capacity, especially in the port of Tartous, to deal with the expected increase of cultivation from new irrigation projects on the Euphrates and the greater use of high-yield seed varieties. An approach from the Syrian Government for help in financing this further expansion was being considered by the Kuwait Fund.

The provision of adequate grain storage facilities, together with the Euphrates Dam and other irrigation schemes, and the development of the railway and the road through Aleppo to Latakia, should go a long way to ensure that the fertility of the Fertile Crescent is not wasted.

Moreover, the Syrian Government's earlier approaches to the Kuwait Fund were a significant indication of economic interest over-riding ideology, while the Fund's response was evidence of its claim to pragmatism, political autonomy and impartiality. For the Syrian Baathists had previously never concealed their disapproval of Arab monarchies or oligarchies especially among the oil states. For foreign aid they had turned chiefly to the Soviet bloc and it was only after the 'nationalist' wing of the Syrian party, led by General (later President) Hafiz el Assad, prevailed over the 'radical' left wing of the party in a bloodless coup in 1970, that Syria began to emerge from her prickly isolation and to improve her relations with the West and with other Arab states. This trend was strengthened by the 1973 war, but, as with Egypt, Jordan and Lebanon, Syria's bright hopes of a more rapid future development with the help of Arab oil money also depend on peace.

12 Iraq

Iraq, the other main component of the Fertile Crescent, was the first independent Arab country to embark on a systematic development programme financed from oil revenue. It is also Kuwait's immediate and most important neighbour. The relations between the two countries have had some sharp ups and downs, not all attributable to the Baathist and army regime which has ruled in Baghdad since 1963.

Relations between Iraq and Kuwait got off to a bad start when Kuwaiti independence was proclaimed in 1961. General Qassim, then the Iraqi military ruler, revived an old claim to sovereignty over Kuwait and seemed to be threatening a military invasion. After a crisis which brought other Arab states, as well as British troops, to Kuwait's support, the Baathist and army regime which succeeded General Qassim dropped the claim. By a happy but judicious coincidence, the Kuwait Government (not the Kuwait Fund) at the same time granted Iraq a £25 million loan. For the next twelve years, despite a more radical policy among the Iraqi Baathists since 1966 and some moments of friction, relations mostly varied from warily correct to cordial.

But neither political differences nor Iraq's own access to oil revenues appear to have been the reason why Iraq did not receive a loan from the Kuwait Fund until 1970, nine years after the Fund began lending operations. The real reason was apparently that the Iraqi authorities at first found it difficult to accept the lending rules of the Fund, and the degree of supervision involved. Once they were convinced that the rules were necessary, useful and standard international practice, the Iraqis relations with the Fund became as smooth and effective as those of other Arab countries.

The Fund then granted loans totalling KD6.8 million (£7.9 million) for two key projects in the Iraqi national development plan: expansion in electric power generation and in the cement industry.

In 1973, however, when the Fund was considering loans for

three other Iraqi projects, there was a serious border clash between Iraqi and Kuwaiti troops. The clash was connected with Iraqi territorial claims designed to improve their control of deep-water access to the new Iraqi Gulf port of Um Qasr. The dispute seemed to put a brake for the time being on further Kuwait Fund lending to Iraq (though Fund officials deny there was any connection). But the Iraqis did not press the matter further. For the Baghdad regime, though having revolutionary ideas about the future of the Gulf which theoretically could mean the end of the rulers of Kuwait, were for the next two years in practice more preoccupied with their internal affairs, especially the Kurdish rebellion, and with their quarrels with Iran and their Baathist colleagues and rivals in Syria, as well as their brief share in the October 1973 war against Israel. After the end of the Kurdish rebellion and the signing of the new agreement between Iraq and Iran in the spring of 1975, attempts were resumed to settle the Iraq-Kuwait dispute through Arab mediation.

Iraq, like Syria, is basically an agricultural country. Its development depends in the first place on being able to use its large surplus of land and water more effectively. But unlike Syria, it has abundant capital available from its own oil revenues. Its oil reserves are believed to be second in size in the Middle East after Saudi Arabia. In the early fifties, when Iraq's planned development began, foreign experts, looking at its resources in oil, water and land and its still comparatively sparse population, saw it as the coming boom country of the Arab world. Its future seemed far brighter than that of those countries like Egypt which appeared to have little oil and too great a population pressing on too little land, or Saudi Arabia which had plenty of oil but few other resources worth developing. If Iraq has not fulfilled all those early hopes it is partly because of political turbulence in a new and fragile state caught up in international, ideological and ethnic conflicts, and partly because of technical obstacles. But it is also because the early planners, mostly engineers in their training or approach, neglected or underestimated the formidable human and social problems involved in transforming the Iraqi economy. Any move for change encountered problems of social structure, land tenure and setttlement, and of the lack of educated and trained people to execute well-intentioned schemes. In 1953 perhaps only three per cent of the population were literate and only 20 per cent of those aged five to nineteen were receiving education, most of them in primary schools. By 1972 about 28 per cent of those over five years of age were literate, though the percentage was probably nearer 50 per cent in urban areas and proportionately lower in the countryside.

Iraq has a harsher climate than Syria and, for technical and geographical reasons, the control of the Tigris and the Euphrates, the great twin rivers of Iraq, and their use for irrigation are particularly difficult. And the social history of Iraqi farmers – many evolved only recently from a tribal organisation through a modern form of feudalism to the latest attempt at socialist-controlled cooperatives – has also hampered stable and efficient agricultural production.

Iraq's oil wealth began to flow in earnest in the early fifties, especially when supplies to the West from Iran were interrupted after Dr Moussadeq's nationalisation of the Anglo-Iranian Oil Company. Between 1950 and 1954 the government's oil revenues rose from £2 million to £67 million a year. From 1952 onwards seventy per cent of these revenues were automatically allocated to a Development Board. This body had been set up two years earlier to supervise the spending of a World Bank loan for the Wadi Tharthar flood control scheme and to prepare a general development plan. From 1953 the Board was subject to the supervision of a Minister of Development.

The Development Board, which included British and American irrigation experts, undertook no detailed economic planning of its own but checked and supervised programmes and projects prepared by the various ministries. It concentrated at first on flood control and irrigation schemes. Their completion has now ended serious flooding in the plains of central and southern Iraq, supplied irrigation water for nearly 800,000 acres in the north-east and provided hydro-electric power through the station at Samarra.

The first six-year plan 1951-6, called for expenditure of £155 million of which £53 million was to be spent on irrigation, flood control and drainage; £32 million on industry and mining and £23 million on roads and bridges. In the first four years only £30 million was actually spent. Then in 1955 a new revised five-year plan was introduced. It was adjusted both to the expectation of expanding oil revenues and to satisfy criticism of its priorities. The Development Board was accused of concentrating too much on big prestige construction projects and neglecting expenditure on housing, schools, health services and effective land settlement. The critics argued that a change of emphasis was needed to prevent the gap between rich and poor from widening instead of narrowing. Otherwise the country risked a social-political explosion.

The new programme envisaged spending £303 million over five years, later increased in 1956 to £500 million for the period ending 1960.

In 1958, before many of the social benefits of the new programme had had time to take effect, the monarchical regime in Iraq was overthrown by the military revolution headed by General Qassim. The revolution had its roots partly in nationalist resentment against the degree of British control of Iraqi affairs and partly in social discontent. Development spending had brought inflation in the towns without doing much to relieve the harsh situation of the rural poor. Successive Iraqi governments had relied on support from big landowners, often tribal sheikhs, to maintain 'political stability'. The labourers and share-croppers on the huge estates in central and southern Iraq (some of them hundreds of thousands of acres in size) were little better than serfs, for it was unlawful for them to leave the land while they were in debt to the landlord: if they did go to the towns to look for work the landlord could destroy their family hut and drive their family out.

The pre-revolutionary governments had made some attempts at land settlement and redistribution on state lands which formed some sixty per cent of the country's cultivable land. By 1958 an area of about a million acres had been thus settled but most of it was not given to small farmers or labourers; half went to powerful sheikhs and some of the rest to retired civil servants or army officers.

In September 1958, after the revolution, an agrarian reform law was passed limiting land ownership to 600 acres for irrigated land and 1,200 acres for rain-fed land. The expropriated land above this limit was, after five years of state management, to be redistributed among smallholders. The new farmers would join state cooperatives which would supply and organise equipment, irrigation, drainage, production and marketing.

The scale of land reform in Iraq was more massive than in Egypt or Syria; in particular it involved the state in supervision and management on a scale which severely taxed and eventually outstripped its technical and administrative resources, a burden which was increased by ideological conflicts between Communists and non-Communists within the revolutionary regime. By the end of 1972 some four million acres had been expropriated and part of it distributed to 100,000 peasant families. Over a thousand cooperatives and 61 collective farms had been formed. But large areas of expropriated and state lands were still being farmed by tenants under government contract.

Because of the strain on government services and on the new and still weakly-staffed cooperatives, especially in maintenance, credit and marketing, there was a sharp fall in agricultural productivity. Yields began to improve again after the agrarian reform programme was brought into the five-year plan in 1965 and more government investment was made in agriculture, particularly in fertilisers.

The second five-year plan of 1965-70, drawn up after the overthrow of General Qassim and the installation of a Baathist-military regime, provided for investment of £446.7 million, of which one-third was to be spent on industry. In July 1964, the new regime had nationalised all banks and insurance companies and 32 of the biggest industrial and commercial firms. The nationalised industries included cement, steel, asbestos, textiles, cigarettes, paper, flour-milling and trading companies. But much of Iraqi industry was still on the small workshop scale and this was left in private hands. The Baathist regime thus moved further to the left at home and established closer ties with the Soviet Union and other Communist countries in trade, economic aid and military supplies (by 1970 Soviet military and economic aid was estimated to have totalled 700 million dollars).

In 1972 Iraq signed a treaty of friendship and cooperation with the Soviet Union. But it also at first suppressed and then limited the activities of Iraq's own Communist Party (which in 1972 was allowed to re-emerge as part of the National Front and given a small share in the government) and maintained its own independent pan-Arab revolutionary line. In foreign trade it began to increase its imports of capital goods from the

West after the expansion of oil revenues in 1973-4. In 1974 the United States overtook the Soviet Union as the chief supplier of Iraqi imports. Moreover, oil continued to provide over 90 per cent of Iraq's exports, with Italy, France and Holland as the chief customers. In 1972, the Iraq government nationalised one of the three main oil concessions operated by the Western consortium of the Iraq Petroleum Company after a dispute over the company's decision to cut back production. The Government had already taken over the previously unused IPC concession area of North Rumelia and made an agreement to operate it jointly with the Russians. The dispute with the IPC was settled in February 1973 leaving the Government in control of the IPC and of its associated company, the Mosul Petroleum Company, but with the other IPC associate, the Basra Petroleum Company still independent. During the Middle East war in October 1973 the Iraq Government nationalised 43 per cent of the BPC comprising the American, Dutch and Gulbenkian interests. This holding was later increased to a controlling share of 60 per cent and the remaining 40 per cent was taken over in February 1976, giving the government effective control over all oil operations in the country..

The big oil price increases originating in 1973 spectacularly transformed the scale of Iraq's oil revenues and her development planning.

In 1970 Iraq's oil revenues totalled some £200 million. By 1975 they had risen to over £3,000 million. The benefits, it is true, had to be spread over a population which had doubled in twenty years from five million in 1955 to an estimated 10.4 million in 1975 and continued to expand at the rate of 3.3 per cent a year. In 1971 per capita national income was still only about £180 a year.

The greater part of oil revenue has gone to development. The third five-year plan which ended in 1974 called for a total investment of £1,100 million. The main emphasis, as in the preceding plans, was on agriculture and irrigation (which was allocated £390 million). The new plan for 1974-9 originally envisaged expenditure of £3,400 million and the sum of £584 million was allocated for the first year ending March 1975. The investment target was then raised to £12,750 million of which £4,550 million was for agriculture and a similar amount for industry, £1,500 million for education, and another £1,500 for transport and communications. But in June 1975 it was announced that Iraq would spend at least £15,000 million on development in the next five years, with the main priority going to agriculture and oil production. Plans for attaining national self-sufficiency in food production (in 1974 Iraq imported £270 million's worth of food) included the expansion of cultivated land area by a quarter and the development of a dozen big dam and irrigation projects. The latter included a £300 million dam at Kirkuk, another £250 to £300 million dam near Mosul on the Tigris and two big irrigation and livestock breeding complexes to be created near Baghdad at a cost of £375 million.

But in the budget for April to December 1975 more than a third of the development allocation of £1,650 million was ear-marked for industry. Industrial development in the earlier five-year plans had included state factories for bitumen, textiles and sugar refining (the latter two at Mosul), an ammonium sulphate fertiliser plant at Basra and factories for paperboard, rayon, shoes and cigarettes. The Russians helped to build eleven new factories, among them a steel mill and plant for electrical equipment at Baghdad, and factories for phar-maceuticals and agricultural machinery. Three new electric power projects totalling 500,000 kilowatts were completed at Kirkuk, Baghdad and Basra, and a hydro-electric power sta-tion was built at the Samarra barrage on the Tigris. Other hydro-electric stations are planned at the Dokan and Derbendi dams. Electric power consumption in Iraq increased from 1965-70 at the rate of 12.5 per cent a year and the rise continued during the seventies. In 1975 the government allocated £36 million for the first stage of a £47 million programme to bring electricity to 9,000 villages.

It was to help finance the Samarra power project that the Iraqi Government approached the Kuwait Fund for a loan in 1970. The project was for three generating turbines with a total installed capacity of 84 megawatts, equal to 15 per cent of Iraq's then power capacity. The cost was estimated at KD17.35 million (£20.24 million) of which just under a third was in foreign exchange. The Fund granted a loan of KD3 million (£3.5 million) for 15 years at four per cent. The Fund also had under consideration in 1973 a loan of KD2.75 million (£4.12 million) for two other power plants in Iraq. The first was an 80 megawatt station at Hilla in central Iraq and the other of the same capacity at Shuaiba in the south.

Cement works are often among the first industrial projects attempted by developing countries, partly to provide for their own growing needs of construction materials for their development plans. Their proliferation is also often quoted as an example of how better regional planning among the Arab states would avoid wasteful overlapping in investment.

In Iraq the cement industry has been fairly long established but it is perhaps surprising to find not only that it supplies Iraqi domestic needs but also that cement is the country's third biggest export after oil and dates (half of its cement exports go to Kuwait).

The industry was launched with the privately owned Iraq Cement Company in 1936 but owing to the Second World War the building of the company's planned 100,000-tons-a-year plant in Baghdad was not completed until 1949. Within six years this plant had quadrupled in size and there was a rush by other investors to emulate a profitable business. Five new plants were established, two of them by the government, bringing the country's cement-making capacity up to 1,200,000 tons a year by 1958. But capacity had temporarily raced ahead of demand, which in 1956 was for about 600,000 tons. The sharp competition, especially in the sluggish market conditions after the 1958 revolution, led some of the cement firms to seek outlets in foreign markets. Lack of experience in exporting led to losses and the closing down of some plants. Then in 1959 and 1960 the government stepped in to fix local prices, promote and subsidise exports and share out the markets in proportion to each plant's productive capacity. These measures, together with the revival of local demand and the increasing imports of the Gulf countries, restored the cement plants to full and profitable working. Soon the export subsidies were no longer needed and were brought to an end.

In 1964-5 after the Baath regime took over in Iraq, the cement industry was nationalised. It was reorganised from six companies into three units with a combined capacity of 1,200,000 tons a year. By 1971 installed capacity had increased to 1,400,000 tons and under the five-year plan for 1970-5 there were four projects aimed at almost doubling cement production capacity by adding another 1,300,000 tons a year.

Iraq has ample supplies of the raw materials used in making Portland cement: limestone, clay, gypsum and iron pyrites. Her reserves of limestone are enormous.

The plan was intended to increase exports to meet unsatisfied foreign demands while also satisfying increasing demand at home.

It was for one of these four projects intended particularly to expand output for export that the Iraq Government in 1970 asked for a loan from the Kuwait Fund. The project was in two parts: to increase production of the existing cement plant at Samawah about 170 miles south of Baghdad by 500,000 tons of clinker a year; and to build a new 350,000 ton cement grinding mill with loading facilities at the new port of Un Qasr in south Iraq, 50 miles south of Basra. Clinker from Samawah would be transported to Um Qasr to be ground there in the new plant and mixed with gypsum to make ordinary Portland cement. The port facilities would be able to load 600,000 tons of clinker and cement a year.

The project was to cost £8,860,000, of which seventy per cent was in foreign exchange.

The Iraq Cement Public Company, which runs the Samawah plant and is in charge of the project, is the largest single enterprise in the Iraqi economy after the National Oil Company. It was earning pre-tax profits of £2.2 million a year and when the Kuwait Fund was approached the company had already spent nearly £3 million, mostly in foreign exchange, on its expansion plans. Although the company's management and staff were experienced and efficient, much obviously depended on estimates of the future market for its increased output.

The marketing prospects at home and abroad were therefore analysed in detail by the Kuwait Fund mission which went to investigate the project in 1970 and 1971.

World production of cement, the analysis showed, had been growing at the rate of over 20 million tons a year; it was 540 million tons in 1969 compared with 36 million in 1920. In Iraq in 1969-70 cement consumption was 1,080,000 tons and this was expected to almost double by 1990. Between 1965-71 Iraq exported between 300,000 and 500,000 tons of cement a year, eighty five per cent of it to Kuwait, Saudi Arabia and the Gulf emirates. But there was an unsatisfied demand from these states of between 1,100,000 and 1,370,000 tons a year. This demand was expected to increase, despite the plans by other Arab countries, including some in the Gulf, to create or expand their own cement production (In 1968 Egypt produced over 3 million tons of cement a year and Syria and the Lebanon each over 900,000 tons).

The local production of the Gulf states was expected to increase from its 1970 level of 500,000 a year to 1.4 million in 1980 and 2.28 million tons in 1990. But by then the cement consumption of these states would have risen from 2.1 million to 4.7 million tons a year of which Kuwait alone would be consuming more than half. So there seemed plenty of room for expanding Iraqi exports.

But what of competition with Iraq from other suppliers in the world market? The world cement market as a whole is expanding with growing consumption by the developing countries. World exports were 22,450,000 tons in 1969 and growing at the rate of 8½ per cent a year.

Iraq's closest competitors in price in the Gulf markets are Egypt and Pakistan, but Iraq has an advantage through nearness in cheaper shipping costs and the ability to use smaller ships. Iraqi cement arrives fresh after a shorter haul and can be ordered in small and regular shipments instead of large cargoes. This saves the customers overheads from storage and means quick delivery in a matter of days. Since April 1971 Iraqi cement has also enjoyed the advantage of having to pay no customs dues in Kuwait, its biggest export market.

It was estimated that the Samawah and Um Qasr project would increase export earnings of foreign exchange by £2,450,000 or eight per cent of Iraq's export earnings other than those from oil. The project would provide only about 100 more jobs but it would add an average of £1.17 million a year to income from the public sector of the Iraqi economy.

On the basis of what seemed to be a sound economic proposition, the Kuwait Fund in 1971 granted the Iraqi government a loan of KD3.8 million (£4.4 million) for 13 years at four per cent. The loan covered half the total cost of the project and seventy per cent of the foreign exchange costs.

Another loan of some KD4.7 million (£7 million) by the Fund was being considered in 1973 for a second cement project. This would have set up a cement factory near Kufa with an initial capacity of 200,000 tons designed to be increased even-

tually to 600,000 tons a year. But loans for this and the Hilla
and Shuaiba power station projects seem to have been victims
of the political strains caused by Iraq's border dispute with
Kuwait.

13 Bahrain

Kuwait is now the wealthiest and most populated of the Arab Gulf states and was the first to become fully independent. But the political and commercial centre of the Gulf for long lay in the islands of Bahrain. It was not until 1971, ten years after Kuwait, that Bahrain became independent. In doing so, she rejected both Iran's claim to sovereignty over her territory and membership of the embryonic Gulf federation, the Union of Arab Emirates. Her treaty with Britain was replaced by a treaty of friendship and cooperation. But Bahrain's modern economic and social development had begun a generation before that of Kuwait or the other Gulf states. She was the first beneficiary of the Gulf oil boom. It was the discovery of oil in Bahrain in 1932 by Standard Oil of California, now operating locally as the Bahrain Petroleum Company (BAPCO), that led eventually to the oil exploration along the Arabian shores of the Gulf and the discovery of the enormous oil fields of Saudi Arabia, Kuwait and more recently of Abu Dhabi and Oman.

In November 1974 the Bahrain Government negotiated a 60 per cent participation in BAPCO, and in April 1975 announced its intention of acquiring full ownership of the company, following the example of Kuwait.

Bahrain's oil production and revenues have never been on the spectacular scale of those of the other Arabian oil producers. But they have been enough to improve the lot of her 200,000 people and ease their way into the modern world without overwhelming Bahraini society with a flood of easy money. And in common with the revenues of the other Gulf oil states they were suddenly quadrupled after the 1973-4 price increases. Oil revenue comes both from local production and from the operations of the BAPCO refinery which also uses oil from the mainland of Saudi Arabia. Since 1958 Bahrain has also had an agreement with Saudi Arabia on sharing the revenues of off-shore oil – the Bahrain islands lie just off the Saudi coast – and after 1966 the off-shore fields of Abu Salafa were operated by ARAMCO, the American company which had the concession for Saudi Arabian oil.

In 1971 Bahrain's oil revenues were £8 million. Expenditure under the state budget for the same year – Bahrain was the first administration in the Gulf to publish its budget and annual report some forty years ago – totalled £21 million, of which £8.1 million was on capital works and development projects.

In 1974 oil revenues rose to over BD (Bahrain dinars) 50 million (about £75 million). The 1975-6 budget anticipated revenues and expenditure at BD134 million (£201 million), a fifty per cent increase on the previous year. BD61.3 million (£98 million) was allocated to development projects of which BD23.5 million (£35 million) was for new projects and the remainder for projects already started.

In addition to its own increased oil revenues, Bahrain has benefited from substantial aid from the richer Gulf states, principally Kuwait, and more recently from Saudi Arabia and Abu Dhabi. It has had KD9.35 million in loans from the Kuwait Fund; and a loan of £11.8 million from the Abu Dhabi Fund. Saudi Arabia is sharing in the financing of a number of joint ventures with Bahrain which may include a project being studied for a 25-kilometre causeway linking the islands of Bahrain with the mainland of Saudi Arabia, to be completed by 1981.

Another big project in Bahrain's development programme is the building of a dry dock for big oil tankers using the Gulf. The dock, expected to cost some £90 million, would be able to take tankers of up to 370,000 tons and was expected to be ready in 1977. It is being financed jointly by the seven countries of OAPEC with most of the money coming from Saudi Arabia and Kuwait.

Bahrainis pride themselves on being the most sophisticated and educated Arabs of the Gulf. They rather look down their noses at the Kuwaitis as *nouveaux-riches* upstarts and see themselves as the mentors of the even later-developing Arabs of the Trucial Coast federation, the United Arab Emirates. The first post-secondary education in the Gulf was created in Bahrain in the sixties in the island's teacher training colleges for men and women. Subsequently the Gulf Technical College was established at Isa Town, the handsome model township with 7,500 houses for various income levels, which has been built with all modern amenities on desert land during recent years.

While social progress has been steady, political evolution has been slow. The Khalifa family which has ruled the island since 1782 still keeps a firm grip on power. But Bahrain is a compact community with a modest, homely and hard-working atmosphere (except for its very expensive new hotels). The warnings of the occasional out-bursts of political protest and minor violence have been at least partly heeded and an attempt has been made to develop local government and to bring more of the educated younger men into running public affairs. The average age of the cabinet in 1971 was less than forty and although five of the eleven ministers, including the prime minister, were Khalifas, it also included outsiders with technical qualifications from the educated middle class. The first National Assembly was formed in 1973. But, as in Kuwait, the prime minister remained a leading member of the ruling family. The Assembly was short-lived: it was suspended by the Ruler in August 1975 after a prolonged and stormy conflict with the government over security legislation and a proposed new labour law that would have legalised trades unions and strikes.

Before the oil boom began, Bahrain was already the headquarters of the British political and military presence in the Gulf – a presence which officially ended in 1971. Its great pearling industry had begun to decline but it was an active trading centre as it had been since the earliest times. From the third millenium BC it was an important half-way house on the trade routes from the Indus Valley to Mesopotamia, and in modern times it has been a centre for trans-shipment and re-export for goods consigned to other parts of the Gulf, especially Saudi Arabia and Qatar. The new port of Mina Sulman, built on the south of Bahrain island in the late 1950s, has berths for six ships of up to thirty feet draught, while the oil port of Sitra can handle 100 vessels a month. Since 1963 there have been ship-repairing and engineering facilities and yards for building ships up to 1,000 tons. Some small-scale industry, mostly for consumer goods and building, also grew up during the fifties and sixties, and there has always been some agriculture.

So Bahrain has never been so heavily dependent on oil revenues as the other Gulf states, but she nevertheless has had to think about ways of sustaining her economy when the oil runs out in an estimated 20 to 30 years' time.

The first step towards a more comprehensive planned development came with the setting up in 1967 of the Bahrain Development Bureau within the Finance Department of the Government. The creation of the Development Bureau, with some foreign experts on its staff, was followed by the formation of a Bureau of Statistics. It was later expanded into a Ministry of Development and Engineering.

One of the main objectives of the Development Bureau was to attract foreign investment. The attractions it had to offer were cheap power from the big but still largely unused reserves of natural gas associated with the oil fields, Bahrain's maritime position and facilities, cheap land, comparatively cheap labour, a fairly literate population, and tax concessions.

The Bureau's first big success was in persuading a consortium of foreign companies, with mostly British capital and with the participation of the Bahrain government, to build a £62 million aluminium smelting plant and ancillary services on Bahrain. Both Kuwait private investment and the Kuwait Fund have contributed to this project. The Kuwait Fund's loan of KD1 million (£1,160,000) for 12½ years at 4 per cent represented only a small fraction of the cost of the smelter. But this was one of those cases where the Fund's main contribution was not so much in providing money (its financial participation was only a token sum), as in helping to organise and ensure the financial backing of others. The Fund's specialists were able to give valuable advice and support to the Government of Bahrain in dealing with the other parties involved.

The main incentive for the building of an aluminium smelter on Bahrain, rather than elsewhere, was the availability of cheap and abundant power from the island's natural gas, together with Bahrain's convenience as a place for a port. Making aluminium requires large amounts of electricity. The appeal of the project was to international companies which have an expanding demand for aluminium and which saw advantage in making the metal themselves, rather than buying it from other producers.

There had been for many years a steadily expanding world market for aluminium with consumption increasing at the rate of eight to ten per cent a year. Out of the world's production of 7,500,000 tons in 1969, two-thirds was produced by six big international companies – three American, one Canadian, one

French and one Swiss – which also controlled 85 per cent of aluminium semi-manufacturing industry in the non-Communist world. Other manufacturers, with requirements of a million or so tons of aluminium a year, were therefore interested in a source of aluminium supply independent of these six big integrated producers. The output of the Bahrain smelter, which has a capacity of 120,000 tons a year, could in any case provide only a fraction of the increasing world demand.

After some complex financial negotiations, in which the Kuwait Fund played a catalystic role, agreement was reached on the formation of a company to undertake the project. This was Aluminium Bahrain (ALBA), a limited but private chartered company controlled by a syndicate composed of six foreign companies, British, Australian, French and Swedish, and the Bahrain Government which holds one-fifth of the shares. About half the financing came from Britain in the form of a loan of £28 million from the British Government's Export Credit Guarantee Department.

The financing was carried out through the Bahrain Government which contracted the loans and re-lent the money to ALBA. The company was given a fifty-year concession by the Bahrain Government for smelting and other operations, as well as a twenty-year exemption from tax and port dues in Bahrain and the free import of raw materials for the same period.

Each member of the syndicate, including the Bahrain Government, buys a certain quota of the smelter's output in proportion to its shareholding in the company. The Bahrain Government can either sell its quota or use part of it eventually in new local industries it has planned to establish, such as the manufacture of aluminium paint and door and window frames. It will also get royalties on the smelter's production after it has been operating for eleven years.

The main contract for the building of the smelter – worth £42,750,000 – went in 1969 to a British firm. Design and construction were coordinated by a Swiss engineering firm, and other European specialists, chiefly Italian and Swedish, advised on special processes.

The smelter is located on the east coast of Bahrain, about 12 miles south of Manama town. It has its own electric power station to provide up to 180 megawatts from 14 gas turbines (more than twice the capacity of the Bahrain Government's power station) and gets water for cooling purposes from its own wells with a daily capacity of a quarter of a million gallons.

Six miles from the plant site and three miles out at sea an artificial island has been created in shallow water with a jetty stretching out 700 feet into deep water. The island, connected with the plant by an overhead ropeway, can store 6,000 tons of the finished aluminium and 32,000 tons of alumina, the main raw material for making the metal. The alumina arrives from Australia at the rate of 172,000 tons a year in tankers which unload at the jetty.

Alumina, for which ALBA has a long-term contract with the Australian producers, is the main ingredient in making aluminium, apart from smaller quantities of cryolite, fluoride, petroleum coke and pitch. The essence of the process is that calcined alumina (aluminium oxide) is chemically reduced by electrolysis to produce aluminium metal. This is done at a temperature of about 900 degrees centigrade, in a series of over three hundred electric furnaces or 'pots', each holding 25 tons. The anodes used in the electrolysis are made from petroleum coke and pitch in a special plant attached to the smelter.

For Bahrain, the main direct benefits of the smelter will come from the profits from the sale of the Government's share of the ALBA output, estimated to reach £625,000 in 1977 and £2 million in 1985, and from royalties rising to £412,000 by 1982-5. Indirectly, Bahrain benefits from more jobs and from the sale of natural gas and other local materials and services. Fifteen hundred to 2,500 workers were engaged on building the plant and the ALBA operating staff consists of 878 Bahrainis and 55 foreign employees, adding over £600,000 a year to the national wage bill. The Bahrain Government gets half the profits from the sale of natural gas which will eventually bring it in another £437,000 a year.

Altogether the project is expected to increase government revenues by an annual average of about £1.5 million during the years 1977-81 and by £2.8 million from 1981-5. During the same periods it will also bring a net foreign exchange gain rising from £1.7 million to £3.1 million a year. Admittedly not very large sums, but a useful addition to Bahrain's modest resources.

The Kuwait Fund has also lent the Bahrain Government another KD8.35 million (£9.23 million) for three other development projects. One was for a grain silo and flour mill in the port of Bahrain, the second for two new bridges and the widening of the causeway linking the two main islands of the group, and the third and biggest for a power and water distillation plant.

Bahrain imports almost all its wheat needs but the poor quality of locally milled flour had led to people preferring to eat more expensive rice. With the aim of improving the flour the government proposed the establishment of a modern mill that would have the monopoly of the flour trade. All the islands' wheat needs from abroad would be imported in the form of grain instead of flour and milled locally. Grain imports would be handled by a new silo of 12,000 tons capacity with provision to expand to 20,000 tons. The project was designed by an Iraqi firm of consulting engineers and the designs were checked and approved, at the Kuwait Fund's request, by a Swedish firm of consultants. A Lebanese firm won the contract for building the mill and silo and a British company supplied the mechanical and electrical equipment.

The total cost of the project, completed in 1972, was about £1.5 million. Part of the financing came from private share capital and a commercial bank loan, while the Kuwait Fund gave a loan of KD500,000 (£583,000) for 12½ years at four per cent to meet half of the foreign exchange cost.

The causeway and bridges which join Bahrain's main town of Manama with the neighbouring island of Muharraq form one of the islands' chief communication links. With increasing traffic – the number of cars in Bahrain doubled betweeen 1961 and 1968 – the link became a bottleneck. Both the causeway and the old bridge were too narrow and the bridge was wearing out and becoming dangerous.

So it was planned to widen the causeway and to replace the old bridge with two new steel girder bridges at a cost of some £1.2 million. A British firm was awarded the contract for building the bridges, with the steel girders coming from Japan. The bridges and work on the causeway have now been completed.

The Kuwait Fund granted a loan for the project of KD500,000 (£583,000) which covered nearly half the total cost and 85 per cent of the foreign exchange cost.

In 1972 the Fund granted a loan of KD7.35 million (£8.12 million) to help finance an expansion of Bahrain's electric power and water facilities. Construction of a dual-purpose project to this end was begun in 1973. It will almost double the islands' generating capacity and also provide for the distillation and distribution of nearly five million gallons of water a day.

It may be long before Bahrain can hope to develop her industry and commerce to the same degree of intensity as bigger off-shore island states, such as Hong Kong and Singapore. But the smelter project shows what can be done, by a combination of imagination, initiative, shrewd calculation and some outside encouragement, to attract substantial foreign investment to what is not at first sight an obvious place for a major industrial venture. Already ambition has been stirred and plans have been discussed for a second aluminium smelter on the island.

Perhaps the biggest benefit from the smelter for Bahrain itself may prove to be precisely in stimulating international interest in investment there, in strengthening business confidence and in gradually contributing to the creation of a local industrial base.

14 Yemen

The Yemen, in the south-western corner of the Arabian Peninsula, is one of those countries, like Germany, Vietnam and
Korea, which were divided by political circumstances and
ideology into two separate sovereign states, while retaining an
aspiration for national unity. The two Yemens include some of
the most economically and socially backward areas of the Arab
world and some of its most lively and sharply intelligent people.
Both states have been plunged in recent years into a struggle for
modernisation and independence, a struggle which in each case
had elements of civil war and outside intervention. But in
neither state is the fact of political separation yet as serious as in
other divided countries: historical Yemen has rarely been
united politically except in moments of crisis against foreign
invaders; but neither has it ever been very rigidly divided in
practice: the borders have been very open, wild and ill-defined.
The Yemen's natural state has been a kind of anarchic confed-
eracy. But this anarchy has existed within a loose but recognised framework of tribal, political, religious and cultural relations.

In the north there is now the Yemen Arab Republic, the
historic heartland of the Yemen, with a population of some six
million (in 1973) in an area of about 75,000 square miles. In the
south is the People's Democratic Republic of the Yemen with a
bigger area of 112,000 square miles but a population of only
about a million and a half, a quarter of whom are concentrated
in the port and capital city of Aden. Following serious border
fighting between the two states in October 1972 they signed an
agreement on a cease-fire and a treaty of political unity. Three
years later, little if any progress had been made towards unity,
and it seemed doubtful how far their ideological differences
would permit their unification to become a reality.

The division between north and south had its roots in the
occupation of the port of Aden by the British 138 years ago and
the subsequent extension of British control inland to the sulta-
nates and sheikhdoms of what became the Eastern and West-

ern Aden Protectorates. While this was happening, the rest of
the Yemen to the north was under Turkish control until 1918
and then under the independent rule of the Zeidi Imamate.
Until its over-throw in the 1962 army-led revolution, the theo-
cracy of the Imans kept the northern Yemen closed to outside
influences, while maintaining a claim to suzerainty over the
British colony of Aden and the protectorates in the south.

After seven years of civil war, with Egyptian and Saudi
Arabian intervention on the opposing Republican and Royalist
sides, a compromise peace was achieved and North Yemen has
been struggling since then to recover and reconstruct. Until
June 1974 it had a moderately conservative republican regime,
backed by some former Royalists, which pursued a free enterprise economic policy and a foreign policy of non-alignment. It
sought aid and support from both East and West, though
leaning politically more towards the West. It also tried to keep
a balance between outside Arab influences, but in practice it
came to be increasingly dependent on Saudi Arabia as Egypt
withdrew, and eventually itself drew closer to the Saudis.

The 1974 military coup was intended, according to its
authors, a group of officers led by Colonel Ibrahim Mohammed
Al Hamdi, to end divisions in the country and get rid of
corruption and indiscipline in government. The civilian
Republican Council under its president, Abdurrahman Bin
Yahya Al Iryani, was replaced by a seven-member military
Command Council (subsequently reduced to four members,
one of whom was the prime minister, a civilian). The constitution was suspended and the Consultative Assembly dissolved;
the Assembly was to reconvene within six months to draw up a
new electoral law. The 'divisions' referred to by the 'coup'
officers were primarily between those elements, led by Al
Iryani, who wanted a conciliatory policy towards South
Yemen, and those who supported the then more militantly
hostile Saudi attitude towards the Aden regime.

The new military regime promised to continue the same
basic economic and foreign policies. The Command Council
declared that it would 'do its utmost to modernise the development bodies in order to develop our local resources and use
them in a manner which will ensure placing them in the right
areas, keeping them from the influence of salaries and allowances and freeing them from disregard and indifference'.

The backwardness of North Yemen is of a rather unusual kind. Unlike most of Arabia it is not a desert or steppe peopled largely, at least until very recently, by pastoral nomads: it is an agricultural country, a land of high mountains, fertile plains, terraced valleys and merchant cities with an antique civilisation and architectural beauty all their own. Until very recently this civilisation was encapsulated in the Middle Ages by prolonged isolation from the outside world. There is nothing in North Yemen as modern as the city of Aden, and its estimated per capita income – not much more than an informed guess – of £55 a year (in 1973) is one of the lowest in the world. But most of the country is less primitive and severe in its way of life than the hinterland of South Yemen.

South Yemen has the only Arab regime that considers itself ideologically (but not militarily) part of the Socialist (Communist) camp, though still fundamentally Arab nationalist in outlook. Its left-wing nationalist revolutionary regime and the state itself were born from a violent struggle for national independence. The state is formed from a combination of the former Aden colony and the Eastern and Western Aden Protectorates, which already, before the British left, had been merged into the short-lived Federation of South Arabia.

South Yemen includes three different kinds of area. Aden and its surroundings are relatively developed and sophisticated with a modern administration and economic basis. Then, not far from Aden, are the more highly developed agricultural areas of Lahej and the Abyan Delta, and a few towns, much less advanced than Aden, along the coast and inland in the Hadramaut, the eastern half of the country. Finally there is the wild and mostly barren hinterland of mountain and desert.

Much of this last is scarcely administered at all and the people there, either nomads or subsistence farmers, live in the simplest and harshest conditions.

Set theatrically between the gaunt Arabian mountains and the vast glittering swell of the Indian Ocean, Aden provides a spectacular backdrop for political drama. When I arrived there in December 1971 the People's Democratic Republic of the Yemen was celebrating its fourth year of independence from British rule. Yet it was then hard to believe that not long before the city had been a place of exploding bombs, guerrilla

ambushes and British military frustration. In its five town-
ships, strung out round the port and oil refinery, its main
sources of livelihood, an air of quiet stagnation prevailed.

Aden's Khormaksar airport was then a homely place where
passengers were first politely received in a charming little
garden courtyard shaded by overhanging leaves. From there to
the Crescent Hotel near Steamer Point is a drive of some twenty
miles. The Crescent is an old-style imperial hostelry, like the
Grand in Khartoum. It has a graceful façade of Belgravian
pillars and pale cream stucco. Inside there are big and lofty
rooms with steadily whirring fans and balconies with lattice
window-shutters where crows hover and hop in and out to steal
bread from the breakfast table. Like most former foreign-
owned businesses in Aden except for the oil refinery, the hotel
had become a nationalised concern. Once crowded with visiting ships' passengers, tourists and businessmen, it was then
half-empty. In the dining-room there were still remains of past
splendour in the plush oval-backed chairs and the enormous
French-worded menu. Alas, on the menu most of the words
were only words – though the best lobster in the world was still
available for less than a pound. A long table was filled with
North Koreans, identically dressed in white shirts, blue trous-
ers, grey-blue caps and little Kim Il Sung badges, and drinking
bottled beer. There were some UN officials, a few Egyptians
and an Indian family. A cluster of sauce bottles less elegantly
recalled the imperial past.

In the streets near the port the tax-free shops had few customers for their Japanese cameras and Swiss watches. Small
children darted out to beg at every corner.

But under its lethargic surface, the town was full of political
rumours, of an abortive coup and secret executions, of a government split and a ministerial reshuffle. The Government of
Democratic Yemen is drawn from the country-bred guerrilla
leaders of the National Liberation Front who fought the British
and crushed the old sultans and their town-based nationalist
rivals. They are left-wing anti-imperialists dedicated in theory
to revolution against the present regimes throughout the oil
lands of Arabia and the Gulf. They actively supported the now
defeated revolutionary guerrilla movement in neighbouring
Dhofar against the Sultan of Oman whose regime is backed by
forces and advisers from Britain, Iran and Jordan. But their

biggest preoccupation is still with the desperate economic situation into which their new state was born. This concern led them in March 1976 to an agreement to normalise relations with Saudi Arabia which would, it was believed, bring them Saudi financial aid in return for keeping their borders quiet.

The problem of reconciling economic facts and political ideals has lain behind repeated upheavals inside the NLF since independence, the most important of which was the 'corrective move' of June 1969 which deposed the former leader, Qahtan el Shabani, and replaced him by the present three-man presidential council under the chairmanship of Salem Rubai Ali. The same conflict was said to have been involved in a rumoured struggle for power within the regime between 'pro-Chinese' and 'pro-Russian' elements. The latter were believed to favour a cautious policy of economic consolidation and stabilisation, and the former a more revolutionary drive for the taking over of all businesses by workers and peasants.

The then prime minister, Ali Nasser Mohammed, also one of the top three (he was still there in 1975), is a burly handsome man in his thirties, intense, serious and courteous. He is a former teacher of Arabic. He works in what was once the British ambassador's office inside a barbed wire compound which now shelters the NLF command headquarters and the presidency.

He told me that while Democratic Yemen considered itself a member of the socialist camp it did not see this as contradicting the aim of Arab unity. Nor would it accept foreign bases, even from Communist countries, on its soil. Despite Democratic Yemen's present isolation from other Arab states, he claimed that 'belonging to the socialist camp will not prevent us from unity with other progressive states. We are trying to get this unity. We are struggling for unity between the two Yemens, then for Arab unity, which we are trying to form on the basis of an Arab progressive front against Zionism, imperialism and reaction.'

The premier said that the 'corrective move' of June 1969 had been concerned not with personalities but with changing social policies. It was a question of building new relations in the community in all fields, in agriculture and agrarian reform, in nationalising foreign banks and other firms, establishing a new constitution, overhauling government departments and building a new national army on an ideological basis.

Before 1967 the economy of Democratic Yemen or South Arabia, as it was then called, was largely based on services provided in the Aden port, the oil refinery and the British military base. Almost 70 per cent of GNP came from trade, transport and other services and only 16 per cent from agriculture.

With the coming of independence, this economic structure was dealt a triple blow. The British withdrawal meant a loss of revenue from the military base and from the spending of the troops and their families, estimated at £10 million a year, as well as a loss of local employment with the military services and civil administration. British economic and military aid to the South Arabian Federation, which was running at the rate of £25 million a year, was stopped, except for what was already in the pipeline, because no agreement could be reached with the independence regime on the terms for the aid's continuation. The third and perhaps heaviest blow of all was the closure of the Suez Canal as a result of the 1967 Arab-Israeli war. The amount of shipping using Aden and its bunkering services was suddenly cut by three-quarters.

Between 1966 and 1969 per capita income actually fell from £62 to £42, while unemployment in Aden rose to about 25,000.

Of total exports in 1968 of SYD55 million (South Yemen dinar then equalled £1) indigenous exports were only SYD 2.3 million or 4.2 per cent of the whole. Of these over half was cotton. Two-thirds of total exports were refined oil products from the British Petroleum refinery, which uses imported crude. The refinery, which in late 1971 was running at about half capacity, has so far been exempted from nationalisation. The rest of the exports were re-exports, such as textiles and foodstuffs. Imports in 1968 totalled SYD84 million, of which SYD37 million stayed in South Yemen.

The trade deficit totalled SYD20 million in 1971 and SYD16 million in 1972. Since 1968 there has been an annual payments deficit averaging SYD2 million, most of the trade deficit being covered by remittances and public transfers. There are no foreign exchange reserves except for the backing for the currency – which means about £21 million in usable foreign exchange. In 1975 the International Monetary Fund allowed South Yemen to purchase 9 million dollars to help reduce the payments deficit, parallel with measures to control inflation through import cuts, increased development expenditure and the freezing of the budget and salaries.

The internal budget deficit in 1971 was £6 million (expenditure of £21 million – of which £9 million went for the armed forces – and revenue of £15 million). The deficit was kept down to this figure and eventually reduced in 1973 by drastic pruning of government expenditure and by seeking other sources of foreign aid to replace British aid. But foreign aid is expensive and has been mostly for projects, not in cash for budgetary support. Russia lent £8 million in 1969 and East Germany gave a loan for the purchase of some equipment. The Chinese provided a loan mostly for road building. The United Nations has given technical assistance in various fields, including 5.4 million dollars from IDA for education projects. Britain has offered scholarships for training.

South Yemen has received no compensation from the Arab oil states for what might be considered her war losses – the effect on Aden port of the closure of the Suez Canal – but she has received payments from the OAPEC fund created to subsidise oil imports of the poorer non-oil producing Arab states. Algeria, Iraq and Libya have given some assistance, and ideology has not prevented the regime's acceptance of help from Kuwait. This Arab aid has shown some other increase since 1973. In 1974 the Kuwait Fund granted a loan of KD4.5 million (£6.75 million) for a big road project and another of KD4.2 million (£6.3 million) for an agricultural scheme, bringing the total of Kuwait Fund loans and grants to South Yemen by 1975 to KD9.08 million (£13.6 million). In its 1975-6 budget Kuwait allocated KD625,000 (nearly £1 million) for schools and health clinics in South Yemen through its General Authority for the Gulf and South Arabia. In 1974 the Arab Fund made a KD3.2 million (£4.8 million) loan for the development of the fishing industry. In the same year Iraq granted an interest-free loan of 5 million dollars (£2.27 million); Libya made a cash grant of LD1.5 million, and paid out a loan of LD1.5 million which had been promised two years earlier.

Apart from dealing with the most urgent problems of stagnation and unemployment, the Government has also had to think of the changes in the long-term structure of the economy that are implied by decreased reliance on Aden's role as a supplier of services. The reopening of the Suez Canal has begun to restore at least part of Aden's lost trade, but even so other resources in the country will need to be developed.

Between 1971-3 a modest three-year development programme was in progress which envisaged expenditure of some £40 million, of which £9.5 million was allocated for industry and £10.5 million to agriculture. The regime claimed that the plan was highly successful in agriculture and had helped to deal with unemployment, education and communications.

The new five-year development plan for 1974-9 envisages expenditure of £115 million. It gives special priority to infrastructure projects and to the development of livestock and fisheries.

The man chiefly responsible for controlling the country's economy when the 1971-4 plan was launched was the then deputy prime minister and Minister of Planning, Mahmoud Abdullah Ushaish. He was a small wiry man with a grey moustache, quiet and thoughtful. He was originally from North Yemen but came to Aden as a child. He studied commerce and accountancy in Khartoum and worked in Aden for British Petroleum. His offices were symbolically in one of the now-nationalised former bastions of private business in Aden, the old Besse Building in the Crater commercial district. A beautiful spacious construction of wood and stone, with broad balconies, high rooms, fanlights of plaster and coloured glass, and cool, dark wood everywhere, it is the epitome of an old-fashioned eastern merchant house. Mr Ushaish said that Democratic Yemen had the difficulties of any under-developed country – lack of capital, of cadres and skilled workers. They were trying to remedy the serious lack of technicians and administrators for the time being by employing foreign specialists and United Nations experts. The economy was, he said, in that stage of the 'National Democratic Revolution' which would lead eventually to 'scientific socialism'. But the public sector did not cover the whole economy, either in agriculture or in industry and commerce. Confiscated land had been reallocated to farmers and there had been no large extension of state farms or of land confiscation. The peasants joined cooperatives and received government aid, but most of the land was still in peasant ownership.

The promotion of investment law made it clear that while

certain 'strategic' industries which related directly to development should be in government hands, there remained a considerable role for 'national capital' in the private sector. Democratic Yemen welcomed foreign investment in non-strategic areas of the economy. A free zone in Aden port had been created to encourage foreign capital to invest in industries there, primarily for re-export.

Aden port itself has remained financially and operationally autonomous under the Port Trust. Yemenis have replaced British and Indians in the top tiers of the port management, under a Yemeni director. British and other foreign specialists continued to be employed in the pilot and engineering services while Yemenis were being trained. The operations remained efficient. Although the port revenue was halved, expenditure was also cut to provide a profit.

To deal with the renewed flow of shipping expected now that the Suez Canal is open, a two-stage scheme for the improvement of Aden port was drawn up. It includes dredging, expanded moorings and a new repair dock. To meet part of the estimated cost of 30.7 million dollars (£14 million) the Government has been negotiating for loans from the World Bank and the Arab Fund.

In trying to attract back more traffic Aden faces stiff competition from Djibouti, and to a lesser degree from Hodeida and Jeddah. It also has to face the fact that the flow of traffic through the Red Sea and the Suez Canal is likely to remain well below the pre-1976 level.

To help prepare studies for the modernisation of Aden port and of Al Rayan airport in the Hadramaut, and also of livestock development, the Kuwait Fund made a grant of KD300,000 (£450,000).

Meanwhile, both the government and foreign advisers have been paying more attention to the possible development of agriculture and fishing. Even if no great increase in export earnings from agriculture could be achieved, it might be possible to substitute more home-grown food, including fish, for the £10 million's worth of foodstuffs imported each year.

The obstacles of climate and terrain are, however, formidable. Most of the 112,000 square miles of the country is mountainous and rugged and with very little rain inland. Only a million to a million and a half acres are considered potentially cultivable with the help of irrigation. Less than a quarter of this area is currently cultivated, but the three-year plan aimed to double the irrigated area, largely by digging some 200 wells.

A senior official of the Ministry of Agriculture, Hussein Bin Saddiq, explained to me the several government reviews of land and agricultural problems that had been made since independence. In March 1968 there was the first agrarian reform law. Land tenure and relations had previously been unregulated. Some landlords owned five to ten thousand acres, but there were very few big landlords. Most were medium owners with 100 to 1,000 acres. This first law fixed land ownership limits at 25 acres for irrigated land and 50 acres for dry farming. The surplus was expropriated and redistributed to landless peasants in holdings of three to five acres for irrigated land and up to twenty for dry farming. But this law did not work well and a new law in November 1970 made many changes. Redistributed land was no longer given into peasant ownership. The State now keeps ownership of the land but the peasant pays rent in the form of a share of the crop. All small land users have to form production cooperatives, on the East German system. The ownership limit was cut from 25 to 20 acres or 40 acres per family (twice these amounts for non-irrigated land). Private renting of land was forbidden: owners have to work the land themselves. Development of the state-aided cooperatives has been held up by a shortage of trained people to manage them and lack of government money to finance them.

In the tribal areas of the north collective farming is the custom, but in the last 20 years the tribes neglected farming in favour of 'other things', in other words, fighting and the money paid to them for it. After independence and the confiscation of the lands belonging to the big landowners, the tribes clung to their old system. The government did not interfere, said Mr Saddiq, but was looking at ways in which the old collective system might be adapted to new farming methods.

The aim was eventually to parallel the production cooperatives by the creation of peasant unions, political bodies controlled by the NLF. Together with local government authorities, the cooperatives and unions would be responsible for social development in agricultural areas.

But outside the Aden area most of the country still has only the sketchiest government administration and little is known about either its people or its resources. The first step towards effective development is to learn more about it.

It was here that the Kuwait Fund made its first contribution to South Yemen development.

In May 1971 the Yemen Democratic Republic signed an agreement with the Fund for a loan of KD330,000 (£385,000) for fifty years at no interest to finance a country-wide agricultural and socio-economic survey and a pre-investment study of agriculture in the Abyan Delta.

The aim of the country-wide survey was to provide the basis for formulating a long-term economic and social plan for agriculture and to work out the priorities to be given in the development of various wadis.

The two studies were to be carried out over a period of two years by an Arab firm of consulting engineers.

The two main agricultural areas of South Yemen are in the Abyan and Lahej deltas, east and north of Aden. They cover some 100,000 acres or about half of the readily cultivable land.

The Wadi Abyan was chosen as the most promising area for an urgent pre-investment study for several reasons. It has usable surface water available that could be better utilised; it is not far (30 miles) from Aden with its heavy unemployment; it is linked with Aden, the main market and export outlet, by a road – rare in South Yemen – which is being improved.

The country needed to launch a productive investment project as soon as possible because of the depression and unemployment since independence, the departure of the British and the closure of the Suez Canal. Abyan was also chosen for study because the agricultural development already established there was showing signs of trouble. Yields were declining because of rising ground water levels, deficient water distribution and soil erosion. The study was intended to help save and restore the country's most productive agricultural area.

The Abyan area has an average of 250 million cubic metres of surface water available from the two wadis. At present the area growing cotton varies between 15,000 and 30,000 acres according to the size of the flood. But with better use of the flood water this figure could, it was estimated, be pushed up to 60,000 acres, and even more with the use of underground water.

Cotton cultivation was introduced into the Abyan area in 1943 by the British who built some canals and water regulators.

It quickly became the country's biggest agricultural area, producing most of its cotton. But more recently yields of cotton and
other crops began to decline. The canals had been allowed to
deteriorate and the irrigation methods used were primitive.
There was no crop rotation and the uncontrolled flood water
made it impossible to use fertiliser. But experts believed that
with a better use of water, and of fertilisers and insecticides, the
cotton yield could be doubled.

A development study, similar to that financed by the Kuwait
Fund for the Wadi Abyan, was undertaken in the Wadi
Tuban area by the UNDP (United Nations Development
Programme) and the FAO (United Nations Food and Agriculture Organisation). These two areas are regarded as the most
suitable for rapid development to alleviate South Yemen's
immediate serious economic difficulties.

The development studies it had financed led the Kuwait
Fund in 1974 to grant a loan of KD4.2 million for 40 years
without interest for the development of the Abyan delta area.
The project involves the improvement and expansion of the
irrigation network in an area of 53,000 hectares, the provision
of farm equipment, and training and consulting services. The
loan covers almost the entire cost of the project.

In 1975 the Fund granted a loan of KD4.5 million (£6.75
million) for 40 years at 1.5 per cent for part of the cost of a
KD9.35 million (£14 million) highway project – most of the rest
of the cost is being met by IDA. This project was for a 350-
kilometre road to link the Wadi Hadramaut, a relatively densely
populated agricultural area, with the port of Mukalla, and
thence to Aden. Although the South Yemen depends for its
main means of communication on its 4,700 kilometre road
network, only 330 kilometres in the Aden area have hitherto
had asphalt surfaces and only 20 kilometres elsewhere in the
country have been macadamised.

As part of the Government's drive to develop the fishing
potential of the South Yemen's Red Sea and Indian Ocean
coasts, the Kuwait Fund granted KD50,000 in 1973 for a
pre-investment study of a fish meal and fish oil plant. This was
followed by the decision of the Arab Fund in 1974 to make a
loan of KD3.2 million (£4.8 million) for fisheries development.
The project includes a 17,100-ton plant for fish meal, a 5.400-
ton plant for fish oil, and six fishing boats. In addition, there is

provision for a power station at Mukalla, a water supply network and the construction of a new road.

North Yemen is a land of startling beauty, deep poverty and enormous charm.

From Aden to Sanaa, the North Yemen capital was a flight of about forty minutes in an old DC 3 of the Yemen Air Lines. There were only four or five passengers on my flight and the rest of the seats had been taken out to fill the space with freight. A young Egyptian smoked placidly as we completed refuelling and waited to take off. A spritely old Yemeni, with no teeth and thin brown legs under a long, chequered kilt, supervised the loading operations.

We climbed over the desert north of Aden and then across a grand wall of rugged mountains. Mud villages and forts clung here and there to hillsides and peaks.

Sanaa is on a plateau, eight thousand feet up, with clean cool air, brilliant light and pale blue mountains round about. Its airport is casual and friendly. Luggage was dumped on the ground beside the plane where it could be loaded straight into a waiting taxi. A polite man in a dark suit took our passports into a small shack, the terminal building. There were no customs to be seen. (By 1976 there was a handsome new terminal and the customs were much in evidence.) The double-track road into the city from the airport was Sanaa's first metalled thoroughfare; there are still only one or two others.

It was the beginning of the Bairam feast and the town was gay and animated. Women and children were in festival costumes. Their robes of purple, silver or gold and the red and blue turbans of the men glowed in the clear sunlight against the soft brown background of the town's fabulous architecture, its walls and towers of mud and stone.

The houses of Sanaa were mostly still set within the ring of the city wall. They are often huge mansions of seven or eight stories. Some have stone on the first two floors and mud-brick above. High carved wooden doors open on to courtyards or deep, narrow unpaved alleys.

The Yemenis have the most extraordinary decorative sense. They blend stone of different colours, grey, green, pink and black and the varied browns of mud-brick and plaster with the utmost subtlety. They set off the brown facades with an edge of

whitewash here and there, or with different coloured window-
frames, and fanlights of carved alabaster and coloured glass.
But they also transform the most mundane modern things.
Metal roll-down shutters for shops and garages are painted
casually with different colours on each section in the most
harmonious combinations – including natural rust! – so that a
street front may sometimes look like an exhibition of Mark
Rothko canvases. Where modern steel gates have replaced the
heavy old wooden doors, the gates are brilliantly painted and
have naive but elegant designs in wrought-iron laid onto the
sheet metal background. The cars and trucks have individual
painted decorations and elaborate convolutions of wrought-
iron on their sides and luggage racks. The concrete or stuccoed
walls of the more modern houses are often decorated with gay
geometric patterns and bright colour washes. Even the cement
step between my hotel bedroom and bathroom had an elegant
floral pattern scratched into it.

Everywhere one looks in Sanaa there is something or someone original or beautiful. There is also often unbelievable
squalor, sometimes in unexpected places; the surroundings of
the presidential palace were littered with old bones and other
rubbish.

In a country both leisurely and pious, the Kurban Bairam
feast is apt to last up to five days. I feared that my chances of
seeing during that time any of the leading Yemenis I had
planned to visit were very small. In fact, my fears proved
groundless. This was not only because of the hospitable infor-
mality of the Yemenis who received me in their homes instead
of their offices, but also largely because of the great help given
to me by a young man from the Ministry of Foreign Affairs,
Fuad Nomaan, the American-educated son of a former prime
minister of the Yemen, Abdullah Mohammed Nomaan. I had
met his father, one of the great names among the movement for
liberal reform in the Yemen, previously in Beirut and London.

It was with Fuad Nomaan that I went to see the then prime
minister, Mohsin el Aini. (later ambassador in London and
then recalled briefly to the premiership in 1974 after the military coup). We walked from my hotel to the premier's house
through dusty streets lined with beautiful old buildings.

On the way we passed the former palace of the Imam where
Al Badr was besieged in the 1962 revolution. The top floor was

shattered by tank shells but the Imam escaped in the darkness through a side door onto the street – incredibly, the rebel troops had not surrounded the palace completely. The top floors were still in ruins but the rest of the palace was being used as a students' hostel.

Down a rough alleyway nearby, a door guarded by a soldier opened into a bare courtyard with a well in one corner and a medium-size house in traditional style. Narrow stone stairs set in the thickness of the walls led to an upper floor. Here the prime minister had two reception rooms. One was in Yemeni style. The other was European with black leather chairs and sofas and on the walls photographs of international statesmen encountered by the prime minister when he was serving as ambassador in Washington, Paris and other capitals.

Mohsin el Aini is from the Beni Jalloul area outside Sanaa. Short, plump and affable, he was wearing a well-cut lounge suit and spoke excellent English, using words with humour, subtlety and often ironic charm.

He said that North Yemen's basic problem in economic development was lack of administration: if the government were able to collect all the taxes and customs duties owing to it, it would be able to cover its financial deficit.

The country had not been ruled by an administration until 1962; it had been ruled only by 'the mysterious power' of the Imam. This power came from a combination of the Imam's personality, the isolation of the country and the simplicity of its life. The Imam had merely collected the zakkat (Islamic tax, a tithe of two and a half per cent on property) and paid a few salaries. There were no hospitals, schools or embassies. There had been no national currency. 'That is how we found the country in 1962 and started to build an administration. Unfortunately the war came. For a few years our friends the Egyptians (a hint of irony just perceptible here) were bearing all the burden of responsibility in the country, due to the military situation. When they left we had to start again.

'During the last three years there has been the beginning of administration in the Yemen. We are now trying to control the customs posts and this has been made effective in Hodeida, Mocha and the North. We have made a start in organising the zakkat. We have not the cadres of qualified people to take care of everything. We are proud of what we have achieved in spite of all the difficulties of war, intervention, poverty and lack of education.

'Now we have a central planning board, just started this month, and connected with the prime minister's office, with the help of experts from the World Bank and the Kuwait Fund. We feel that with these experts we can start planning and coordinating all the aid projects of the United Nations and others.

'Since 1968', said Mr Al Aini, 'we have been concentrating our efforts on building this state, stopping the fighting and normalising our relations with the rest of the world. We have had to bring about national unity, face a serious drought, reorganise the armed forces, finish the constitution and begin the experiment of the Consultative Council and Republican Council.

'But even in development many things have been done – schools, roads, water systems, hospitals. This has been due not to the government but to the Yemenis themselves. They have money and with peace they have seized the opportunities to build and start projects. Foreigners cannot appreciate what they see, but those who knew Yemen before know that things have changed. When you yourself arrived at Sanaa airport you probably said to yourself "What kind of an airport is this?" If you had come a few years ago you would have spent two weeks at least trying to get into the country. Now there is a flight every day to somewhere. Cables used to take two weeks. Now we have telex and telegrams and you can telephone to Peking or Paris.

'The last three years have convinced the Yemenis that by themselves they can coexist and prosper.' Unity, peace and the structure and powers of the state had not been imposed by force. 'People all over the country are armed – sometimes better armed than the government's forces, but they don't use their arms. There are still parts of the country that are not administered. But this is not a separation by force: people go to and from Sanaa and do what they please. But we have not been able to send governors and officials to these areas, mostly in the north, because it costs too much to do it, the local price is too high (the premier meant by this the demand for government subsidies from some tribal areas or groups, payment of which helps to keep the peace.) So we are playing a waiting game with them. We tell them we can live without them for twenty years, but meanwhile they won't get the schools and hospitals they want. We shall wait and see who gets tired first. But there are no offensive operations by either side. It is mostly a question of roads.'

North Yemen has suffered not only from seven years of bitter civil war but also from two subsequent major droughts. The Government's expenditure regularly exceeds its revenues by as much as a hundred percent 'The Yemen is a country where the people have money and the Government has none', was the comment of one UN expert. In 1970 the budget deficit was £12.5 million. By 1975-6 it had risen to YR210 million (£20 million) out of an estimated expenditure of YR778.5 million (£74 million). The gap has hitherto been filled by inflation and by aid from many countries, though with the help of the International Monetary Fund the inflation has been brought under control and the currency stabilised. The government also hopes for some increase in revenue from better tax collection.

The international aid is mostly project aid and not direct budgetary assistance, except in the case of Saudi Arabia which has helped to finance the government's peace-keeping subsidies to the tribes. The country's three principal roads were built by the Russians, Americans and Chinese – one each. Other sources, including the Kuwait Fund, with a loan of KD284,000 (£426,000), the Netherlands and the World Bank have helped to finance other roads. The Russians equipped the Republican Army and both Russians and Chinese have supplied hospitals, doctors, and factories. In the past Russian and Chinese aid was in the form of loans bearing interest – said to total £35 million out of a total foreign indebtedness which was estimated by some sources at £75 million in 1972. Britain and West Germany have also helped with aid during the drought and in technical assistance programmes. But, especially since 1973, the main sources of foreign aid have been the World Bank, (chiefly through IDA) and the Arab countries. Loans from IDA in 1975 included 10 million dollars (£4.5 million) for rural development in the provinces of Ibb and Taiz, and 6.25 million dollars (£2.8 million) for the water supply of Sanaa.

Among the Arab countries, apart from Egypt's past commitment and continuing technical assistance, the chief financial contributors until 1972 were Iraq with a development loan of £3.5 million, and Saudi Arabia with a loan of £4.2 million. In that year six Arab states also gave educational aid. Kuwait, which had already financed the building of schools, hospitals and other public services through its Fund for the Gulf and South Arabia, provided £300,000 for higher education and a hundred teachers for schools. Abu Dhabi paid for 150 teachers and allocated £200,000 to set up an institute of Yemen studies. Qatar offered £100,000 for a teachers' training institute in Sanaa. Saudi Arabia was to pay for 250 teachers and 80 university and technical scholarships. Syria and Egypt each sent teachers to work in the Yemen. This form of aid has continued and in 1975 Kuwait allocated another KD1.5 million (£2.25 million) to North Yemen through the General Authority.

In 1974 the Arab states provided North Yemen with 34 million dollars (£15 million) to compensate for the inflation of world prices of imports including oil prices, and Saudi Arabia gave budgetary support amounting to SR120 million (£13 million). Iraq helped to finance the development of Hodeida port. The Abu Dhabi Fund gave two loans jointly with IDA, one of 10 million dollars for rural development and the other of one million dollars for the Sanaa water supply.

The Kuwait Fund at first lent North Yemen about KD1 million for two projects, one for irrigation in the Wadi Zabid and the other to modernise the Salif salt mines. But before considering larger project aid the Fund decided to concentrate on helping the Yemen Government to work out a development plan and to create the rudiments of an economic planning organisation.

The Yemenis and foreign experts agree that the building up of an efficient public administration, especially in financial matters, is now the paramount task in the country. Lack of such an administration is the biggest barrier to economic development. This is also the view of the United Nations Development Programme which has an extensive operation in both Yemens. In the North it had in 1972 a budget of three million dollars and a staff of sixty UN experts with headquarters in Sanaa. One of its projects was an Institute of Public Administration, which would be responsible for training civil servants and reforming government machinery, and which would cost £350,000 over three years.

The state of public administration in North Yemen in the early seventies when the Kuwait Fund World Bank mission began its work, was described in one of the UNDP reports in the following blunt terms: 'There is no national economic and social development plan. A start has been made on collecting statistics, but there is no systematic coordination of projects and aid. There is no understanding of administrative order and structure or hierarchic control. There are no corporate loyalties and no decisions at middle levels. There is no respect for laws and regulations and copies are often not available to the staff who should implement them. There is no system for measuring the value of work or staffing needs. There is an acute shortage of qualified personnel but a large number of employees who are unqualified, unspecialised and untrained. There is no proper system of incentives; salaries are low and ministries are housed in insanitary, dark and unhealthy buildings. There is a lack of the most elementary equipment, no filing system or even paper and paperclips.'

There was in fact, an almost total lack of government machinery at lower levels. Outside the two main towns of Sanaa and Taiz the country was run, if at all, by local notables. In the more remote areas taxes were still collected, if at all, through tax farmers. Where government machinery did exist below the level of the minister's own office, it was difficult for it to take decisions. Depending on the ministers' personalities some ministries were relatively efficient. But often they were little more than titles on paper borne by men with good intentions but little means of carrying them out. The Ministry of Agriculture, for example, consisted in 1972 of three rooms in an old building, one for the minister, one for his staff and the other room empty. When a foreign expert went to the newly-created government statistical office to ask for information about the Ministry of Health, the head of the office pulled an old school exercise book out from under his chair to look up the details. Decisions or laws when formulated take a long time to be put into effect. Life is leisurely, with long dreamy afternoons spent chewing qat, a mildly narcotic leaf; there is no money in the treasury, ministers are often inexperienced and governments change rapidly. Much of the country is inaccessible to motor transport outside the areas reached by roads linking Sanaa, Taiz and Hodeida.

Project aid to the Yemen is sometimes limited in value because it goes into outwardly impressive but little used buildings, such as hospitals without enough staff to run them properly, staff which the Yemenis cannot yet provide or pay for. But already by 1976 ministries had begun to acquire some trained staff and real functions.

The Kuwait Fund's aid in establishing a plan and planning organisation took the form of a joint technical assistance project with the World Bank. This was the first joint operation of its kind undertaken by the Bank with a national aid institution.

In November 1971 the joint Fund-World Bank mission began work in Sanaa. It consisted of four experts – two economists, one agronomist and one engineer, and was due to spend two years on the job. The chief of the mission, nominated by the Fund, was a Sudanese engineer and a former civil servant, Mr Abdullah Ghandour. The other Fund representative working with him was a Syrian economist, Dr Adel Akel, who was formerly in charge of the Syrian Government's planning department and later Dean of the Faculty of Economics at Aleppo University. In 1973 the mission was extended for two years and the membership increased to six with an additional allocation of KD100,000 (£150,000). A further extension and grant of KD125,000 (£187,000) were authorised in 1975, bringing the total amount granted for the project to KD296,400 (£445,000).

The main task of the mission was to draw up a coordinated development plan, economic priorities and organise investment resources. Its chief problem was to create a workable administration, for the bottleneck at all points is the lack of qualified people. Trained people are needed especially in statistics, accountancy and planning, and the mission aimed to train Yemenis on the job.

The mission began by reading through piles of dusty untouched files in government departments, and talking to people in every ministry, as well as to the United Nations experts and the new Institute of Public Administration.

The mission saw three chief factors affecting an improvement of the administration. One was stability and continuity of government. Another the provision of adequate incentives, and the third a question of mentality, of attitudes to work.

Because of low government salaries, the best-educated or most enterprising people were attracted to the private sector of the economy or went to work abroad. At the same time the pool of trained talent available in North Yemen had increased in the past two or three years; many came from South Yemen because they were afraid of 'socialism' there.

Until the Government issued a decree raising civil service salaries the private sector was paying three or four times the government salaries. Ministers used to get £70 a month, under-secretaries £33 a month and a school teacher only £12.50. The under-secretaries' salaries were doubled and the ministers' salaries were also raised to a figure to be fixed by the Republican Council.

In changing the mentality to one of greater working efficiency much depends on the example of those at the top, from the minister downward, and of the educated or qualified few. The Minister for Development in 1972, for example, was himself a qualified engineer and a man of energy. He worked twelve hours a day and set an example in punctuality and application. In other ministries the staff came and went as they pleased. But change has begun in Sanaa in the last few years. In most offices there are now one or two efficient people and the pace is being set by institutions outside the ministries. The Central Bank, for example, has a reputation for being more efficient than any government office.

A United Nations expert has been helping the government draw up a new tax system and United Nations mission was reorganising the customs office. Ten Yemeni customs officers were trained in Syria which has similar problems of difficult borders and extensive smuggling. Taxes so far have come mostly from government employees, with taxes on private business among the lowest in the world. A new income tax law was being drafted. In rural areas the problem of modernising the zakkat or replacing it with some other tax system is complicated by the religious implications. The religious problem also arises over the introduction of a more modern credit system for farmers, because of the Islamic objection to usury. At present, peasants get credit in the form of goods from merchants and repay them in kind, often several times over in value. Most land is privately owned and in the most fertile coastal areas it is often owned by absentee landlords who rent it out through middlemen to share-croppers.

With the help of the Kuwait Fund – World Bank mission, the Yemen Government produced its first development plan in 1973 for the period 1973-6. The plan envisaged development expenditure totalling YR936 million (£88.2 million) of which transport would get YR292 million (£27.8 million); education YR195 million (£18.6 million); and agriculture YR138 million (£13.1 million). The allocation for development in the 1975-6 budget was YR210 million (£20 million), all to be financed from foreign aid.

While helping the Yemen Government to improve its administration, so as to enable it to use aid more effectively, the Kuwait Fund made loans for two projects which were already going concerns but appeared capable of quick development. However, progress on both projects was held up by management and technical problems.

The first was an agricultural project for the expansion of irrigated farming in the Wadi Zabid area, one of the most important of several wadis which bring water down to the Tihama or coastal plain. The second was for the modernisation of a salt mine, one of North Yemen's few non-agricultural export activities, at Salif on the Red Sea coast, 52 miles north of Hodeida.

The Wadi Zabid project was undertaken in conjunction with the United Nations (UNDP/FAO). The first phase was to be a two-year survey of the land and water resources in the area. This was carried out by a Hungarian firm and completed by May 1971. The United Nations provided 1.34 million dollars (£558,000) of the cost. The Yemen Government's contribution of 450,000 dollars (£187,500) plus the local operating costs were financed from a Kuwait Fund loan of KD190,000 (£223,500).

The survey showed that there was good land and considerable surface water resources. But the experts disagreed over the best irrigation and water control plan.

The original concept was criticised by some experts for putting too much emphasis on a big dam and reservoirs. So a third year was spent on surveying what some regarded as more promising ground water which could be used in a series of smaller irrigation and flood control works.

In the second phase of the project the United Nations is to provide 248,000 dollars (£103,000) and the Yemen Government 407,000 dollars (£186,000). Most of the Government's share is being financed by a further Kuwait Fund loan of KD115,000 (£135,000). The Fund has also lent another

KD20,000 for an agricultural project in the Wadi Mawr area.

A pre-investment study financed by the Kuwait Fund led in 1973 to the Fund's granting a bigger loan for agricultural development in the Wadi Zabid area. The loan was for KD1.9 million (£2.85 million) for 40 years without interest. The total costs of the project, to be completed by mid-1978, were estimated at KD5.37 million (£8 million). The foreign exchange costs of KD3.34 million (£5 million) are mostly being covered by IDA, with the local costs being met by the Fund loan.

The project aims at modernising the irrigation system in about 17,000 hectares of the Wadi Zabid. It is expected to increase agricultural production in the area by nearly KD1.5 million (£2.25 million) a year through bigger crops of food grain, cotton, oil seeds and vegetables.

Salt mining in the Yemen, the subject of the other main project loan, has a long history. The Salif mine exploits huge rock salt deposits of very pure quality, hundreds of millions of tons in an area stretching many miles in length and breadth and over a mile deep. Mining at Salif began commercially when Yemen was under Turkish rule but it stopped in 1915 when the Turks left. It was not resumed until 1951 when a group of Yemeni businessmen took it over. From 1953 onwards the entire output of the Salif mine was sold to a Japanese company and Japan is still the sole market for Yemeni salt. In 1963 after the Republic replaced the Imamate, the mine was nationalised and was run as a joint operation with the Egyptian national mining organisation. When the Egyptians left the Yemen this partnership ended and in 1969 the operation reverted to the control of a Yemeni state firm, the Yemen Salt Mining Company, or Yemsalt.

By that time total capacity of the mining plant was 450,000 tons a year, working on two shifts. But the equipment both for mining and for loading the salt on ships for export was eighteen years old, and beyond repair. This made loading the ships slow and difficult, putting up costs and adversely affecting export possibilities.

In 1969 Yemsalt approached the Kuwait Fund for a loan to modernise the mine. Yemsalt had then already bought a new 100-tons-an-hour production line from a Rumanian company. But they had made no arrangements for improving shipping facilities and had not carried out any studies of feasibility or profitability of the project. Because of the lack of qualified specialists in the Yemen, the Fund made its own feasibility study. It also asked for a study to be carried out on a modern ship-loading and stockpiling system, including the building of a jetty to take 50,000-ton ships. (The Company also provides facilities for the staff and workers in the shape of a water desalination plant, electricity and medical, school and police services.)

Without modernisation the mine would probably have lost its export market and gone out of business, for there are huge supplies of salt available in the world, and the market, while expanding rapidly, is keenly competitive. World salt production has tripled since the Second World War, reaching 124 million tons in 1968. This has been largely because of consumption by the chemical industry and the increased use of salt in road de-icing, food preserving and water-softening. Only about three per cent of production is for table salt. But only nine per cent of total production goes into export markets because the main consumers are also mostly producers. Japan is the world's biggest salt importer, using about 7.5 million tons a year but producing only a million tons herself. She buys chiefly from Australia, Mexico and China, so that to hold even her small share of the Japanese market, the Yemen has to remain competitive with these countries.

Yemen's salt has three advantages. It is rock salt which needs no treatment except crushing and grading. It is of high quality, and its location by the seashore means there are no land transport costs. But its low cost of production is partly offset by the long sea journey to Japan – 2,000 miles longer than from Australia.

The modernisation project was to completely replace the old equipment and introduce modern loading facilities in place of the former loading of ships by hand.

It was hoped that the use of bigger ships, of bulk carriers, would cut the transport costs and that sales could be pushed up to 300,000 tons a year. This would bring a net gain in foreign exchange of seven million dollars over ten years – an average of 600,000 to 700,000 dollars a year or twenty per cent of all Yemen's exports in 1969. The cost of the project was at first estimated at just over KD1 million – later revised to KD2 million – of which 83 per cent would be in foreign exchange. In 1970 the Fund granted a loan of KD700,000 for twenty years at 1½ per cent interest. The loan was to the Yemen Government which re-lent it to Yemsalt at four per cent. In 1972 and 1974 the Fund granted two further loans of KD1.2 million and KD1.1 million for the Salif mine.

Progress in getting the hoped-for results from the project appears to have been slow because of the rising costs of equipment, and management difficulties.

The Fund also made a grant of KD85,000 for a geological survey of the rock salt at Salif. This was one of eight outright grants made by the Fund to the Yemen Government. Three others totalling KD296,400 were for the Fund – World Bank joint technical assistance mission; another of KD25,000 was for studies connected with the spinning and weaving industry; KD50,000 was granted for a study of agricultural development in the Tihama; a grant of KD80,000 was for techno-economic studies of livestock development; and in 1975 a grant of KD70,000 was made for a study of increased cement production.

By 1975 the Fund's loans and grants to North Yemen totalled KD6.1 million (over £9 million).

15 Conclusions

Travelling through the Arab countries in the early seventies before the latest oil super-boom, one was left with the impression of a substantial and increasing effort of economic and social development, but one which was not yet commensurate with the resources then available or which even then were about to become available on a bigger scale through increasing oil revenues during the following ten or twenty years.

Since 1973 these revenues have already achieved much higher levels than were expected, amounting to tens of thousands of million of pounds a year, and they will go on accumulating on a vast scale. What is happening, and what will happen to this cataract of money? Will it go to finance yet more industrial expansion in the already wealthy West? If it stays in the Arab world how wisely and productively will it be used? How widely will its benefits be shared? What harm as well as benefit will it bring to Arab society?

I hope that the preceding chapters will have shown that many people in the Arab world, both in government and outside, were actively concerned with these questions even before 1973, though at that time the concern was neither as urgent nor as widespread as it should have been and as it has since become. For now in 1976 a visit to the Arab countries reveals a tremendous acceleration in economic development programmes, in some cases perhaps outstripping the ability of existing political and social institutions to carry out such a huge transformation.

But at a time when the rich nations have been increasingly questioning both the value and feasibility of their long-accepted goals of maintaining economic growth, the Arab states, like most countries of the developing Third World, remain undeterred by the new fears and doubts about affluence: they seem uninhibitedly committed to following as fast as possible the path of 'modernisation' which the industrial countries have already trodden. And it has to be remembered that even with the new oil revenues the Arab world as a whole still lags far behind the developed countries in wealth and, moreover, that oil is a wasting asset which needs to be replaced by other resources. The majority of Arab countries, including at least two of the oil producers, Algeria and Iraq, have per capita incomes far below those of the desert oil states with their relatively small populations. But even if the oil revenues were equally distributed among more than 100 million Arabs they would still be poorer than the industrialised countries.

According to the Secretary-General of OECD, the cumulative surplus of the OPEC countries, Arab and non-Arab, will probably reach a peak in the early eighties of about 225 to 250 billion dollars at 1974 prices. This sum represents about six per cent of the combined GNP of the twenty leading industrialised countries of OECD in 1974.

Great changes are, however, taking place and will continue in both the physical and mental environment of the Arab world: their impact on natural and man-made beauty and on the quality of human relationships is not always an improvement. Nor is there anything like enough attention being paid to reducing the economic and social inequalities within Arab societies, parallel with efforts to increase production.

The critics of Western industrial society are concerned with the quality of life as reflected not only in greater social justice but also in the state of the physical environment, the nature of work and a meaningful role for the individual human being in society. For the Arabs, as for other former colonised peoples, there has been another concern which has complicated and sometimes limited their economic choices. This is their concern to achieve and maintain political independence and revive their cultural identity. It has a double and contradictory effect. On the one hand, it drives them along the road of material development and social change at a faster pace, sometimes faster than can be easily assimilated. On the other hand it sometimes imposes political and social conditions which limit the most efficient use of their economic resources.

There have been some obvious obstacles to the best use of Arab resources: the continued disruptive effects of the Arab-Israeli conflict and the wastage caused by high defence expenditures; the newness of many states, their unstable recent history and the tensions caused by their sometimes conflicting international allegiances; the conflict between the need for

foreign help, especially technical help, and the assertion of
national independence; the persistence of archaic political and
social structures in some countries; the pressure of demand for
social justice before the fruits of development are ready for
sharing; finally, the vast problem of merging different cultures,
which is often involved in 'modernisation'.

But many of the difficulties can no longer be blamed on
others. The Arabs, if they are prepared to help each other, now
have it in their grasp to transform their civilisation and to do it
in their own way, in their own style, taking what they want from
the modern world without necessarily destroying those values
they cherish most. They have the intelligence, they are beginning to acquire the skills, they have the resources and now they
have the capital, if it is properly used.

The significance of the Kuwait Fund in this situation is vital.
It is a pioneer example of the intelligent use of Arab capital,
brains and experience on a scale covering the whole Arab world
(and now extended to other developing countries) in a manner
which puts basic needs before differences in ideology. It has
helped to establish other Arab development institutions at a
time when they are most needed and it provides a model for
development funds set up by other Arab oil states, such as
Saudi Arabia and Abu Dhabi.

The value and influence of the Fund are disproportionately
great compared with the money it spends. Beside the rapidly
growing oil revenues of the Arab world, the Fund's development
investment of an average of some £10 million a year in the first
eleven years of its existence up to 1973, will seem small, and even
the current rate of £150 million a year may appear modest. But in
the first decade – the last part of it after the 1967 war – the
Fund authorities were content to establish the Fund's credentials, to learn from experience and earn the confidence of the
Arab governments and international institutions. These aims
the Fund has undoubtedly achieved, and so laid the indispensable foundation for serious development work and for the use of
the expanded funds now at its disposal. At the same time, as I
hope the preceding chapters have shown, the Fund has invested its funds effectively in nearly sixty carefully-chosen projects.

This achievement contrasts with the wastage sometimes
associated with less well-conceived Arab development operations.

The expansion of the Kuwait Fund, together with the other forms of inter-Arab aid coming from Kuwait, still represents only a relatively small proportion of the surplus oil revenues of the Arab countries which could be made available for investment in the Arab world and in other developing countries during the next few years. More is already coming from the new inter-Arab Fund for Economic and Social Development and from the Abu Dhabi and Saudi Arabian development funds on whose readiness to make substantial contributions much will depend.

But if increased development funds from oil are to be used effectively they need serious, intelligent and incorruptible management. The establishment of such high standards in an inter-Arab institution is perhaps the most important contribution made by the Kuwait Fund to the development of the Arab world. It was the first of many such development institutions that will be needed at different regional, national and local levels if the great opportunities opened up by oil wealth are not to be frittered away and if the dream of an Arab renaissance is to be given a solid material foundation.

The Kuwait Fund for Arab Economic Development

LOANS TO ARAB COUNTRIES 1962-75

Country and Project	Amount (KD000)	Status
ALGERIA		
Oil pipeline phase I	7,500	Completed
Oil pipeline phase II, III	2,500	Completed
Total	10,000	
BAHRAIN		
Aluminium smelter	1,000	Completed
Flour mill and silo	500	Completed
Causeway and bridges	500	Completed
Sitra power and water plant	7,350	Under way
Total	9,350	
EGYPT		
Suez Canal expansion	9,800	Completed
Suez Canal reopening/repairs	10,000	Under way
Cargo ships construction	3,500	Completed
Abu Qir gas project I	4,500	Under way
Abu Qir gas project II	3,500	Under way
Talkha fertiliser plant	7,000	Under Way
Abu Qir power project	10,000	Under way
Total	48,300	
IRAQ		
Samarra hydro-electric	3,000	Completed
Samarra, Um Qasr cement project	3,800	Completed
Total	6,800	
JORDAN		
Yarmouk Valley	1,900	Completed
Phosphate mines	3,000	Completed

Jerusalem electricity		240	Completed
Jerusalem Hotel		175	Completed
Jordan Hotel		85	Completed
Zerqa River		4,600	Under way
Hussein power station		3,020	Under way
Industrial Development Bank		1,000	Under way
	Total	14,020	

LEBANON

Joun electricity		1,670	Completed
Grain silos		800	Completed
	Total	2,470	

MAURITANIA

Road maintenance		1,150	Under way
Nouakchott-Kiffa Road		5,800	Under way
	Total	6,950	

MOROCCO

Tessaout agricultural project		7,350	Under way
Tadla agricultural project		2,700	Under way
Sucrafar sugar factory		860	Completed
Phosphate plant		2,400	Under way
National Development Bank		6,000	Under way
Quneitra electricity		3,350	Under way
	Total	22,660	

SOMALIA

Mogadishu power project		6,200	Under way

SUDAN

Sudan Railways		7,000	Completed
Sugar plant		1,700	Completed
Agricultural development		4,210	Completed
Mechanised dry farming		1,600	Under way
Rahad irrigation scheme I		3,300	Under way
Rahad irrigation scheme II		11,200	Under way
Sennar sugar		4,500	Under way
Industrial Bank		1,500	Under way
	Total	35,010	

SYRIA
Grain silos	7,000	Under way
Oil refinery	2,000	Under way
Mehreda power station	9,900	Under way
Total	18,900	

TUNISIA
La Goulette electricity I	3,800	Completed
La Goulette electricity II	4,600	Completed
Medjerda Valley I	2,000	Completed
Medjerda Valley II	3,200	Under way
Gas pipeline	900	Under way
Fishing ports	2,850	Under way
Phosphate mines	2,000	Under way
Development Bank	2,500	Under way
Carthage Airport project	4,000	Under way
Total	25,850	

NORTH YEMEN
Wadi Zabid	325	Completed
Salif salt mine	3,000	Under way
Highway project	284	Under way
Tihama agricultural project	1,900	Under way
Total	5,509	

SOUTH YEMEN
Abyan project	330
Abyan Delta project	4,200
Mukalla – Hadramaut highway	4,500
Total	9,030

Grand total 221,049

TECHNICAL ASSISTANCE GRANTS TO ARAB COUNTRIES 1962-75

Country and Project	*Amount*
	(KD 000)
MAURITANIA	
Exploitation of mineral resources	175
SOMALIA	
Livestock development and irrigation	200
SUDAN	
Livestock development study	50
Sennar sugar factory and grain silos studies	100
Transport study	300
	Total 450
NORTH YEMEN	
Technical assistance I, II, III	296.4
Textile plant factory	25
Geological study: Salif salt	85
Tihama agricultural project	50
Livestock development	80
Expansion of cement production	70
	Total 606.4
SOUTH YEMEN	
Fish meal plant	100
Aden Port; Rayan Airport;	
Livestock development	300
	Total 400
ARAB PLANNING INSTITUTE	
Training programme in economic	
planning	78
UN ECONOMIC COMMITTEE FOR WEST ASIA	
Cooperation between committees	
and development funds	50
	Grand total 1960

LOANS TO OTHER DEVELOPING COUNTRIES
1974-75

		KD 000	*Status*
BANGLADESH			
Rural electrification		6,400	Under way
Manu River project		2,300	Under way
	Total	8,700	
MALAYSIA			
Palong land settlement		7,600	Under way
RWANDA			
Tea plantation		1,000	Under way
SRI LANKA			
Urea plant		7,500	Under way
TANZANIA			
Textile plant		4,500	Under way
UGANDA			
Livestock development		5,750	Under way
SENEGAL, MALI, MAURITANIA			
Senegal River basin programme		10,000	Under way
	Grand total	35,050	

TECHNICAL ASSISTANCE GRANTS TO OTHER DEVELOPING COUNTRIES 1974-75

(KD 000)

AFGHANISTAN
Sugar industry and exploitation of Farah- Rud River   400

MALI
Agricultural development and cement plant   200

NEPAL
Dairy products plant   90

UGANDA
Sugar and power development   230

GUINEA
Technical Study of Road Construction   150

GUINEA BISSAU
Technical study of Port and Airport Construction   200

OVERALL TOTAL LOANS AND
GRANTS: KD259,000,000

Index